CATHOLIC EDUCATION:
HOMEWARD BOUND

CATHOLIC EDUCATION: HOMEWARD BOUND

A Useful Guide to Catholic Home Schooling

by
KIMBERLY HAHN
and
MARY HASSON

IGNATIUS PRESS   SAN FRANCISCO

Cover by Roxanne Mei Lum

The Hahn Family:
Photograph by Olan Mills

The Hasson Family:
Photograph by Alan Porter
Focused Images Photography, Inc.

© 1996 Ignatius Press, San Francisco
All rights reserved
ISBN 0–89870–566–5
Library of Congress catalogue number 95–78090
Printed in the United States of America ∞

We dedicate this book first and foremost to Jesus Christ, our King, with love and gratitude for the opportunity and the strength to serve Him in this work—may all praise and honor be His;

and also

with love to Mary, His Mother, our best example as mother and teacher. In the words of John Paul II, "Mary had a unique relationship with her divine Son: on the one hand she was a docile disciple, meditating on his words in the depths of her heart, on the other, as his mother and teacher, she helped his human nature to grow in 'wisdom and in stature, and in favour with God and man'." It is our hope that all who read this book will follow her example as disciple, mother, and teacher.

WITH DEEPEST THANKS . . .

to my beloved, Scott, who has fortified me with the right combination of helpful hints, hugs, and humor, for dreaming with me about the possibilities of home education and helping those dreams come true; and to our children, Michael, Gabriel, Hannah, Jeremiah, and Joseph, for your many sacrifices to complete this book, and for treasured times together each day, learning about the Lord, Latin, literature . . . and life.

Many thanks also to Marilyn Grodi, Michaelann Martin, and Pia Crosby for reviewing our manuscript and offering invaluable suggestions; to the members of the Heart of Mary Home School Support Group in Steubenville for their prayers and encouragement; for all of the personal support from our family members in the Hahn and Kirk clans both for this project in particular and for our home education in general; and special thanks to my sister, Kari Harrington, my constant companion on the trail of home education since our first-borns were babies—curriculum confidant, prayer partner, fellow strategist, and overall troubleshooter. Finally, heartfelt thanks for my parents, Jerry and Pat Kirk, for their consistent encouragement in our marriage and family, especially in our adventure of home education. You are a constant witness of the joy of being lifelong learners.   K. K. H.

With tender love and deep gratitude, I want to thank my husband, Seamus, for all his love, his tireless patience, unfailing support, encouragement, and invaluable wisdom in helping me complete this book; to our children, Mike, Mary Kate, Jim, Brigid, and Peter ("PJ"), who bring joy, mischief, and wonder to our school days—you are my motivation and inspiration. "*¡Muchas gracias!*"

With admiration and encouragement, I wish to thank the scores of mothers who shared their time, experiences, and wisdom to provide the concrete ideas woven throughout these chapters. I am indebted in particular to Debbie Brock, whose initial inspiration and continued support culminated in this work; to Lisanne Bales and Elizabeth Foss for their countless hours spent editing and improving our efforts; to Miki Hill for her priceless friendship and humor; to Father Richard Gill, L.C., and Father William Izquierdo, L.C., for their invaluable guidance, prayer, and insights during the peaks and valleys of the past few years; and finally, to my parents, Charles and Mary Rice, who began my own adventure in home education years ago, inspiring me to share the fun with my own children.   M. R. H.

CONTENTS

FOREWORD

As an avid reader, I am committed to the proposition that all books are NOT created equal. In this case, however, I cannot feign any neutrality or impartiality of judgment. Nevertheless, I still make bold to declare my strong conviction that *Catholic Education Homeward Bound* is far and away the best book on the subject of Catholic home education, and this for several reasons.

First, it is *reliable* as a guide for Catholic parents who want to stay close to the heart of the Church in the schooling of their children. The authors demonstrate that home schooling cannot be regarded as some sort of fringe movement on the Church's periphery; instead, it is squarely based on Catholic teachings drawn straight from natural law, Sacred Scripture, and the writings of Doctors, saints, and popes, all of which point to the inalienable right and duty of parents to decide what is the best education for their children. As deeply committed mothers (and no, they're not "supermoms"), the authors—along with many thousands of others—share a sense of divine calling. Moreover, they are ready and willing to learn from —and support—parish schools; at the same time, they show why Catholic home schoolers deserve respect and consideration.

Second, in its treatment of topics and resources, this book is nothing if not *thorough*. Indeed, you would be hard pressed to find anything more complete, especially among titles written by teachers with a daily load of lessons. Just about every angle is covered: from lesson plans and child discipline to field trips and spiritual formation.

Third, this book is *balanced*. In tackling controversial issues like socialization and standardized testing, or in treating practical questions like selecting curriculum material while avoiding burnout, Kimberly and Mary consistently display sanctified common sense. Indeed, readers will find here just the right combination of secular and sacred, theoretical and practical. In striking such a remarkable balance, these two full-time homemakers and teachers simply write the way they live.

Fourth, *Catholic Education Homeward Bound* is *useful*. Whether you're looking for advice and encouragement, language resources, aids for teaching the multiplication tables—or the Ten Commandments—you're sure to find this book to be a very functional tool. And you never get the feeling that it's being handed down to you "from on high" by experts who never experience frustration and failure; the anecdotes they share are proof positive of that. Sure, there's a great deal of wisdom and experience between these covers; but it was acquired by Mary and Kimberly the same way it reaches most of their readers: through the "home school of hard knocks". Indeed, the many truths in this book are not the only things to have been tried and tested.

Let me close by testifying to the integrity and dedication of these two women—and I speak of "women" deliberately—because they are more than simply home-schooling moms and full-time homemakers; they are faithful wives and best friends to their husbands. Rest assured, this book represents a real labor of love, one performed for thousands of present (and future) Catholic home educators; but I must bear witness to the fact that it is only one among hundreds of other "labors of love" that Kimberly and Mary have showered upon their husbands, children, neighbors, and friends. It seems fitting, then, for me to share the words that just came to mind as I paused, wondering how to close: "A good wife who can find? She is far more precious than jewels. . . . She opens her mouth with wisdom, and the teaching of kindness is on her tongue. She looks well to the ways of her household, and does not eat the bread of idleness. Her children rise up and call her blessed; her husband also . . ." (Prov 31:10–28).

Scott Hahn
Feast of All Saints, 1995

PART ONE

FACT FINDING

I

When It Comes to Catholic Education There's No Place Like Home

An Overview

What's this home education all about, anyway?

—a concerned grandmother

Home education? It's about "parents who want to nurture their children and allow them to mature at their own pace in all areas of their lives: spiritually, intellectually, and physically" (Kari Harrington, mother of seven). It's about offering an "unlimited variety of subjects" with which to pique our kids' "interests and talents" (Anna Akis, mother of four). And it's about teaching our kids "who they are, what they have been created for, and where they are going—that this life is a journey back to God the Father, who created them" (Clyde Gualandri, father of four).

Home education is about all these things: academic success, creative and happy kids, cohesive and intimate family relationships, and a deep and lively faith. But what *is* it? And, specifically, what is *Catholic* home education? That is the question this chapter addresses.

Undoubtedly you have other related questions, too. Why should you consider home education? And how much time, energy, and knowledge does it take to do it successfully? And finally, is it *really* worth it? Later chapters answer each of these questions in detail. For now, though, let's begin at the beginning. What *is* Catholic home education?

3

Parents—Teachers in Training

If you are a parent, you *are* "home educating" already. Your role as educator began the day your firstborn loudly announced his arrival and demanded your attention and love. And you will teach your children for years to come—until they are well into adulthood. As a mom or dad, your teaching grows out of, and is perfected by, your love for your kids. The natural bond between you provides the best foundation for teaching and learning: a foundation built on love, acceptance, trust, and encouragement.

Yet, for most parents, teaching their child how to hold a spoon or how to get dressed or how to master a thousand other simple but important details of childhood comes so naturally that they probably never stop to consider themselves "teachers". It's just part of the job description of being a mom or a dad. In fact, though, it is hard to think of anything you do as a parent that is not in some measure "educating" your child—whether it is teaching your son proper manners, showing your daughter how to spell her name, or discovering bugs under rocks together. This *is* home education.

When, as parents, we are uncertain how best to teach a particular thing, we draw upon the wisdom of others who have already done it successfully. Your friends will tell you their latest theories on how to get your infant to sleep through the night; Grandma shares the secrets of potty-training your first toddler; your sister gives you suggestions for disciplining and training your preschooler. We learn from others and find the best way to go about it for ourselves and our children.

Teaching academic subjects to our children, as we will discuss in greater detail throughout this book, is exactly the same. It is really a very natural extension of the teaching (and learning) we already do as parents. In the words of Kari Harrington, who has been home-educating for nine years, "Home schooling is basically a continuation of what we have done during the first five years of our children's lives. We've just added some specific curriculum to our nurturing environment." Attentive parents easily create a stimulating and encouraging atmosphere for their babies and toddlers that serves as a gentle springboard for later academic learning—both in the home and outside the home.

So, you have actually been home educating all along, whether you knew it or not! The question to ask yourself, then, is not "Should I *begin* home educating my son or daughter?" but rather "Should I *continue* to do so?"

Parents' Irreplaceable Role

Many parents focus on this question for the first time when their eldest child nears kindergarten age and that first ride on the yellow school bus approaches. But parents of older children often find themselves reconsidering their role in their child's education when their child's school has failed him intellectually or, more critically, proves dangerous to him spiritually, morally, or even physically. Some parents wake up one day to discover they have relinquished too much control over their son's or daughter's education to "experts" who are either inept or untrustworthy.

Whenever you first confront this question, the answer begins with your identity as parents. The Catholic Church has long considered parents "the first and foremost educators of their children".[1] In speaking about marriage and families, the Church links the responsibility of having children with the need to ensure their education.

> As it is parents who have given life to their children, on them lies the greatest obligation of educating their family. They must therefore be recognized as being primarily and principally responsible for their education. The role of parents in education is of such importance that it is almost impossible to provide an adequate substitute.[2]

[1] *The Christian Family in the Modern World* (*Familiaris Consortio*), apostolic exhortation by Pope John Paul II (November 2, 1981), no. 36, quoting from the Second Vatican Council's *Declaration on Christian Education* (*Gravissimum Educationes*), no. 3.

[2] *Declaration on Christian Education*, no. 3. Numerous Church documents closely link procreation and education, most notably *Humanae Vitae* and the encyclical of Pius XI *On the Christian Education of Youth*. In addition, *Casti Connubii* states: "For the most wise

Parents play a crucial role in shaping and teaching their child—it is in family life that a child's education really begins.

Pope John Paul II urges us to remember that the parents' role in education is "irreplaceable and inalienable, and therefore incapable of being entirely delegated to others or usurped by others".[3] That is due to "the uniqueness of the loving relationship between parents and children".[4] Parents have a unique advantage over any teacher in the classroom. The love and trust between the parent and child opens the child's heart and inclines him to be more receptive to the truths he must learn.

Our love makes us want the best for our children, including the best education we can provide. Not surprisingly, this desire impels many parents to teach their children themselves at home. Parents of nearly a million children have discovered, as we have, the wonderful benefits of home education. We truly think it is the best way, not merely the only available option or our "stopgap" until the schools improve (if they ever do).

Home Educating for Excellence

As an academic matter, home education is really the time-tested, well-proven art of personal tutoring, but with an important twist. In home education, the tutors are those who know the child best and love him the most—his parents. Motivated by their child's best

---

God would have failed to make sufficient provision for children . . . if He had not given to those to whom He had entrusted the power and right to beget them, the power also and the right to educate them" (no. 16).

In the *Pastoral Constitution on the Church in the Modern World* (*Gaudium et Spes*), the Second Vatican Council stated: "[B]y its very nature the institution of marriage and married life is ordered to the procreation and education of the off-spring. . . . When they are given the dignity and role of fatherhood and motherhood, [parents] will eagerly carry out their duties of education, especially religious education, which devolves primarily on them. . . . Married couples should regard it as their proper mission to transmit human life and to educate their children" (nos. 48, 50). Pope John Paul II affirms this teaching in his 1994 "Letter to Families".

[3] *The Christian Family in the Modern World*, no. 36.

[4] Ibid.

interests, parents can choose or tailor a curriculum that lets their child learn much more than he otherwise would—and at his own pace.

The statistics, not surprisingly, are impressive. Home-taught children consistently score well above their institutionally educated peers on standardized tests in all subjects.[5] And children get that advantage regardless of their parents' own educational background,[6] income,[7] or educational approach.[8]

Academic success occurs for the simple reason that nothing can beat a teacher working one-on-one with a child whom she loves and understands and whose personal success is her priority. This observation motivated former teacher Brenna Heffernan to teach her own four children at home.

> With a background in education and some time as a teacher at a traditional school, I became increasingly convinced that I could provide my children with an education that equalled or surpassed that which I provided for my students.

The love and attention she gives her own children far surpass what any other teacher would give, and these contribute to the educational success she desires for them.

But the personal tutoring of home education is not simply the best technique for getting high SAT scores. At heart, home education is really about love—the love that inspires mothers and fathers to listen, to nurture, to form, to correct, and to encourage long after an institutional teacher would have given up and moved on to one

---

[5] Brian D. Ray, *Marching to the Beat of Their Own Drum: A Profile of Home Education Research* (study conducted by the National Home Education Research Institute and published by the Home School Legal Defense Association, 1992), pp. 7–10. See also: "A Nationwide Study of Home Education: Family Characteristics, Legal Matters, and Student Achievement", released by the National Home Education Research Institute in November 1990, and reported in the *Home School Court Report*, December 1990.

[6] Ray, p. 10, citing three separate studies; see also "A Nationwide Study", p. 6.

[7] Ray, p. 10, citing two studies showing no relationship between family income and achievement and two studies showing a weak, but not causal, relationship. "A Nationwide Study", p. 7.

[8] Ray, pp. 6–10; "A Nationwide Study", p. 5.

of the other twenty-six[9] pupils in the class, or labeled a child hyperactive, learning disabled, or worse. Mothers and fathers are simply far less likely to overlook or ignore a young heart eager for knowledge, encouragement, and love.

Home Educating for Heaven

Still, *Catholic* home education means more. As Catholics, we want our children to know that life holds something better for them than merely accumulating material things, achieving a productive professional life, or even enjoying a satisfying personal life. We yearn for the knowledge and love of God Himself. "Our hearts are restless until they rest in thee, O Lord", said St. Augustine.[10] Pursuing the best for our children means not only academic excellence but the deepest possible relationship with our Lord and His Church. Home education offers Catholic families a compelling opportunity to make loving God and serving His Church an integrated part of their lives.

Within the heart of the family, parents can give their children consistent discipline and formation, genuine spirituality, and the strong emotional support they need to become the men and women God wants them to be. More parents cite religious or spiritual reasons for their choice to home educate than any other reason.[11] While Jesus plants the seed of faith, it is our responsibility to till the soil—to make our child receptive to that gift. Rose Grimm, from Ojai, California, is a home-educating mother of seven children ranging in age from two to eighteen years. Her eleven years of teaching and forming her children have convinced her that faith

[9] The most recent statistics from the National Education Association, "Status of the American Public School Teacher, 1990–91", show the average class size in elementary grades is twenty-four students, while in secondary schools it is twenty-six.

[10] St. Augustine, *Confessions*, 1, 1, 1.

[11] Pat Lines, "Home Instruction: The Size and Growth of the Movement", in *Home Schooling: Political, Historical, and Pedagogical Perspectives*, edited by Jane Van Galen and Mary Ann Pitman (Norwood, NJ: Ablex Publishing Corporation, 1991), pp. 16–17. Lines, a researcher in the U.S. Department of Education, cites several different studies to support this conclusion.

is the most valuable thing in the world, and you can't give it to your children in one chunk. You have to do it little by little. If you're with them, you can show them . . . here's a moment to pray, now is the time to hold your temper, here's a chance to be really charitable. You have to give it to them in pieces. . . . The chances of them loving God and growing in Him are so much greater if you're with them than if they are away from you all day or with a teacher who won't share that with them.

Home education allows us to surround our children with an atmosphere rich in faith and love for God. The time we spend together offers so many natural opportunities to share our faith with our children—and to live it more fruitfully.

The spiritual life we live, according to Pope John Paul II, cannot be "a matter only of disposing oneself to hear a teaching and obediently accepting a commandment. More radically, it involves *holding fast to the very person of Jesus.*" [12] Our own faith life, typified not merely by assent to certain intellectual propositions about our Faith but rather by the depth of the relationship we have with God, holds the promise for our children of a mature relationship with the Lord—one that will lead them to that true happiness we so desire for them. In short, our children's openness to faith is cultivated by our own.

But often, the reverse is also true: our children's simple faith encourages us to deepen our own. Frequently, the parents' decision to home educate helps turn their own hearts back toward the Lord as they focus on teaching their children the truths of the Faith. They often learn Scripture and the traditions of the Church for the first time right along with their children. It's never too late to learn.

Real Character Formation

In addition to enriching a family's faith, home education is an effective way to form our children's character. (Unlike at most

---

[12] *The Splendor of Truth (Veritatis Splendor)*, encyclical letter of Pope John Paul II, August 6, 1993, no. 19.

schools, character training at home is not a pseudoacademic subject like "values clarification".) Character formation begins with a recognition of the dignity of the human person. It builds on the specific and practical applications of God's Word to our lives. And it plants the seeds of virtue, which take root and flourish in daily living.

Character building and moral training take time and consistency and, as statistics attest, are often shortchanged because of the hectic schedules and lack of family time that most schoolchildren experience. Yet the time and parental involvement afforded by home education allow the parents to make their child's character development a top priority.

We want each of our children to become a fully balanced human being, not just the clone of his peers. Each child has unique gifts and talents and a personality all his own. As Mary Madden from Steubenville, Ohio, notes, "Home schooling has given me an opportunity to get to know my children as they grow. I find them very interesting people, and I really enjoy being with them!" Through home education, a child spends more of his time in a supportive and nurturing family atmosphere—the best place for him to develop his intellectual capacities and talents, to allow his personality to unfold, as well as to receive comprehensive moral training and character formation.

Building Family Unity

The beauty of home education is that it gives a family more time together—time to solidify relationships, to communicate values, and to focus on each child's individual needs in a consistent and unhurried atmosphere. "When kids are in school", comments Laura Berquist, a California mother of six,

> there's a lot of tension in the morning. You're looking for things they need, one child will tell you about the report he forgot to do, another needs money, lunches for all . . . and the last thing you say to them as they're going out the door is "You're going to be late!" [Our] children had almost no unstructured time at all [in school], and a lot of that time was pressured.

In contrast, when they began teaching their children at home, "the morning rush stopped", and the family's focus changed. The stress was off, and the family simply enjoyed being a family together. As another mother phrased it, "Life is very peaceful. . . . We're *here*."

The common goals and shared vision that grow out of home education contribute to a greater sense of family unity within families who home educate. "One of the most important things about home schooling", Laura Berquist continues, "is that the family is central in everybody's consciousness. . . . That's what sold my sister on homeschooling. She saw that everyone in the family sees that the family's good is his own good."

When a family works, studies, and plays together, it grows in closeness and purpose. Rather than having a number of different teachers with various perspectives each year, our children receive from us, year after year, a unified vision for all of life. Cathy Gualandri, a mother of four, came to realize that "after home schooling for the third year, our family is more unified by living the values we so treasure together." The best hours of the day—ours and our children's—are spent together, instead of trying to squeeze in time for each other after car-pooling, attending activities, doing homework, and cooking meals. As a result, parents and children really know and enjoy each other.

Creating a Family Culture

Increasing the amount of time your family spends together means more than just coziness. It means you have the opportunity to establish a strong family culture. A family culture, like a national culture or a "corporate culture", is really a series of details that all work together to highlight the important aspects of lives lived together and the values underlying them. Birthdays celebrate a child's (or adult's) uniqueness and "specialness" to the family; feast days celebrate personal heroes and inspire holiness; traditions such as chopping down a Christmas tree together build family unity.

Family culture has an even greater importance now than before, as the prevailing secular culture has not only abandoned its Christian underpinnings but proved openly hostile to the values Catholic families are trying to instill in their children. It is only common sense that the more time a family has to spend together, the richer its family culture will be.

Family Flexibility

In addition to time, home education also offers the advantage of flexibility in scheduling not only each day but also each week and the entire school year. Family vacations, daily schedules, and long-term plans are no longer dictated by the school bureaucracy's calendar. Each family is free to accommodate family needs and emergencies according to what works best for it—and to change its plans as circumstances warrant.

Home education gives parents the ultimate in school choice. In their desire to give their children the best education and to create the ideal circumstances for harmonious family life, home-educating parents choose the schedule, curricula, and activities that accomplish their family goals. Thus, in an era when time seems to move so fast and events spin out of our control, home education allows the most important choices to remain with those to whom they matter the most—the family itself.

Home—The School of Choice

All the benefits of home education—strong academics, greater time and flexibility, enriched relationships with each other, and deepened faith—have led thousands of parents to conclude, in the words of Susan Waldstein, a home educator from Notre Dame, Indiana, "Even if there were the best, most perfect school in the world, I wouldn't want to give up home schooling because of what it does for our family."

This book sets out the "why" and the "how-to" of home education. We hope to encourage all parents, whether they choose to educate their children exclusively at home or not, to embrace their unique opportunity as parents to inspire their children's intellects, form their characters, and inflame their hearts with love for God.

2

Home Education Makes the Grade

Is Home Education Good *Education?*

Statistic: Nationally, only 25 percent of fourth graders in public and private schools and 28 percent of eighth graders are reading proficiently. Just 25 percent of eighth graders are proficient in basic math skills.[1]

Statistic: The 1994 standardized test scores of over 16,000 home-educated children showed average reading scores in the 79th percentile (better than 79 percent of the students taking the test), written language and math scores in the 73rd percentile, and composite scores in the 77th percentile.[2]

Statistic: A recent study of over 10,500 home-educated children found that they averaged 15 to 32 percentage points higher on standardized tests in math, reading, and language skills than their public school peers.[3]

[1] *The National Education Goals Report*, vol. 1: The National Report (1993), pp. 55, 62; reporting findings of the U.S. Department of Education National Education Goals Panel.

[2] "Advocates Hail Test Scores of Home-Schooled Students", *The Washington Times*, January 17, 1995, p. A3.

[3] *Stanford Achievement Test Group Summary Scores by Grade* (Home School Legal Defense Association, 1992). Achievement test scores were compiled by the National Center for Home Education, a division of the Home School Legal Defense Association, for the Spring of 1992. Reported scores were from 10,750 students affiliated with the HSLDA. This 15–32 percentage point advantage for home-taught children is consistent with the majority of studies on the achievement of home-educated children. See also: "The Academic Achievement and Affective Development of Home-Schooled Children", by Brian D. Ray and Jon Wartes, in *Home Schooling: Political, Historical, and Pedagogical Perspectives*, edited by Jane Van Galen and Mary Anne Pitman (Norwood, NJ: Ablex Publishing Corporation, 1991).

Why try home education? The short answer is "Because it works!" The goal of education is understanding—not perfect attendance, "passing", or even getting straight A's. Home education, with tutoring as its basic method, naturally fosters real understanding in its students. In addition, it gives parents the opportunity to tailor the curriculum and select the best resources to help their child discover what is true, whether in algebra, science, or theology.

Common Sense Tells Us
Tutoring Is the Best Approach

Think about it: if a friend came to you and said her son was consistently having trouble understanding his math homework, would you recommend he double the time spent in class or that he find a math tutor? Common sense tells us that when a child has difficulty in school, the remedy probably isn't more hours spent in large classes but rather intensive, personal instruction—tutoring. Similarly, everyone knows of bright children who, given individual instruction on interesting topics, have been spurred on to incredible achievement. Tutoring offers parallel benefits to bright and average students alike.

School—A Stark Contrast to Tutoring

The typical student in school receives less than eight minutes of individual attention during a six-hour school day.[4] The average public-school class size is twenty-six students, some of whom, because of disciplinary, motivational, or personal problems, will require disproportionate amounts of time, leaving little for the rest of the class. It is simply impossible for even the most highly motivated, talented teacher to come close to providing the amount of feedback and personal encouragement that a child receives when he is tutored—especially by a loving parent.

[4] Raymond and Dorothy Moore, *Home Style Teaching* (Waco, TX: Word Books, 1984). For a more in-depth analysis of the limitations of American schools, see John Goodlad, *A Place Called School* (New York: McGraw-Hill, 1984), p. 29.

Even the entrenched education establishment recognizes the benefits of one-on-one instruction and continually seeks more money in order to reduce class sizes and decrease the student–teacher ratio. Declining test scores amid ever-increasing education budgets provide good evidence that something is wrong with the mass-produced, "fast-food" approach (limited menu, billions and billions "served") of institutional education. Examples abound: Newark, New Jersey, for instance, has the dubious distinction of spending the highest amount in the country, $9,760 per pupil, while producing abysmally low test scores year after year.[5]

Even when faced with the stark results of nationwide failure of the public-school system, school districts and the National Education Association continue to oppose home education. The National Education Association has repeatedly adopted a position that home education

> cannot provide the student with a comprehensive education experience. . . . Instruction should be by persons who are licensed by the appropriate state education licensure agency, and a curriculum approved by the state department of education should be used.[6]

In reality, their objection seems to be that home education eliminates the school bureaucracy's power over each child's education and returns it to his parents. The N.E.A. maintains this position in spite of the fact that the public education system has failed in the duty it has undertaken.

The 1993 report of the National Education Goals Panel,[7] established by the U.S. Department of Education, decried the fact that nationally only 25 percent of fourth graders read proficiently. State

[5] "Contrary to Gingrich, D.C. Schools Not Most Expensive", *The Washington Post*, March 11, 1995, p. A11. See also: "Mayor of Jersey City Is New Republican Hero", *The Washington Times*, September 28, 1993, pp. A1, A15, discussing Jersey City's greater than 60-percent drop-out rate in spite of the city's $9,200 per-pupil expenditure.

[6] National Education Association's 1990 position statement on home schooling: Resolution C–39. This position was reaffirmed in 1992: Resolution B–55.

[7] *The National Education Goals Report* (1993), publishing report of the U.S. Department of Education National Education Goals Panel. Vol. 1 provides the national report, and vol. 2 gives the state reports. Available from the U.S. Department of Education.

statistics vary widely. Virginia, for example, was on the high end with 28 percent of its fourth graders achieving proficiency, while the District of Columbia showed only an 8-percent proficiency rate. And the national statistics are hardly improved by additional years of schooling, for by eighth grade only 28 percent have demonstrated proficiency, and at twelfth grade (after 11 percent of the class has dropped out), only 37 percent can read proficiently. American students are equally ill prepared when it comes to math, as nearly the same percentages demonstrate that the majority of American students are deficient in math.[8] So, after twelve years of institutional education, parents can only hope their child is in that 37 percent that have actually learned something!

Gifted children, while generally not deficient in skills, suffer from the lack of challenging material offered them in institutional education. Statistics released in 1993 by the U.S. Department of Education[9] highlight American schools' failure to make our best students competitive against the best students in the world in most subjects. Bright students, the research indicates, typically have mastered up to half of the year's curriculum *before the school year even begins*. Yet, "Eighty-four percent of assignments for gifted students were the same as those made to the whole class."[10] The two or three hours afforded weekly to visit the resource room or participate in an enrichment project simply aren't enough to motivate or challenge our best students to reach their highest academic potential. Interestingly, the report recommends that schools try to let children move at their own pace through more challenging material—exactly the prescription offered by home education.

Bureaucracy, not the child's best interests, determines whether he will be challenged or held back by the pace of others less intelligent. One mother recounted how her child's bus route, not

[8] Ibid. District of Columbia statistics are in vol. 2, p. 35, while Virginia statistics are found in vol. 2, p. 187.

[9] "Gifted Pupils Bored, Study Says", *The Washington Post*, November 5, 1993, p. 1.

[10] "U.S. Schools 'Squander' Gifted Students' Talents", *The Washington Times*, November 5, 1993, pp. 1, 16

his intellectual ability, determined whether he would be allowed to attend an advanced reading program.

> For two years our son attended a special public school pre-school program called National Gifted Educators. When he went to kindergarten, they [school officials] told us he couldn't be in the reading program because the bus route for our suburb put him in the afternoon kindergarten, while all the reading classes were in the morning. Our son ended up bored, not excelling as he could have, and set back from what he accomplished in the pre-school program.

Unfortunately, stories like this are not uncommon, as schools are ill-equipped to respond to individual needs.

Public and private schools share common pitfalls, although private-school students as a group do better academically than their public-school counterparts. In fact, however, home-educated students have consistently outscored both private- and public-school students alike on one standardized test after another.

Statistics Show Home Tutoring Works Best

As the home-education movement expands, more and more research confirms what most parents discover for themselves: home-educated students consistently learn more and learn it better than their institutionally educated peers.

Several nationwide, in-depth studies highlight the academic success of home-taught children. The most recent study analyzing the test scores for home-educated children compiled data from the 1994 Iowa Achievement Tests. It confirmed numerous earlier studies that show home-educated children repeatedly outscoring their public-school counterparts by wide margins. (See the statistics at the beginning of this chapter.) Similarly, 1992 test data on 10,750 home-educated children in kindergarten through twelfth grade revealed that their scores in math, reading, and language skills were 15 to 32 percent higher than the scores of their public-school peers.[11] These results confirm an earlier (1986) survey that showed 73 percent of home-taught children reading at least one grade level ahead and an additional 18 percent reading at grade level. Similarly, half of the students tested a year or more above grade level in mathematics, with another 29 percent at grade level.[12]

Numerous states have also collected data showing the achievement of home-taught children. Oregon, Alaska, and Tennessee all report home-educated children consistently scoring significantly above average.[13] Studies conducted in such diverse states as Texas, California, Alabama, Washington, Pennsylvania, and North Dakota confirm generally higher scores for home-educated students compared to their institutionally educated peers.[14]

Interestingly, one study measuring intellectual development, as opposed to achievement test scores, "suggested that home-educated students move into formal thought between the ages of 10 and 11, which is far earlier than the national average at ages 15 to 20".[15]

While the statistics are persuasive, what matters most for home-educating parents is the actual, positive result they see in their own son or daughter. So, ask the parents of a home-taught child, and they'll tell you—their child is learning and learning well!

[11] *Stanford Achievement Test Group Summary Scores by Grade*. Reported in *The Teaching Home* magazine, October/November 1992, p. 26. See also: "A Nationwide Study of Home Education" (1990), Dr. Brian D. Ray, National Home Education Research Institute. This report analyzed data from a 1990 sampling of nearly 1,500 children and showed home-educated children scoring, on the average, at the 80th percentile or higher in all subjects on the major achievement tests.

[12] Brian D. Ray and Jon Wartes, "The Academic Achievement and Affective Development of Home-Schooled Children", in *Home Schooling: Political, Historical, and Pedagogical Perspectives*, edited by Jane Van Galen and Mary Anne Pitman (Norwood, NJ: Ablex Publishing Corporation, 1991), p. 47.

[13] Ibid., pp. 44–52.

[14] Ibid., pp. 47–52.

[15] *Marching to the Beat of Their Own Drum! A Profile of Home Education Research* (Home School Legal Defense Association, 1992), p. 10.

Why Home Education Works: Attention Is the Key

The basic reason tutoring, specifically home tutoring, succeeds when other methods may fail is that the teacher has the time and the focus to discover exactly what a child already understands, what he still needs to learn, and how best to teach it to him. Tutoring is a superior method of teaching because of the one-on-one attention and the ability to vary the pace of learning according to the child's ease or difficulty in mastering a subject.

Because the parent, as tutor, gives her child individual instruction, she has more flexibility to adapt her teaching to her child's academic needs. For example, if her child grasps a new concept easily, then she doesn't need to belabor the point. She can elect to skip over repetitive exercises and move on to the next concept. Similarly, if her child is "stuck" and unable to make progress in the workbook, the mother can put the book aside and play creative games, do oral drills, or use a different resource to help her child move past that plateau.

Parents have the freedom, unlike a classroom teacher, to choose what parts of their curriculum to emphasize in order to balance their child's physical and intellectual readiness. Boys, for example, mature more quickly in their large motor skills than in their fine motor skills. Girls develop their fine motor skills much earlier. While the average first-grade girl may progress equally well in reading and writing, a boy may benefit from focusing just on his reading skills until he is physiologically ready to write. Yet in a school setting, where the curriculum mandates reading and writing at the same pace for all students, a boy may unfairly be marked down for his physiological immaturity.

The individual emphasis of home education also allows the parent to accommodate "delight-directed learning".[16] Delight-directed learning motivates a child by structuring academics around a topic he finds particularly interesting. A girl who loves horses, for example, will be more highly motivated to write a

---

[16] "Delight-directed learning" is a phrase popularized chiefly by Gregg Harris, who conducts seminars on Christian home education for Christian Life Workshops.

report on horses than on spaceships. Marsha Jacobeen, the mother of five sons, discovered that her ten-year-old son's fascination with birds sparked his creativity in many subjects at once. "Home schooling lets me consider my children's interests when planning their studies. One of my sons has a great interest in birds, so I tie that interest into his reading, writing, and science assignments." As a parent, she has the flexibility to respond to her child's natural curiosity and to incorporate his interests into the curriculum.

One-on-one attention also allows the parent to be more demanding of her child than a classroom teacher might be. In learning a foreign language or math facts, for example, the child can't hide the holes in his knowledge behind the other students' answers. He doesn't have the option of ducking his head behind his book so that the teacher will call on someone else in the class when he doesn't know the answer. His teacher will *know* he doesn't know the answer.

In home education, because the parent keeps abreast of whether or not her child understands the material, grades are far less necessary than they are for institutionally educated students. Schools must rely on tests to measure how much a student has learned; grades become the only reliable indicator of understanding. Julia Fogassy of Seattle, Washington, became acutely aware of how little grades reveal when she decided to take her children out of school and teach them at home.

> When they were in school, I imagined I was on top of their progress. When I brought them home, I realized how far out of touch I was. I didn't know what they knew or what they didn't know.

While a parent may choose to grade and record her child's progress (for example, to comply with state requirements, to prepare a transcript for later school admission, or to motivate a child conditioned by school experience to expect a grade as a reward), her real assessment of his progress is based on personal knowledge, not numbers in a grade book.

Obstacles Overcome by Tutoring

One of the earliest advocates of the modern trend toward home education, John Holt, identified three stumbling blocks to real learning—stumbling blocks he felt most institutional education reinforced rather than eliminated. These stumbling blocks, the fear (or dread) of boredom, fear of failure, and fear of misunderstanding,[17] too often become the defining elements of a child's educational experience. They lead to foot-dragging in the morning, chronic lateness, endless refrains of "I hate school", anxiety, academic difficulties, and discipline troubles in the classroom.

The fear of being bored arises when a bright student knows he'll be sitting for hours listening to repetitive explanations of material he grasped from the first. What takes him two minutes of concentration may take the rest of the class a full forty-five-minute period to master. The intelligent child tends either to try to avoid the situation (for example, dragging his heels about leaving the house in the morning and constantly ending up late for school) or to occupy himself with something more interesting when he gets there (doodling, daydreaming, or mischief making), while the teacher tends to the other twenty-five students in the class. One Midwestern twelve-year-old girl, for example, dealt with the "incredible waste of time" she experienced in school by perfecting her ability to read a favorite book balanced on her lap, all the while keeping her textbook opened to the correct page and an ear cocked to the teacher's lesson. "At least I got to read something interesting and I still got A's", she explained. At best, the situation results in a waste of time and a dulled interest in true learning. At worst, it can lead to behavioral problems, academic failure, and genuine unhappiness in the child.

The fear of failure is experienced not only by the child at the bottom of the class but also by the child stuck in the middle. He is not advanced enough to learn things quickly and on his own, yet not behind enough, or so obviously confused, as to attract the

---

[17] See generally: information provided by Holt Associates, 2269 Massachusetts Ave., Cambridge, MA 02140; telephone (617) 864-3100.

individual attention he needs. Test anxiety (and attendant physical symptoms such as headache or stomachache) strikes if the student's perception is that nobody is worried about giving him the time or additional help he needs to understand the material—and he knows he hasn't mastered it yet. The bureaucratic concern, instead, is to complete the requisite pages in the specified time. When most students complete the material with at least C work (which incidentally illustrates something less than real proficiency, otherwise they would all have A's), everybody moves on to the next unit of information. The child's fear of failure intensifies when the class moves on even though his own grasp of the material is very tenuous. The student knows, even if the teacher doesn't, how hard it is to build on a shaky foundation.

The fear of misunderstanding exhibits itself in different ways. For example, a shy child may be afraid to ask questions in front of an entire class and thus worries continually about whether he understands the material. A boy's anxiety may ratchet up when the teacher announces instructions, as he knows she will give them only once. What if he doesn't understand them? His stomach may turn into knots as he tries to figure the instructions out himself, knowing all too well the reaction he will get if he asks to have them repeated.

These three obstacles to true learning—the fear of failure, fear of boredom, and fear of misunderstanding—often cast a shadow over a child's entire educational experience. Yet, this is not at all an inevitable part of education. Tutoring, especially as experienced in home education, minimizes these obstacles and then offers a ready means of eliminating them entirely.

Why Parents Are the Best Tutors

One of the main reasons home education is so successful is that the parents guide the child's education. Having the parent as tutor is not a liability that needs to be diminished nor a drawback that is outweighed by the other benefits of home education. On the contrary, parental commitment, love, and involvement are the crucial ingredients that make home education so successful.

David Guterson, a teacher at a public junior high and the father of three home-taught sons, explains why even the most dedicated teacher cannot educate the way a mother or father can: "They [parents] love their children with a depth I can't match. . . . And finally teaching is an act of love before it is anything else."[18] A parent's love for her child is, quite simply, her best teaching qualification. This love, in turn, provides the foundation for trust and credibility between teacher and pupil, parent and child. It is a relationship that endures without needing to be established anew every September or severed every June.

Parents, from the moment of their child's birth, occupy ringside seats from which to observe their child's learning patterns. Most mothers and fathers find that much of their child's personality was evident right from infancy, and the rest has been unfolding before their eyes ever since.

Especially during the early childhood years, parents have an unparalleled chance to discover their child's temperament, learning style, and initial aptitudes—the keys to that child's future academic success. Every mother who has taught her toddler to use a spoon or her four-year-old to count his blocks as he puts them away in the toy box, and every father who has taught his six-year-old to ride a two-wheeler, knows something about how that child learns and what motivates him. Is he aggressive? Does he like to watch others before trying a new skill himself? Does he learn more quickly by observing or by hearing an explanation first and then watching a demonstration? Is he better at expressing himself verbally or through action and participation? Does he respond to competition or become discouraged by it? Does he like to try things in private first, without anyone watching his efforts, or is he motivated by having an audience? All of these observations are important because they reveal to parents what kind of support, structure, motivation, and approach will help their child learn best.

Every mother who has had a child in school has, at one time or another, thought to herself, "They just don't understand him", or

[18] David Guterson, *Family Matters: Why Homeschooling Makes Sense* (New York: Harcourt, Brace, Jovanovich, 1992), p. 10.

"Her teacher just isn't giving her what she needs", or "If they could just give him a little more attention or encouragement. . . ." The bottom line is this: no one knows your child like you do; no one will give him the love, encouragement, and support that you will; and no teacher has the time (assuming he has the interest) to discover and appreciate all the wonderful things about your child that you already know. After all, you've spent the better part of his first five years teaching him, motivating him, disciplining him, and loving him. It is simply impossible for a teacher to know him well enough to respond to him as you would.

Guterson describes the advantage of having parents undertake the academic education of their children in this way:

> Uninhibited by the inherent inertia of schools—their uniformity of content and pedagogy—and intimately connected to their child's educational needs, home-schooling parents are able to invent and reinvent, learn from error, modulate as their understanding deepens, and finally nurture their child's intellectual growth from the advantageous position of one who loves that child deeply. In short, parents are natural teachers, positioned by the very structure of life to tend to the learning of their children.[19]

Most parents unselfconsciously teach their child everything he needs to know in his first four years without ever giving a second thought to whether they are "qualified" or "certified". Suddenly, when their child turns five, it's different. With academics looming ahead, parents are made to feel that only education "experts" can teach their child, in spite of the fact that the parents have been teaching their child successfully for years, that they know their child better than anyone else, and that they have firsthand knowledge of his temperament and learning style—knowledge that it may take a classroom teacher all year to discern, if she ever does.

Formal classroom-teaching experience is not what makes a parent a good teacher. In fact, some home educators describe their former careers as teachers as a hindrance. Maggie Murray, a former elementary-school teacher who now teaches her four daughters at

[19] Ibid., p. 22.

home, described her years of classroom experience as more of a drawback than a help in teaching her daughters. "You have to unlearn everything you've learned about teaching." Because so much classroom instruction occurs in large groups, following a uniform sequence and curriculum, she found little of it helpful.

Several studies on the backgrounds of home-educating parents affirm that teacher certification, income, and educational background are not decisive factors in the success of home education. One study, for instance, reported "no significant differences" in academic performance between home-educated children with a teaching-certified parent and those without a "certified" teaching parent.[20] Similarly, several studies have shown "no significant relationship"[21] between the educational background of the teaching parent and the achievement of the child. In fact, children whose parents' education stopped at the twelfth grade still score higher than the national average on achievement tests.[22] Finally, family income level seems unrelated to achievement in home-educated children.[23]

All these statistics point out that the best education for a child is ensured, not by the teacher's advanced degrees, the money available to spend on curriculum, or even the number of hours spent in formal, structured learning. Rather, success depends on the teacher's awareness of the child's real needs, talents, and deficits and on the teacher's own commitment, attention, encouragement, and love—all of which are more easily found in a parent than in a classroom teacher.

Home Education Provides a Personalized Curriculum

Although later chapters in this book cover in greater depth the question of how a parent knows what to teach, it is important to consider here why choosing an individual curriculum makes such

[20] Ray and Wartes, p. 47.
[21] Ibid., pp. 46–47. See also: *Marching to the Beat of Their Own Drum!*, p. 10.
[22] Ray and Wartes, p. 46.
[23] Ibid.

good sense. Home-educating parents provide their children with a significant advantage that even the best private school would be hard-pressed to duplicate: a personalized curriculum. The parent usually teaches from a curriculum chosen or fashioned to suit a particular child's intellectual level and interests, learning pace and learning style, and the parents' vision of a complete, integrated education. As tutors, the parents provide their child with an individually tailored program designed to answer the questions, "What does he already know?" and "What should he learn next?"

Parents may choose materials from various grade levels in order to accommodate their child's real educational level. For example, an eight-year-old might have math skills commensurate with a third grader, reading comprehension skills of a fourth grader, spelling skills of a second grader, etc. In a school situation, it would be impossible for a teacher to customize the curriculum, in each subject, to the varying levels of each one of her students. The home educator, in contrast, consciously chooses curricula with her student in mind.

An individually tailored program keeps the excitement and enthusiasm in learning and eliminates the boredom inevitable in sitting through repetitive explanations of materials already mastered. In contrast, the classroom teacher usually does not get to choose the curriculum from which she must teach. Nor does the schoolteacher have the flexibility to drop the curriculum or substitute a text if the one chosen by the school board is not working for a particular child. Unlike a parent, the teacher can't begin anew with one that works.

Finally, a personalized curriculum gives the parent the opportunity to choose materials that conform to the child's learning style. For example, an auditory learner (one who learns most easily by *hearing* the material to be taught) could use audiotapes extensively in her subjects so as to retain the facts better. A tactile learner might benefit from a hands-on approach to science or math, relying heavily on manipulatives to reinforce the concepts studied in the texts. The ideal curriculum offers a combination of hands-on, visual, and auditory instruction, but with the balance tilted toward the most effective method for each particular child.

Yes, Home Education *Is* Good Education

Home education gives families an incredible opportunity to offer their children the best academic education. The tutoring that is at the core of home education provides the best education for our children. The chief reasons home education is so successful can be summarized as follows:

1. Tutoring is the most effective teaching method. One-on-one instruction, especially by a teacher (parent) who knows the child intimately, promotes real understanding of the subjects studied and at a pace suited to the child.

2. Personalized curriculum challenges the child at the right level. Parents choose the curriculum that best suits their child's intellectual abilities, learning style, and interests. Parents can adapt the curriculum as they recognize new needs or goals. Boredom, discouragement, and fear of failure are greatly reduced or eliminated. Parents retain flexibility to decide what their children will study at a particular age (e.g., Latin for third grade, astronomy for fifth grade, logic for eighth grade). The possibilities are limitless.

3. Home education ensures greater thoroughness and depth of learning. Because understanding is the goal, and the child's needs set the pace, children really learn what they are taught (e.g., in a parent–child dialogue about a story the child has read aloud, the discussion time is limited only by the topic being explored, not by a bell at the end of a forty-five minute class period). The child avoids learning gaps that inevitably occur when he misses something and the teacher moves on to the next topic.

4. Home education exposes children to a greater breadth of education by providing variety and flexibility in the choice of subjects to be studied as well as field trips and in-depth projects. Budget cuts, liability concerns, and the diminishing availability of

parents to accompany classes on field trips have resulted, all across the country, in drastic cutbacks in or elimination of school field trips. For example, Fairfax County, Virginia (one of the top five school districts in the country and one of the wealthiest counties in the country), provides one field trip a semester for elementary students. In contrast, one local Catholic home-education support group in the same county averages one field trip a month plus a variety of speakers.

5. Tutoring allows better use of the child's time. Time wasted in the classroom is greatly reduced (no lines to stand in for water or bathroom breaks, and the parent—even in a large family—has far fewer children who need her attention). A child still has a real need to play that is ignored in the hours spent in traditional institutional education. Because tutoring accomplishes learning more efficiently and effectively, the child has a greater amount of time to "be" a child and enjoy childish pastimes at an unhurried pace.

6. Tutoring avoids the unwanted "extras" provided in public education. Parents retain control of the child's sex education and avoid the unwelcome aspects of drug, death, sex, and AIDS education imposed by the public schools.

7. Tutoring gives much more than a private-school education but at a fraction of the cost. Home education exceeds many of the benefits of private education (lowest student–teacher ratio, personalized curriculum, high test scores) and provides them less expensively. Unlike public education, there is some expense (curriculum, books, possibly advisory services, testing), but it typically doesn't exceed four hundred dollars per child each year and is often much lower.

3

At Home with Catholic Education

Is Home Education Catholic *Education?*

As a convert (from Protestantism) who began home schooling a kindergartner and was received into the Church nearly simultaneously, I was and continue to be surprised by the volume of Church teachings and traditions that we must know and transmit to our children. The teachings about the sacraments and vocation of marriage state that parents are the primary educators of their children. What a responsibility and great joy to be learning about the fullness of the Faith alongside my children and to know that the Holy Father and the Church approve of and encourage our choice of education for our children. It's also reassuring to have the grace of the sacraments to enable us to fulfill this duty!

— Marilyn Grodi, home-educating mother of three

Now that we're home schooling, we actually have time to do Christian formation that just didn't fit in the schedule before. Every day we go to Mass as a family, because now we're free to choose *our* priorities in educating our children.

— Cathy Cutler, first-year home educator

I did not want to send my children away from me at such a young age. I knew that I wanted to be the primary influence giving them roots in their Catholic Faith. Home schooling has provided the opportunity for each of us to grow in understanding the history of our Faith, the heroes, the customs.

— Brenna Heffernan,
schoolteacher turned home educator

[We] receive great spiritual direction that is just as applicable to the practical sides of home schooling as it is to the spiritual life. After all, we want to sanctify our daily work. What a great gift it is for us to raise, teach, and form the consciences of our children as our number-one daily task.

— Curtis and Michaelann Martin,
home educators of four

Catholic education in the United States today is receiving mixed reviews. Some Catholic schools provide an excellent Catholic education, faithful to the Church and to the parents who have entrusted children to their care. Other Catholic schools, however, have lost sight of their mission either by becoming so watered down in the Faith that they are simply nice private schools or, worse, by permitting teachers to undermine the Church's teaching in many areas. Their pupils question the Church and distance themselves from their parents, who have not been educated "critically".

Some CCD programs try to make up for the lack in the Catholic education of their youths who attend public schools by giving them at least a basic foundation in Catholicism. But there are CCD programs that are overly concerned with being "relevant" and fun for the children. The little doctrine they do impart, moreover, can be enough to inoculate the children from ever being serious Catholics.

Parish schools and CCD programs need the support of our prayers, wisdom, and finances, where appropriate. The question remains, however, whether or not we as Catholics are obligated to support them by sending them our children. Many people assume they must do so because it is their tradition, regardless of whether or not the education now being provided is truly Catholic.

Perhaps they have too narrow a definition of Catholic education. Real Catholic education encompasses more than classes taught by priests and nuns. It is much more than education taking place in our particular Catholic parish.

What Is Catholic Education?

What makes education Catholic or not is its foundation in the fullness of the Catholic Faith and the degree to which the Faith is integrated into the education of the whole person: mind, heart, and soul. Catholic education forms our children as fully integrated human beings with a loving relationship to God and a desire to serve Him faithfully in whatever way He asks. In his "Letter to Families", Pope John Paul II states, "The 'heart' of our redemption is the starting point of every process of Christian education, which is likewise always an education to a full humanity."[1]

According to the Vatican II document *Declaration on Christian Education*, all of us have a right to "true education". "True education is directed towards the formation of the human person in view of his final end and the good of that society to which he belongs and in the duties of which he will, as an adult, have a share."[2]

Teachers involved in Christian education are obliged to

> ensure that young people are never deprived of this sacred right
> . . . the right to be stimulated to make sound moral judgements
> based on a well-formed conscience and to put them into practice
> with a sense of personal commitment, and to know and love God
> more perfectly.[3]

As important as academic training is to the development of our children's minds, even more important is spiritual and moral training for the development of our children's souls and character.

St. John Chrysostom, Patriarch of Constantinople from 398 to 404 A.D., reminded parents of their Christian duty in the total education of their children in his homily on Ephesians 6:1–4:

> Do you want your child to be obedient? Then from the beginning
> bring him up in the discipline and instruction of the Lord. Don't
> think that it isn't necessary for a child to listen to the scriptures;
> don't say, "Bible-reading is for monks; am I turning my child into

---

[1] Pope John Paul II, "Letter to Families", no. 16.
[2] *Declaration on Christian Education* (*Gravissimum Educationis*), no. 1.
[3] Ibid.

a monk?" No, it isn't necessary for him to be a monk. Make him into a Christian! Why are you afraid of something so good? . . .

We are so concerned with our children's schooling; if only we were equally zealous in bringing them up in the discipline and instruction of the Lord! (And then we wonder why we reap such bitter fruit when we have raised our children to be insolent, licentious, impious, and vulgar.) Let us heed the blessed Paul's admonition to bring them up in the discipline and instruction of the Lord. Let us give them a pattern to imitate; from their earliest years let us teach them to study the Bible. . . .

Don't surround them with the external safeguards of wealth and fame, for when these fail—and they will fail—our children will stand naked and defenseless, having gained no profit from their former prosperity, but only injury, since when these artificial protections that shielded them from the winds are removed, they will be blown to the ground in a moment. Therefore wealth is a hindrance, because it leaves us unprepared for the hardships of life.

So, let us raise our children in such a way that they can face any trouble, and not be surprised when difficulties come: let us bring them up in the discipline and instruction of the Lord.[4]

For the wellbeing of our children's souls as well as their minds, let's carefully consider the choices we have for their education. For we are the ones God will hold accountable, first and foremost, for the training they receive.

Choices in Education for Catholics

In his "Letter to Families", Pope John Paul II echoes the *Declaration on Christian Education* in two important teachings: the role of parents in education is primary, and the role of the Church and state in education is secondary and subsidiary. In this section, we will take a brief look at these roles and their implications in choosing a Catholic education for our children.

[4] St. John Chrysostom's homily on Ephesians 6:1–4, "On Marriage and Family", trans. by Catharine P. Roth and David Anderson (St. Vladimir's Seminary Press, 575 Scarsdale Rd., Crestwood, NY 10707).

Parents as Primary Educators

From the moment we held our first newborn until the present day, we have been teaching our children about everything we know, from God and family relationships to colors and numbers. Many of us realize we play a part in our children's Catholic education, but we may not realize that we are primarily responsible to provide generously for it.

Whether or not we delegate the task of formal intellectual training to others, we are still the ones who will answer personally to God for the education of our children.

> It is therefore the duty of parents to create a family atmosphere inspired by love and devotion to God and their fellow men which will promote an integrated, personal and social education for their children.[5]

The atmosphere of love for God and each other in our homes is a vital part of educating our children.

Canon 1136 in the 1983 *Code of Canon Law* states, "Parents have a most grave duty and enjoy the primary right of educating to the very best of their ability their children physically, socially, and culturally, and morally and religiously as well." A brief commentary on this passage by Edward N. Peters clarifies that "the Church in no way intended to deprive of their natural, vocational, and canonical right those parents who elect to educate their children at home. . . . Canon 798, indeed the whole canonical treatment of education, is concerned *not* that parents send their children to Catholic *schools*, but that parents see to the *Catholic* schooling of their children" (emphasis in the original).[6]

In partial fulfillment of our duty as parents, we have the right and responsibility to be involved in choosing where our children are educated. "Parents, who have a primary and inalienable duty and right in regard to the education of their children, should enjoy the

[5] *Declaration on Christian Education*, no. 3.

[6] Edward N. Peters, *Home Schooling and the New Code of Canon Law* (Front Royal, VA: Christendom Press, 1988), pp. 45–46.

fullest liberty in their choice of school."[7] We believe this freedom of choice includes, among other choices, home education.

The Church and the State as Secondary Education Providers

For most of our country's history, tutoring or home education was the norm. According to historian Dominic Aquila,

> Education before the mid-nineteenth century was unsystematic and informal, and deeply enmeshed in the world of adults. Apprenticeship was a common means of education; reading, writing, and the general transmission of culture from one generation to the next were the responsibilities of families, church, and the community.[8]

Education was understood by Americans in the broadest sense of how we learn, encompassing all of life.

In contrast to Europeans, attendance at formal schools for Americans was not yet mandatory. Did this mean education was unimportant to Americans? On the contrary, Americans placed a very high value on education. They simply believed that it was shortsighted and narrow-minded to reduce education to institutional schools. In fact, many were concerned that centralizing education would produce impoverished education.

Largely due to the influence of Horace Mann, the public, or common, school system became mandatory in Massachusetts in 1852, amid strong criticism from Roman Catholics, among others. Says Aquila, "Gradually other states followed Massachusetts' example so that by the end of the Civil War, education in America had become restricted to specialized institutions (schools) which were segregated from the mainstream of adult life."[9]

In the common schools promoted by Mann, virtue, rather than religious truth, was taught. Mann consciously allowed religion,

---

[7] *Declaration on Christian Education*, no. 6.

[8] Interview with Dominic Aquila, Professor of History, Franciscan University of Steubenville, Steubenville, OH, March 1995.

[9] Ibid.

limited to a watered-down nondenominational set of common beliefs, to the extent that it served as a handmaid for politics. "For Mann, schools were above all else necessary for the development of those virtues that sustained republican government." [10] At the time, Catholics and some groups of Protestants objected to the division of religious and moral education.

Catholics wanted *more*, not less, in the way of religious and moral education.

> In the 1840s Bishop John Hughes of New York City led Catholics in a political counter-offensive against the Protestant state school monopoly from which emerged a separate Catholic school system wherein children took instruction in the Catholic Faith intermingled with their education in arts and letters, and the sciences. [11]

Thus the rise of Catholic schools came about, in large part, as a defensive maneuver against a public educational system founded on humanistic moralism with an anti-Catholic bias.

Whether the Church or the state provides education for children, the institution must understand its fundamental responsibility to serve the parents. Repeatedly in his "Letter to Families", Pope John Paul II calls on both the Church and the state to support parents and to cooperate with them in their child's education. Parents may

> share their educational mission with other individuals or institutions, such as the Church and the state. But the mission of education must always be carried out in accordance with a proper application of the principle of subsidiarity. This implies the legitimacy and indeed the need of giving assistance to the parents, but finds its intrinsic and absolute limit in their prevailing right and their actual capabilities. The principle of subsidiarity is thus at the service of parental love, meeting the good of the family unit. . . . Subsidiarity thus complements paternal and maternal love, and confirms its fundamental nature, inasmuch as all other participants in the process of education are only able to carry out

[10] Ibid.
[11] Ibid.

their responsibilities in the name of the parents, with their consent and, to a certain degree, with their authorization.[12]

We need to understand this principle of subsidiarity in order to see the genuine freedom we have to educate our children.

Simply stated, the principle of subsidiarity means, first, that whatever we as parents can do for our children, we should do. Next, the Church and the state are involved in education to the extent that we delegate that responsibility to them.

> Whenever the family is self-sufficient, it should be left to act on its own; an excessive intrusiveness on the part of the state would prove detrimental, to say nothing of lacking due respect, and would constitute an open violation of the rights of the family.[13]

This is the principle of subsidiarity applied to education.

Public or Private Secular Schools

Is it possible to send our children to public or private secular schools?

> In accordance with the principle of subsidiarity, when the efforts of the parents and of other organizations [the local Catholic schools] are inadequate it [the state] should itself undertake the duty of education, with due consideration, however, for the wishes of the parents.[14]

In other words, public schools are an option in the event Catholic schools, at home or in the parish, are found wanting. However, the public schools must not teach values contrary to the values of the Church. Is this the case today?

Sometimes public education seems like the best option for families because of finances or proximity to their home, yet these families share concerns about the morality of what is taught. Nevertheless, they say they would rather tell their children not to

[12] Pope John Paul II, "Letter to Families", no. 16.
[13] Ibid., no. 17.
[14] Declaration on Christian Education, no. 3.

believe the values they hear at school that contradict what they are taught at home than send their children to a supposedly Catholic school where they may not recognize how their faith is being undermined.

But is it a good option to risk a child's exposure to the harm of false moral teaching received in a public school, particularly when a young child may not discern harmful values when they are taught?

Some people respond by saying that information is neutral—facts are facts, they aren't moral or immoral. Science is science, history is history, and math is math. Besides, the children get plenty of teaching about morality at home, so why can't they pick up the intellectual training at a secular school?

We must examine our choices carefully before we delegate to others our responsibility to teach our children. As good parents, we take care of the physical needs of our children and would never offer them a real choice between food and poison. Their bodies will die, but their souls will live forever. Will we take as great a care that they are not offered poison for their souls?

First, what some teachers believe children should know may or may not be true. For example, one science teacher taught the theory of evolution as if it were a fact, without a mention of the creationist theory of the universe's origin. One child asked him why abortion was wrong, then, if people were merely animals descended from the apes. The teacher said that was a good point —precisely because we are just animals, there is nothing more wrong about abortion than about getting rid of unwanted baby animals, especially in the face of "overpopulation" or severe deformities.

Often history in the public-school classroom is skewed in such a way that the students are not told of the significant contributions made by Christians through the ages. The perspective of good and evil is missing, because there is no objective basis for analysis. In fact, there is such a serious drive by the politically correct crowd to marginalize or eliminate the influence Christians had in the founding of our country that even professors at secular universities have decried the current history textbooks' inaccuracies.[15]

In contrast to Catholic school classrooms, God has, for all intents and purposes, been banished from the public-school classroom. Some public-school teachers go so far as to teach principles contrary to the Christian Faith on a regular basis, challenging the basic presuppositions their students have been learning at home.

There are even those in the public educational system who are pursuing an agenda—through Outcome-Based Education, for instance—that runs roughshod over the concerns of parents. (For an explanation of Outcome-Based Education, see Appendix A.) This represents a major shift in educational philosophy. Instead of learning objective material that can be taught and tested, the students work in groups and advance as a group by fulfilling subjective criteria for promotion based on psychological and social objectives.

Second, information given in an indiscriminate way, without regard for the maturity of the children, can be very detrimental. Moral errors *are* spread. Under the guise of a frank discussion of "facts" in the public-school classroom, moral teachings the children receive at home are contradicted. Issues such as contraception, abortion, homosexuality, and euthanasia are addressed with the expectation that students should separate the "facts" about these issues from the "opinions" they may have about right and wrong. Liberal environmentalism is presented as if man were the animal who is out of control. And relativism (which dogmatically opposes the concept of dogma) is pervasive as the basis for analysis. We can readily see the consequences of supposedly value-free public education when vital issues are discussed as if there were no objective moral standard by which to judge them.

Third, there is the danger that education apart from faith will lead children to think that faith is not very important. One of the most problematic aspects of public education is that for six or seven

---

[15] Paul Vitz, *Censorship: Evidence of Bias in Our Children's Textbooks* (Ann Arbor, MI: Servant Books, 1986).

hours of the day, the Faith, indeed, even the acknowledgement of Jesus' redemption and love, is banished, ignored, truncated from the students' lives—as if the context for their entire lives were irrelevant.

Though many Christian instructors who teach in the public-school systems would prefer to include their faith in their instruction, they have been gagged by fears of lawsuits or job loss. Unwittingly, they teach the children that their faith is "opinion", while they are studying "fact" in school. The idea that God is not welcome in the classroom but allowed at home indicates to the child that when he is studying "real" things—the physical realm that God created for His glory and of which man is the highest creature—the Creator does not fit in.

Artificially cutting Jesus out of the day sends our children the wrong message. Its effect may go unnoticed in the short run, but it's real. This subtle message teaches children to compartmentalize their faith, making a sharp distinction between their family's faith and what teachers at school label "truth". Value-neutral education does not exist, however. The only question is on whose values will the studies presented be based: the Christian parents' or secular society's?

Remember St. Paul's caution that " 'Knowledge' puffs up; but love builds up" (1 Cor 8:1). This is one of the reasons Solomon repeatedly writes "The fear of the Lord is the beginning of knowledge" (Prov 1:7). According to the Sacred Congregation for Catholic Education document entitled *Catholic Schools*, "Reference to Jesus Christ teaches man to differentiate between the values which ennoble man and those which degrade him." [16]

Though some families acknowledge there are difficulties, they hope their parish CCD classes can provide the necessary balance to the secular approach of the school. Is this realistic? Can a CCD class adequately counter the attack on faith and family values that may be occurring at the local public school? Unfortunately, one hour per week in most CCD programs cannot accomplish the task

[16] Sacred Congregation for Catholic Education, *Catholic Schools* (*Malgré les declarations*), June 24, 1977, no. 11.

of fortifying a student for the challenges he faces day in and day out in a public school.

Parochial and Private Catholic Schools

Whenever possible, it is our duty to provide a Catholic education through a Catholic school[17]—our Catholic home school, a private Catholic school, or a local parish school. If we opt to send our children out of the home to a Catholic school, we must know the school is faithful to the mission given the school by the Church: specifically, the Catholic school "so orients the whole of human culture to the message of salvation that the knowledge which the pupils acquire of the world, of life and of men is illumined by faith."[18]

> The Catholic school should teach its pupils to discern in the sound of the universe the Creator whom it reveals, and, in the achievements of science, to know God and man better. In the daily life of the school, the pupil should learn that he is called to be a living witness to God's love for men by the way he acts, and that he is part of that salvation history which has Christ, the saviour of the world, as its goal.[19]

This is the mission of Catholic schools.

Yet many Catholics today say they spent between eight to twelve years in Catholic education and did not learn the Faith. Many people have even left the Church, after years of "Catholic" education, without really understanding the Faith the Church teaches. Parents are dumbfounded to discover, after sacrificing greatly to provide a Catholic education for their children, that their children now reject the Church's authority in their lives, intending to live life however it best suits them.

In fact, many people recount horror stories about the "faith" their children have learned at Catholic schools. They anticipate

[17] *Declaration on Christian Education*, no. 8.
[18] Ibid.
[19] *Catholic Schools*, no. 46.

their children will be taught the Faith and are not aware that particular teachers are undermining the Faith on a daily basis.

How can this happen?

First, some families teach their children the Faith as best they can and assume their children are receiving an education supportive of the Faith, just as they had decades ago—and those teaching in the school are not telling the parents differently. One mother thought she was making the right choice when she sent her daughter to her parish school.

> My oldest daughter spent six years in a diocesan Catholic school until it finally dawned on me she was not receiving a Catholic education. To receive a Catholic education, I had to leave a Catholic school.

Unfortunately, this is not an isolated case.

Second, some families are not taking responsibility for training their own children in the Faith. They are relying on the Catholic school to do the job for them.

> Certainly one area in which the family has an irreplaceable role is that of religious education, which enables the family to grow as a 'domestic church'. Religious education and the catechesis of children make the family a true subject of evangelization and the apostolate within the Church. We are speaking of a right intrinsically linked to the principle of religious liberty. Families, and more specifically parents, are free to choose for their children a particular kind of religious and moral education consonant with their own convictions. Even when they entrust these responsibilities to ecclesiastical institutions or to schools administered by religious personnel, their educational presence ought to continue to be constant and active.[20]

Though the school is to be a support to the families, it is the parents, not the school, who are primarily responsible for the religious education of the children. Delegating the responsibility is not the same as abnegating the duty.

[20] "Letter to Families", no. 16.

Third, many Catholic schools are not being faithful to the mission the Church has given them:

> Mindful of the fact that man has been redeemed by Christ, the Catholic school aims at forming in the Christian those particular virtues which will enable him to live a new life in Christ and help him to play faithfully his part in building up the kingdom of God.[21]

This document of the Sacred Congregation for Catholic Education goes on to say that the Faith must "be imparted explicitly and in a systematic manner to prevent a distortion in the child's mind between general and religious culture".[22]

A vital part of the Catholic education of our children is academic training from an authentically Catholic perspective. Some Catholic schools, however, have substituted time-bound, current ideologies for timeless Catholic values. They have wanted to appear "relevant for today". In so doing they have relativized the Faith, watering it down at best or diluting it with poison at worst.

Some teachers in Catholic schools, in the course of their education, have had their own faith gutted; but they have been trained to be teachers. So what are they to do? Admit they no longer believe the Catholic Faith and start over vocationally? Or continue to teach in a Catholic school anyway, "enlightening" the children with values clarification, amoral sex education, one-sided historical–critical approaches to Sacred Scripture and a laissez–faire attitude toward the Church's teaching on any issue the child wants to challenge?

Before we entrust our children to a Catholic school, we must know how faithful it is to the Church's teachings. Some Catholic schools are shamefully pretending to be something they truly have no intention of being. In fact, it can be dangerous to send our children to Catholic schools that do not accurately represent the Faith—it can subject them to the risk of rejecting a Faith they were never given a real chance to know.

Understandably, many Catholics do not want to abandon the parochial school system; at the same time, however, they are deeply

[21] *Catholic Schools*, no. 36.
[22] Ibid., no. 50.

concerned with the impact a particular school is having on their children. Parents who elect to home educate are exercising their right to choose the best education for their children. Vatican II's *Declaration on Religious Liberty* states, "The civil authority must therefore recognize the right of parents to choose with genuine freedom schools or other means of education."[23]

Is it necessary for Catholic parents to send their children to Catholic schools in order to support parochial education for those children who cannot be taught at home? No! On the one hand, we do not want to spoil Catholic education for others, nor, on the other hand, do we need to feel compelled to send our children to those institutions. (For some practical suggestions about how we can be involved in local Catholic schools as a support without sending our children, please see Chapter 14.)

The question is not whether we will undertake the responsibility for our children's Catholic education, but how. Twenty-five years ago Catholic parents sacrificed greatly (often acquiring a second job) to be able to pay for their children to attend a parochial school. Is it possible that today the sacrifice that Catholic parents are being called upon to make is not only financial but also a personal commitment of time in home education?

Catholic Home Education

Home education is one way to educate our children within the Church and for the Church, with proper care given to spiritual, moral, and intellectual development. Our homes can be a rich environment in which children learn about the nature of the Church as God's Family in the context of their own family!

God reveals Himself as Father, Son, and Holy Spirit—a community of persons constituting the foundational Family of which we are a part. God made man, male and female, in His image. Then He called them into the family relation of marriage to be "fruitful and multiply"—to reflect His image by becoming a family.

---

[23] Vatican II, *Declaration on Religious Liberty* (*Dignitatis Humanae*), no. 5.

When Adam and Eve sinned, they lost the grace of sonship. The sonship lost in Eden because of sin has been restored in Christ through His faithful Sonship. Through Him we are reestablished as sons and daughters of God. This makes us brothers and sisters in God's Family.

The Catholic Faith helps us to see this family blueprint for the Church throughout the structure of the Church: we acknowledge our Holy Father as the visible head of the Church on earth; we look to Mary as our Mother; we see the saints in heaven as our older brothers and sisters; and we even refer to nuns, monks, and priests as sisters, brothers, and fathers. This is not just a quaint way to refer to each other. This is an expression of the very nature of the Church as the Family of God!

The Church carries out her educational mission through families. In the sacrament of Matrimony God calls us to the wonderful role of having children and educating them. When we stand before the priest and witnesses, we pledge to the Lord and each other that we will be open to the gift of life. This includes our commitment to the education of each child.

> The fruitfulness of conjugal love extends to the fruits of the moral, spiritual, and supernatural life that parents hand on to their children by education. Parents are the principal and first educators of their children. In this sense the fundamental task of marriage and family is to be at the service of life.[24]

It is the grace of the sacrament of Matrimony that will strengthen us in Christ to do what we cannot do on our own.

We vow in front of witnesses who represent the Church—the priest and the people—precisely because of our need for their love, prayers, and support, to be faithful to the task of building a godly family.

> If it is true that by giving life parents share in God's creative work, it is also true that by raising their children they become sharers in his paternal and at the same time maternal way of teaching. . . .

---

[24] *Catechism of the Catholic Church*, no. 1653.

The Church wishes to carry out her educational mission above all through families who are made capable of undertaking this task by the sacrament of matrimony, through the "grace of state" which follows from it and the specific "charism" proper to the entire family community.[25]

What a glorious task!

What better context can there be for us to live the reality of the Church as the Family of God than the natural context of family life? The authority we have as parents, exercised prudently, prepares our children to love, respect, and obey God as Father, to follow the Pope as our Holy Father, and to listen to the local bishop and priests as fathers. When we guide our children's sibling relationships to be caring, supportive, and helpful, we teach them how to care, support, and help others in the Body of Christ who have become real brothers and sisters through the flesh and blood of Jesus Christ.

Family life offers us the opportunity for the intellectual, moral, and spiritual development of our children in preparation for their life of service to God in the larger Family of God. This complete education of the child *is* the mission of Catholic education. For us to take advantage of the opportunity, though, we must be committed to our own intellectual and spiritual formation—we can't give what we don't have.

Fr. John Hardon, a noted theologian, urges parents to consider carefully whether or not we should educate our children at home.

In today's increasingly de-Christianized America, secularized American culture, and paganized American society, parents, I repeat, you've got no option. You must under God, and with His light and strength, become the principal teachers of your children. Of course, this presumes that you parents know your Catholic Faith. It is not only that you are to teach your children as the academic world understands teaching, because Catholic education is no mere teaching of academic subjects. Teaching of the Catholic Faith is communicating Divine Grace from mind to mind, from

[25] "Letter to Families", no. 16.

believing mind to believing mind, from believing will to believing will. You parents are no mere teachers when you teach the Catholic Faith. You are the conduits of Divine Grace; no less, indeed more, than you were conduits of human life to the children whom you conceived and gave birth to.[26]

We teach our children more effectively when we develop our interior life with God, learn the Faith better through ongoing scriptural and catechetical instruction, and grow in virtue.

It is one thing for us to know about God and quite another to know Him. Our Faith is not reducible to a system of dogmas. Rather, our Faith centers on the Persons of the Trinity and their love for us as sons and daughters. It is in these relationships that we best understand the dogmas as gracious gifts from our heavenly Father and our Mother the Church. Through the sacraments, Sacred Scripture, and Sacred Tradition, we are called to respond to God's grace, both individually and in the larger Family of God.

Sometimes education with a religious bent can appear to elevate the spiritual realm over the material to the extent that academic training is hindered. The goal of Catholic education is not to focus on the spiritual realm to the neglect of the physical world around us, nor is it to focus on the practical skills needed to "make it in this world" to the exclusion of the spiritual. Good Catholic education blends education for the intellect and the soul so that neither is neglected.

Likewise, good Catholic home education offers a balanced approach of training the soul and body, strengthening the will, and challenging the intellect in submission to the Will of God and to the praise of His glory. This involves learning the Faith, living the Faith, and applying the Faith to all areas of life, including academic studies. This well-rounded education of the heart, mind, and soul of each child will enable your child to become a self-directed, lifelong learner of Truth.

[26] Fr. John Hardon's talk, "Home Schooling, the Soul of Catholic Education", delivered at the NACHE Catholic Homeschooling Convention in Manassas, VA, on June 13, 1992.

Yes, Catholics Home Educate

1. Catholic education forms our children as fully integrated human beings with a loving relationship to God and a desire to serve Him faithfully in whatever way He asks.

2. Parents are the primary educators of their children.

3. Applying the principle of subsidiarity, the Church and the state are secondary providers of education. As such, they serve the family.

4. Parents have a right to choose where their children are educated—at home or in a school.

5. When parents delegate the education of their children to schools—whether public or private, secular or Catholic—they retain primary responsibility for the true education of their children.

6. Catholic home education is a natural context whereby we educate our children within the Church and for the Church with proper care given to their spiritual, moral, and intellectual development.

4

Back to the Blackboard

Basic Goals of Catholic Home Education

Our chief desire for our children is to see them form a deep personal relationship with God that will lead them, ultimately, to eternal happiness. In addition, we want them to be effective apostles, to acquire the best intellectual training in their respective fields, to lead rich family lives (or lives of dedicated celibacy), and to support themselves while contributing to society. How is it possible to work toward achieving these goals?

The basic areas of an integrated Catholic education include the following intellectual and moral challenges: learning the Faith—knowledge about and love of God; living the Faith—character formation; and applying the Faith—academic training, not as a means to religious ends alone but to full intellectual development as a person, and training in life skills. Let's look briefly at each of these areas. (For a more detailed examination of each basic area, including a number of illustrations, see Part 4, below.)

Learning the Faith—Loving and Knowing God

One of the most important passages of Scripture for the Jews—so important that they put it on their doorposts as a daily reminder (and still do today)—was Deuteronomy 6:4–7:

> Hear, O Israel, the Lord our God is one Lord. And you shall love the Lord your God with all your heart, and with all your soul, and with all your might. And these words which I command you this day shall be upon your heart; and you shall teach them diligently to

your children and shall talk of them when you sit in your house, and when you walk by the way, and when you lie down, and when you rise.

This passage speaks of our primary task as parents: to teach our children to love God with everything in their being.

Notice *when* we are to teach our children about loving the Lord: "when you walk by the way, and when you sit in your house, and when you lie down and when you rise"; in other words, throughout the day. Teachable moments come during both structured and unstructured time. Home education enables us to have enough quality time with our children so we can instruct them about the Lord throughout the day, during their best hours.

And *how* are we to teach them to love God so completely? Diligently. In other words, this is a full-time job. We do not see our Catholic Faith as the cherry on the top of our character cake, making us feel good that we have religion in our lives. Rather, our Faith is at the core of who we are, why we are on earth and where we are destined to be—heaven.

What are we to teach our children? Jesus answered with this passage from Deuteronomy when he was asked for a summary of the law: "And he said to him, 'You shall love the Lord your God with all your heart, and with all your soul, and with all your mind'" (Mt 22:27). Jesus herein interprets "strength" in Deuteronomy 6:5 as primarily "mind". This verse not only summarizes the law but helps us see the fullness of our educational efforts with our children: knowing God with our hearts, loving God with our souls, and serving God with our minds and strength.

In order for us to love God, we must know Him and learn how to please Him. Both Sacred Scripture and Sacred Tradition reveal how best to love and serve Him.

Jesus declared, "And I tell you, you are Peter, and on this rock I will build my church, and the powers of death shall not prevail against it" (Mt 16:18). Jesus has built (and is building) His Church by the Holy Spirit in two ways: the Spirit inspired the apostles to write Sacred Scripture (1 Tim 3:16–17) and, through the Church, to select what texts constitute the canon; and the Spirit preserves the Deposit of Faith by leading the Church in her interpretation of Sacred Scripture through Sacred Tradition (2 Pet 1:20–21) and the Magisterium.

Sacred Scripture

Both Sacred Scripture and Sacred Tradition are vital to our intellectual grasp of the Faith; however, religion classes in Catholic schools may rarely refer to Sacred Scripture. Though there are a number of classes taught under the title "Religion" that legitimately would not have the Bible as a central text (such as Church history or liturgical music, to name a couple), most religion courses in Catholic schools are sadly lacking in their treatment of Sacred Scripture. One mother recounts this story:

> When I attended public school I expressed my jealousy over religion classes offered at the Catholic school nearby to my friend who attended that school. I said, "I can't believe you get to study the Bible every day and you even get class credit for it!"
>
> "Oh, no", she quickly corrected me. "We don't study the Bible. I've never studied the Bible in six years of religion class. We study religion."

This lack has contributed to the number of children who have completed years of Catholic education without having much experience with or knowledge of the Bible. This is not as it should be.

As is clear in the various documents from Church councils throughout history, the Church does more than give us the Word of God. She submits herself to it and expounds it as the basis of the Faith. Our beloved Church gives us a steady diet of the written Word of God in the Liturgy of the Word at every Mass as food for our souls. She calls us to read Sacred Scripture regularly, not only in Mass as a community, but as individuals. She even offers indulgences when we read Sacred Writ a few minutes daily! She urges us through the words of St. Jerome to remember that "Ignorance of Scripture is ignorance of Christ."

Unlike any other book that describes Catholic doctrine, the

Bible gives us the very words of God. "For the Word of God is living and active, sharper than any two-edged sword, piercing to the division of soul and spirit, of joints and marrow, and discerning the thoughts and intentions of the heart" (Heb 4:12). For that reason, the Holy Father urges us "to draw attention to the fact that catechesis must be impregnated and penetrated by the thought, the spirit and the outlook of the Bible and the Gospels through assiduous contact with the texts themselves."[1]

We need to study the Bible to be faithful to God: "Do your best to present yourself to God as one approved, a workman who has no need to be ashamed, rightly handling the Word of truth" (2 Tim 2:15). Not only do we need to know the Bible to know Christ, but so do our children.

It's not enough to know a priest who can answer our children's questions about the Faith from the Bible. St. Peter commands us, "Always be prepared to make a defense to any one who calls you to account for the hope that is in you, yet do it with gentleness and reverence" (1 Pet 3:15). This includes answering questions our children ask, even if we have to search for answers. If we will not take time to answer their questions, our children may wonder whether or not belief is worth the effort.

Sometimes we are so concerned that we might be led into heresy by reading the Bible on our own that we neglect to read it at all, keeping it like a family heirloom on the coffee table. But the warning of Mother Church is to read it correctly, not to ignore it. Remember: our Lord is not looking for servile faith that simply parrots a priest's thoughts (which may or may not be faithful to the Church). Rather, He is looking for sons and daughters who so value His word that they read it, study it, and know it.

Sacred Tradition

God has not given us His Word and then abandoned us to interpret it as we will. He has graciously given us His Holy Spirit, who

[1] Pope John Paul II, *Apostolic Exhortation on Catechesis in Our Time* (*Catechesi Tradendae*), October 16, 1979, no. 27.

empowers and guides His Church into all truth. The development of Christian doctrine throughout the history of the Church is a tremendous gift to us. It is important that we not neglect so great a gift, which will strengthen and inform our faith.

We must understand the Church's teaching—Sacred Tradition—so that we can be faithful to our Lord. Many doctrinal battles have been settled long ago, such as those concerning Jesus being fully God and fully man, the Blessed Trinity being three Persons in one, and whether or not Scripture is inerrant. As we study our Faith, we learn the reasons the Church has embraced certain positions and rejected others. There are no new heresies. Hence, our understanding of the Deposit of Faith and the reasons for the Church's pronouncements will strengthen us in the midst of the battles of our day. If we neglect understanding what we as Catholics believe and why, either we will cease to be Catholics or our children will.

If we read Church documents and conciliar decrees with care, prayerfully submitting our hearts to our Lord and hearing His voice through the Church, we will deepen our love for the Lord and our understanding of what obedience to Him means. It is especially helpful to read the Scripture texts to which documents refer while we read the documents themselves.

For instance, we have a great opportunity to demonstrate to our children our filial love and obedience to the Church in our response to the *Catechism of the Catholic Church*. This catechetical instruction has been written for our good and for the good of the worldwide Catholic family. Will we take the time to read and respond to it, or will we ignore this gift from God?

Home education enables us to schedule time for studying the Scriptures and Sacred Tradition with our children. When we oversee their catechetical instruction, we know they are in fact learning what the Church teaches. We further enrich that instruction by our observance of the "fasting and feasting" of the liturgical calendar in our homes. The great acts of God recorded in Sacred Scripture and documented in Church history through the liturgical calendar are illustrated in living color through the lives and deaths of the saints.

The question we need to ask ourselves is: What kind of formal education will best train our children's hearts in the truths of Sacred Scripture and the treasures of the Faith?

Living the Faith—Family Mission and Individual Character Formation

A Catholic vision for life is more than learning about the Faith; it's living the Faith. More than pious exercises isolated from the rest of our lives, our Faith must be woven into the fabric of our daily living. Thus true education will be that which teaches us that to be fully human is to follow Christ wholeheartedly.

Years ago Catholic schools offered Mass daily or at least weekly for schoolchildren and regularly provided opportunities for Confession. Today many Catholic schools do not, though some parents may assume they do. In Catholic home education, we have the flexibility to work the academic schedule around time for attending Mass, going to Confession, and praying, rather than the other way around.

Through the sacrament of Matrimony, God has blessed our union with offspring. We then have the joyful duty of baptizing them and, in turn, bringing them to the sacraments of Reconciliation, First Eucharist, and Confirmation. (See Chapter 15 for a much fuller explanation of how each of the sacraments draws us closer to God individually and as a family.)

According to the Vatican II *Decree on the Apostolate of Lay People*,

> Christian husbands and wives are cooperators in grace and witnesses of faith on behalf of each other, their children, and all others in their household. They are the first to communicate the faith to their children and to educate them; by word and example they train their offspring for the Christian and apostolic life. They prudently help them in the choice of their vocation and carefully promote any religious calling which they may discern in them.[2]

---

[2] *Decree on the Apostolate of Lay People* (*Apostolicam Actuositatem*), no. 11.

As we teach our children how to live the Faith, we train them to respond to God's grace faithfully and prepare them for their own vocations. In fact, says Lisanne Bales, spokesperson for National Association of Catholic Home Educators (NACHE) and home-schooling mother of six, "I have no doubt the efforts home educators have made to reinforce a positive view of the priesthood will bear much vocational fruit for the future."

In addition to the sacraments, we should develop our interior life through individual prayer and catechetical formation. This is essential not only for us but for our children as well. Remember: more is caught than taught. If we want our children to have an interior life with God, we must set the example.

It can be difficult trying to squeeze in family prayer time before school in the midst of dressing, getting breakfast, and hurriedly gathering books, supplies, and coats to get out the door on time. It isn't easy to grab a few minutes for prayer with our children at the end of the day between extracurricular activities and homework. In contrast, home education allows schedule flexibility for the priority of prayer.

We encourage our children's love for God by praying with them and leading them in their own prayers. We can guide our children with a mixture of memorized prayers (which help them learn how to pray) and spontaneous prayers (which are heartfelt expressions of love).

Just as we express love in our families by listening carefully and responding to one another, so we love God by listening and responding to Him. The essence of prayer is just that—conversation with God. There is a time when we share our thoughts of adoration and thanksgiving, feelings of sorrow for sin, and requests for that which we need. There is also a time to be quiet in His presence and listen to Him, especially during visits to our Lord in the Blessed Sacrament, when we have the opportunity for Eucharistic Adoration, loving our Lord simply by being with Him.

Regardless of what form of Catholic education we select for our children, we need to prioritize time as a family for sacraments and prayer. Catholic home education enables us to plan our academic schedule around this priority.

The Family on Mission

Our service to Christ flows out of our knowledge of Him and our love for Him. As individuals, when we live the sacramental life and grow in our knowledge of the Word of God and Tradition, our hearts are trained in holiness. Then the grace we receive from the sacraments and prayer empowers us to reach out to others in acts of true charity.

The Lord is the One who calls us as a family—both parents and children—to the mission of testifying to the world about Jesus Christ:

> It [the family] will fulfill this mission if it shows itself to be the domestic sanctuary of the Church through the mutual affection of its members and the common prayer they offer to God, if the whole family is caught up in the liturgical worship of the Church, and if it provides active hospitality and promotes justice and other good works in the service of all the brethren in need.[3]

The Church is on a mission to Christianize the entire world, and we are preparing our children for their vocation as a part of that mission.

For our children to incorporate a Catholic view of the world, let's guard the way we present home education. We do not want to foster a fortress mentality, constructing walls so no one can get to us and cause trouble. Rather, our aim should be for our homes to become embassies of Christendom—places of refuge in a foreign land, to be sure, but offering the treasure we have found to all who will receive it. Thus, we will nurture children who will be bold apostles to change men's hearts rather than timid people who fear man rather than God.

---

[3] Ibid.

Character Formation

Sometimes we do not see the essential place of character development in the education of our children. We may relegate it to something important but done in our spare time when our children are not busy doing something urgent. Yet character formation is a necessary part of an integrated Catholic education. At times it has been neglected with grave consequences, even in the midst of a Catholic school education, leaving children with the form of religion without their knowing its power to change their lives.

In a typical school, a teacher spends little time each day giving each child personal attention. This time typically involves teaching and evaluating academic concepts rather than training the child's character. As much as we might wish that teachers could lovingly point out character flaws and work with our child on them, such an undertaking is simply beyond the scope of the teacher's work. In contrast, home educator Barb Saxton is available to give her four sons time throughout the day. "What I treasure is extra time to influence my sons—to interact with them on a variety of ideas as we live life together."

In order to help our children live the Faith they are learning, we need to form their Christian character, specifically, fostering virtues and subduing vices. We do not opt for home education because we want to get away from sin; any family will vouch that there's more than enough within our homes. Rather, we want to deal with sin—our own as well as our children's—to assist our children in forming habits by which their souls can grow.

As parents, we are the ones intimately involved in our children's lives. We have the desire and commitment needed to provide the consistent "teaching, correction, reproof, and training in righteousness" (2 Tim 3:16) that will form the character traits that God desires to see in them (and us). Joan and Paul Wise have noticed the effect of home education on the character development in their two sons.

> Home schooling has provided our family with ongoing opportunities to learn from each other. We are most pleased with the empha-

sis we are able to place on character training, enabling our sons to become strong Christian men.

For the Wises, character formation is not a nebulous phrase or a theoretical concept. Rather, it involves training specific attitudes, ways of speaking, being, and thinking that produce moral character.

One person has said that habits are what you do when no one is looking. Habits, good or bad, are the responses of our hearts to all different kinds of situations—they demonstrate our character. This is true for our children as well.

When we talk about character formation through good habits, we mean much more than training a child to be polite. We can train animals to be mannerly. But we guide children to develop as children of the Most High, both with right actions and right motivations. We want them to mature in their love for God the Father so that they are more motivated by their love for Him than by their desire to avoid the pains of hell.

How can we guide the character formation of our children? As we encourage the development of their own interior life through prayer and the sacraments, we nurture the theological virtues (faith, hope, and charity). In addition, we take advantage of situations daily to develop the moral virtues (prudence, justice, fortitude, and temperance) in our children. And we look for their growth in the fruits of the Holy Spirit (Gal 5:22–23—love, joy, peace, patience, kindness, goodness, faithfulness, gentleness, and self-control). (There are many more specific guidelines given in the development of virtue in Chapter 16.)

We bolster good habits through consistent practice of our Faith: worshipping God and partaking of the grace of the sacraments; expressing devotion to our Blessed Mother (celebrating feast days, praying the rosary); venerating the saints and invoking their prayers on our behalf; and regularly acknowledging the work of our guardian angels. We learn how to love our Father better by the example of the saints' words and deeds—they resisted sin and pursued holiness, and they point the way for us to become saints, too.

Throughout this journey of faith, not only are we developing virtues, but we are also struggling to resist vices. To help our children resist vices, we need to help them identify the bad habits they have that need to be corrected. Character flaws are often strengths out of balance or, put differently, the flip side of a child's genuine virtue or strength. For example, a child's hypersensitivity may reveal true sensitivity, compassion, and empathy that just need development. A child's bossiness may in fact be leadership in the raw, so to speak. Only a parent's intimate involvement in his or her own child's life can provide the consistent correction, reinforcement, and overall sense of what character traits are desirable. A parent is uniquely able to speak the truth in love to the child.

The parents' role in character formation is irreplaceable. Even the best teacher who wants to cultivate strong moral character in her students cannot possibly do the job well by herself, since the teacher has many academic tasks to accomplish each day with a large group of children. However highly motivated the teacher may be, he or she cannot be expected to do the impossible.

Character training should include the following: fostering right attitudes, such as having a thankful heart (toward God and others); requiring obedience to rightful authorities (obedience to parents opens the child's heart to accept the authority of God and His Church in their own lives, especially as they mature); being open to and seeking the gifts and fruits of the Holy Spirit; and helping our children see the practical examples of the Holy Spirit's work in our lives.

The question we need to ask ourselves is: What kind of formal education will best enable our children to live the Faith with appropriate guidance in developing godly character traits?

Applying the Faith—Training in Academics and Life Skills

Academics

St. Paul says that we are to "take every thought captive to Christ" (2 Cor 10:5). Consequently, no purely secular subject area can be studied in such a way that Christ cannot receive glory; for all truth is His, whether it be history, science, or math. He made it all. At the same time, intellectual formation is not limited to those subjects related directly to theology.

Academic training consists in forming the mental disciplines and habits of intellect for analysis and communication of truth in a variety of fields. Core subjects refer to the liberal arts and fine arts, which enable the children to understand and appreciate beauty and Catholic culture. The core subjects include reading, writing, arithmetic, history, and science; the fine arts include art, art appreciation, music, music appreciation, drama, and dance.

The purpose of pursuing excellence in academics for our children is not primarily so that they can get a job. (Though that certainly will be one consequence for most of them.) Its primary purpose is to equip our children with a well-developed intellect, trained talents, and acquired skills—the education of the whole person who is mature in Christ.

When we speak of service to Christ, some of us think only in terms of ecclesiastical vocations. But every one of us is called to serve the Lord, no matter what our occupation. "And whatever you do, in word or deed, do everything in the name of the Lord Jesus, giving thanks to God the Father through Him" (Col 3:17). After all, it is the Lord who has graciously given whatever intelligence, talent, and skill we have, and He has wonderful purposes for their development to further His Kingdom on earth. Let's be sure the intellectual formation of each of our children is accomplished with the utmost care, considering the total well-being of the child.

Life Skills

Another aspect of an integrated Catholic education that often is neglected by us due to time constraints is training in life skills. Often our children are so busy with school, homework, and activities that we hesitate to burden them "unnecessarily" with such things as cleaning, laundry, or yard work. Are these skills really unnecessary burdens?

Since all that we have belongs to the Lord, we must be good stewards of our possessions as an act of service to God. Home education gives us the opportunity to teach a variety of practical life skills in the management of our homes. Life skills can be listed in two categories: maintaining our homes and property, and beautifying our homes and property.

We are good stewards of our homes and property when we clean the house, do the laundry, cook, care for our children, clean and maintain the car, and care for the lawn and garden. These are skills our children need in order to help the family now, to offer service to others, and to prepare for their own families and homes.

In addition, there are numerous skills the children can learn at home that will not only assist the family to beautify the home and property but will also be a potential source of revenue for the child in the future. Some examples of these skills include wallpapering, painting, woodworking, decorating, and landscaping.

These skills are not taught quickly; however, spending the time with our child as he or she learns the skill not only helps us do a more thorough job in training but also gives us opportunities for quality time together. The result of a job well done together can produce a wonderful sense of companionship and pride (in the good sense). The child's sense of self-worth receives a legitimate, healthy boost as he or she realizes the valuable contribution made to the family.

As our children get older, there is the possibility of apprenticeships in the areas of plumbing, electrical work, construction, roofing, and a variety of arts and crafts. If these are not skills we possess, we can swap skill training with others who can teach our children while we teach theirs, or perhaps we can learn from the tutor together.

All of this kind of training takes time and effort on the part of parents and children. Catholic home education enables a family to set particular goals for what life skills each child wants to learn in the coming year and then take the practical steps to plan the training as part of the educational goals for the family.

Training our children in life skills is a vital part of their Catholic education for a life of service to the Lord. This may not seem like a very "spiritual" undertaking, but love for God and service to others go hand in hand. Jesus Himself took time to learn the trade of carpentry and certainly assisted at home with Mary after St. Joseph died.

The question we need to ask ourselves is this: What is the best kind of formal education that will provide the academic formation as well as time for important life-skills development to prepare our children for their unique service to God?

Conclusion

Catholic home education can provide an excellent Catholic education as we train each child to love and serve the Lord with his or her heart, mind, soul, and body. Through the natural love and God-given authority we have as parents and with the proper tools for the tasks, we can instruct our children in the Faith in both word and deed, develop their character, teach them academics, and train them in life skills. The Lord is the One who has blessed us with these souls in our care. He will enable us to be faithful to His call on *our* lives, so that our children may be faithful to His call on *their* lives.

1. We are called to love God with our whole heart, soul, mind, and strength. These areas correspond to the four aspects of Catholic home education: spiritual, character, intellectual, and life-skills development.

2. Spiritual development involves our intellectual grasp of the Faith, through Sacred Scripture and Sacred Tradition, and our heartfelt love for God. Through home education, we can make time in our family schedule for those priorities that develop the interior life: the sacraments and prayer. The more we each grow interiorly, the better able we are to fulfill our family's mission in the world.

3. Formation of Christian character—developing virtues and subduing vices—is vital in the education of our children.

4. Academic training consists in forming the mental disciplines and habits of intellect for analysis and communication of truth in a variety of fields.

5. Training in life skills is part of an integrated Catholic education that is often neglected due to time limitations.

6. Catholic home education enables families to balance the development of our children in each of the four basic areas of education so that they mature as well-rounded young adults.

5

Monitoring the Playground

What about Socialization?

[P]eer obsessiveness and the clique mentality are the natural responses of children to mass schooling, which in essence removes adults from their lives or rather puts them there at a ratio of one to thirty and in an authoritarian role not entirely conducive to the forming of meaningful relationships.[1]

> — David Guterson, public school instructor
> and home educator

We have found that one of the greatest blessings of being with our children has been a stronger and deeper relationship with them. Their respect for us and our opinions has grown.

> — Barb Hoyt, mother of five

When a home-schooling mother of eleven was asked, in all seriousness, how she provided for the socialization needs of her children, she broke into laughter. "There are thirteen of us!" she responded.

Here comes the whopper-stopper question: What about socialization? When people ask that question, will they see us falter in our praise of home education? After all, isn't that the insurmountable objection? Catholic home education may be good academically and even more thoroughly Catholic than most other options; but

---

[1] David Guterson, *Family Matters: Why Homeschooling Makes Sense* (New York: Harcourt, Brace, Jovanovich, 1992), p. 69.

63

doesn't the obvious lack of socialization make home education inherently incomplete and undesirable?

When critics of home education think of socialization, they tend to reduce it to sociability—the ability of people to get along. They assume institutional schools offer better socialization because there are more people, and more people mean more opportunities for social interaction. However, sociability is more a product—than the process—of socialization.

The process of socialization in institutional schools is, for the most part, carried on by peers with general oversight by teachers. Sheer numbers of peers do not mean that children will be socialized in a way that is pleasing to God. More is not necessarily better when it comes to peer interaction.

The process of socialization in home schools is begun, nurtured, sustained, repaired, and matured under the watchful care of parents with particular oversight in the developing relationships between siblings.

Critics imply that if our children are educated in a home environment, they could become social morons, unable to cope in the real world. But nearly the reverse is true. What our concerned friends and family members are about to hear (from you) will astound them—socialization is one of the primary reasons for home education. Really.

Social Pressures in School

Your Experience

Let's look briefly at a case in point—you are an expert about your own experience in an institutional school. On the one hand, when you think back on your social experiences in the classroom, your memories, like those of most of us, are probably a mixture of great friendships and difficult relationships. Not all social experiences are created equal.

Some of you entered the class shy and insecure. You may have learned to be more outgoing. Perhaps you learned to follow the crowd in your own quiet way. However, you may have become painfully shy, feeling more and more left out.

Some of you were opinionated, even at an early age. If you had a strong sense of what you believed, you might have become a leader in the class. But your convictions might have caused you to be ostracized if your opinions ran contrary to the crowd. Or you may have chosen compromise, just to survive; then you had to cope with ambivalent feelings about compromising your convictions. And if you compromised your convictions often, you ran the risk of losing your sense of conviction altogether, just to conform to the group.

Some of you were part of the privileged few—the "in" crowd— or somewhere on the periphery of the inner circle. You needed to maintain your status. You may have felt pressure to keep up with fashion, language, and hairstyle trends, so you could stay at the head of the pack. You may have struggled with insecurities, never knowing when others might think you had fallen out of step with the clique. And you had to be careful who your friends were.

Whatever your situation, you learned: best not to stand out— not too smart and not too dumb, not too talented and not too dull, not too talkative and not too shy. If you did well academically, you learned to minimize or hide it—not out of sensitivity to others, trying not to be boastful or arrogant, but because it was a dreadful thing to become the one who was envied. It was easier to settle for mediocrity than to stand out in the crowd.

Peer Socialization

No matter how strong a Catholic family might be, children educated in institutional schools run the risk of peer socialization, according to their peers' collective values, good or bad. Note the warning of the writer of Proverbs: "He who walks with wise men will be wise, but the companion of fools will suffer harm" (Prov 13:20, RSV).

Peer-dominated education often results in copycat objectionable behavior and speech. And peer pressure in the classroom, when misdirected, as it often is, leads to all kinds of problems, including illegal drugs, premarital sex, and random acts of violence. "Do not be deceived: Bad company corrupts good morals" (1 Cor 15:33, RSV).

Without meaning to do so, institutional schools, whether Catholic or secular, create a peer-dependency problem. They segregate children by age out of the sheer necessity of providing instruction for a large number of children. In doing so, they establish a peer-dominated environment. This may be a primary reason for the excessive aggression and competitiveness seen at times in classroom situations among peers.

Peer dependency can lead a child to adopt his peers' values as a reference point instead of those of his family. As Lisanne Bales, home educator of nine years, states, "Simply put, peer socialization by those as immature as one's child is clearly not the cultural socialization I am looking for as a parent. I prefer more early control over the influences and attitudes that will mold my child's world and life views."

Though peer pressure is a potential problem, isn't it needed to help some children become social? What about the child who is shy? Will he be properly socialized outside an institutional classroom?

First, shyness is not a sin. Not every person has to be the talkative sort. Second, if a child is shy because of low self-esteem, a wounded spirit, or a self-righteous attitude, we must address those specific needs. However, they are probably better addressed at home than in school. Finally, in a classroom a child with a quiet spirit who does not need to be the center of attention might be exhibiting godly behavior. Yet a teacher might give him low marks or misperceive him as being backward socially.

On the other hand, the more talkative children are not necessarily better socialized. Scripture warns, "When words are many, transgression is not lacking, but he who restrains his lips is prudent" (Prov 10:19). Though the classroom may seem like an ideal place for making friends, large classes limit the amount of socializing children can do.

Besides, classroom conversation can be very hurtful. Children speak unkind words that teachers cannot always detect or correct. And some children use foul language both in the classroom and on the playground that damages the innocence of other children.

Far from giving the children a taste of the "real" world, the schools have created an environment that is artificial in comparison to other social situations. Where else do you find segregation by age? The other social environments in the "real" world—the home, the neighborhood, the workplace, and the church—are examples of a mixture of ages working together. They necessitate age-integration rather than age-segregation.

Consequently, it is the home, rather than an institutional school, that provides an age-integrated environment for healthy socialization in preparation for social interaction in the world. Guided by their parents rather than their peers, children who are home educated will be better prepared for mixing socially, both as individuals and as part of a group, in other environments. In contrast, children who are schooled almost exclusively with peers are often the ones limited in their social skills.

What Is Socialization?

Jesus' Example

Today people misdefine socialization as the ability to get along with others. Certainly, social skills are one of the products of good socialization. However, we limit our understanding of what God desires for us and for our children if we construe socialization so narrowly.

Jesus, for instance, did not always fit in with others. Often his teachings drove away the crowds. His rebukes offended the religious leaders. And he reached out to all kinds of sinners, which alternately increased or decreased his popularity. With social skills like these, should Jesus be our model?

Yet, Jesus' interaction with others is a model for guiding our children in godly social behavior. As a boy, he "increased in wisdom and in stature with God and man" (Lk 2:52). He knew how to relate appropriately to others, unafraid to go against the status quo. He was firm in conviction, loving and respectful to his parents, kind to children, thoughtful toward the sick and infirm, respectful toward women and foreigners (in ways that countered his culture), and humble toward authority.

Like Jesus, we want to grow in our ability to love and serve others. So much more than jockeying for position among peers, socialization means responding appropriately to people of varying ages out of love for Christ. Socialization, from a biblical basis, is learning how to function within the Body of Christ as an individual and within a group by "loving your neighbor as yourself".

The Civilization of Love

Pope John Paul II, in his encyclical *The Christian Family in the Modern World*, speaks of the contrast between our culture, which emphasizes individualism and selfishness, and the community of love within families, which promotes community through self-giving.

> The family is the first and fundamental school of social living: as a community of love, it finds in self-giving the law that guides it and makes it grow. The self-giving that inspires the love of husband and wife for each other is the model and norm for the self-giving that must be practiced in the relationships between brothers and sisters and the different generations living together in the family. And the communion and sharing that are part of everyday life in the home at times of joy and at times of difficulty are the most concrete and effective pedagogy for the active, responsible and fruitful inclusion of the children in the wider horizon of society.[2]

Thus the family is the social entity at the heart of the "life and mission of the Church" and the "development of society".[3]

---

[2] John Paul II, *The Christian Family in the Modern World* (*Familiaris Consortio*), no. 37.
[3] Ibid., no. 17.

Individual Socialization

Through the life-giving power of marital love, God blesses us with a particular child to love and nurture. From the earliest moments we know the child is there, we care for him. Daily we nurture his body, mind, and soul. "This warm, responsible relationship on a consistent basis is the best foundation a young child can have . . . for social development."[4]

As parents, we lay the foundation of a strong self-concept in our children day by day through our unconditional love and consistent discipline. Upon this foundation, we build their self-confidence by letting them know they are wanted and needed.

As we depend more and more on our children to strengthen the family unit and keep it functioning well, their own sense of self-worth and value grows.

> In fact, the child who remains at home with a mother and shares the tasks of the home appears to develop self-respect and a sense of responsibility and values not shared by the child who started school earlier. These values, in turn, seem to bring with them a certain social and emotional stability that is difficult otherwise to achieve.[5]

Note the consequence of giving tasks to children as a part of family life. The child does not feel devalued, as if his worth were based on what he can produce; rather, the child feels a deeper sense of belonging, since he is contributing to the well-being of the family. This may be a primary reason home-schooled children have consistently scored higher on self-concept tests than their peers in public school.[6]

[4] Raymond S. and Dorothy N. Moore, *Better Late than Early* (New York: Reader's Digest Press, 1975), p. 37.

[5] Ibid., p. 92. The Moores quote Margaret Gott's study "The Effect of Age Difference at Kindergarten Entrance on Achievement and Adjustment in Elementary School" (unpublished dissertation, University of Colorado, 1963).

[6] Raymond S. and Dorothy N. Moore, *Home School Burnout* (Brentwood, TN: Wolgemuth & Hyatt, Pub., 1988), p. 47. They refer to an important study by Dr. John Wesley Taylor, *Self-Concept in Home Schooling Children* (Ann Arbor, MI: University Microfilms Int'l, Order No. DA 8629219).

Our children are a vital part of our household, and they know it. Their cooperation with housework makes home education possible. When people ask how both housework and home education get done, we share how essential our children are to the entire family venture.

Each child has various talents and spiritual gifts that bless the family. We help identify them and suggest how they can best be used in the family. For example, we nurture a child's gift of a sensitive spirit for others in pain by teaching him intercessory prayer. We encourage a child's strong sense of justice over political issues and point out various professions in which the child may serve God for greater justice in our society. We praise a child's generous heart through his donations of time or money.

The secure, loving environment of our homes prepares our children for independence. Independence is balanced by a healthy interdependence (rather than peer dependence) in our children. As noted psychologist Dr. David Elkind says, "parenting practices that encourage children's sense of belonging to the family also facilitate their acceptance by the group and thus the sense of peer-group belonging."[7]

It is this kind of a strong self-concept that helps our children enjoy peers without being controlled by them. Studies have shown that home-educated children are less aggressive than institutionally educated children[8]—their secure self-concept gives them the inner strength to work toward more peaceful resolutions to conflict.

At the same time, a mature self-concept enables our children to take courageous, unpopular stands, especially in defense of the weak and innocent people in our world. Not fitting in may be the better response when our children are called upon to follow Christ's example rather than the example of peers.

---

[7] David Elkind, *Miseducation—Preschoolers at Risk* (New York: Alfred A. Knopf, 1987), p. 127.

[8] Dr. Brian D. Ray, *Marching to the Beat of Their Own Drum! A Profile of Home Education Research* (Paeonian Springs, WA: Home School Legal Defense Association, 1992), p. 12. Based on the study "Adjustment between Home and Traditionally Schooled Students" (University of Florida, 1992).

Socialization within the Family

The heart of Christian socialization is the commandment "Love your neighbor as you love yourself." We show love of neighbor in our families by honoring each other in big and little things. We demonstrate respect for life when we welcome a new little one into the family or when we care for elderly members of our family. We take care of one another's property. We teach good manners and polite conversation.

Home is where we train our children to show unconditional love for one another in imitation of our love for them. For our families to be faithful to the call from Pope John Paul II to be a community of love, the members of our families must know each other and genuinely care for each other. Our children need to see the quality of self-giving love we have for our spouse, which issued forth in their very existence. And in response to our love, they should reflect the same sacrificial love for each other.

Certainly this kind of true socialization can occur in the pockets of time families have together outside of school time. And most families look for quality time with family members in the midst of hectic school, sports, and work schedules. In reality, finding it can be rather hit or miss.

Through home education, we can take advantage of a generous quantity of quality time together. Our families have more opportunities to build this kind of community of love because we have more time together for study, work, and play. It won't happen on its own; but the opportunity is there, if we want to make the most of these relatively few and precious years.

We guide the interaction of our children with us, their siblings, and others in order to develop community within our family. This kind of community, or "civilization of love", according to Vatican II, helps strengthen the Church and build a civilization of love into our culture beyond our family and Church.

Our children have opportunities to serve their brothers and sisters daily. They share their possessions. They offer their time in service and play without necessarily seeing an immediate reward (as with really young ones). They learn respect for others, regardless of age.

Our children learn to appreciate, rather than envy, one another's successes without comparisons with their own accomplishments. One way we do this through home education is training our older children to help us teach the younger ones. This "trickle-down" tutoring builds mutual respect—the older ones serve the younger ones by teaching well and with love, while the younger ones respond with respect.

Even play time can be an expression of love of neighbor. Since home-educated children tend to be comfortable with a broader range of ages than children formed socially in an age-segregated institution, they include younger children in play rather than avoid them. At the same time, they speak easily and respectfully with college students and other adults, including the elderly. One home-educated teen, a member of the teen panel at a conference on home education, offered this thought,

> [It was] my idea to be home schooled. . . . [In school] you're all thrown together and just understand people your own age. You can't relate to adults. Now I talk with and relate better with people of all ages.[9]

Home education helps us become more consistent in our discipline, training our children in conflict resolution, which strengthens their friendships with us and each other. As parents, we guide them, correct misbehavior, explain right attitudes and actions, and help them interact respectfully with others.

Under ordinary circumstances, conflicts with siblings or friends remain unresolved due to the lack of time needed for resolution or because there is no consistent way of dealing with the negative behaviors that caused the conflicts. However, as part of our home education, we can intervene constructively, helping our children understand their vices and work on virtues.

---

[9] Anonymous teen who had been home schooled through high school. She was part of a teen panel at the Home Instruction Support Conference, Sterling, VA, June 1993.

We can take the time that teachers cannot afford to deal with sin when it occurs. For example, our children grow in humility when they ask for forgiveness; they in turn learn to forgive. They replace tattling, complaining, or criticizing one another with speaking the truth in love to each other in a helpful way. None of this training is done quickly or simply, but the time allowed through home schooling our children gives us many more opportunities to social-ize them truly.

Overall, there is more time with home education to create family culture, preparing all of us to serve our Lord better in the Church and society. Our children can relate better to each other because they know each other better. With parental guidance, they can enjoy their similarities and appreciate their differences. And good communication at an early age leads to good communication in the teen years and beyond.

Our children not only become better siblings as they interact in these sacrificial ways—they learn how to be caring brothers and sisters to others in Christ. They are consciously loving their neigh-bor as themselves under our guidance.

These aspects of Catholic socialization are rarely addressed in a public-school classroom and may be marginalized in many Cath-olic classrooms due to lack of time. Yet these are the very principles that show our children who they are as individuals within the Church and how they can love and serve the Lord as part of the Family of God.

Socialization for the Church

True socialization involves not only our actions as individuals but also our service as a family to the Church. When we develop a family ministry, we demonstrate to our children how the Body of Christ functions in meeting the needs of others. Our family has visited retired nuns, taken meals to families who have just had a baby, purchased food for donation to Thanksgiving food baskets for the poor, and opened our home to college students who have become part of our extended household. These family ministries are not major undertakings; they are expressions of service and love accomplished together.

When we recognize our children's gifts in the family (or "domestic church") and teach them the value of others' gifts, we help them grow in their ability to give and receive within the larger Family of God, the Church. They learn to reach beyond the family through prayer for others, by caring for others, and by giving generously to others.

They see how their gifts complement others' gifts within the family and extend that to the Church. For example, one child may be very creative in thinking of ways the family can show hospitality; another child's organizational skills will put those creative suggestions into practice. Or one child may be sensitive to a lonely child in the neighborhood, while a sibling might invite that child to join their activities.

One aspect of socialization within the Church involves leadership training. Children should be taught both by word and example how to lead by serving, rather than trying to dominate others to make them follow. Our children's primary role model is Jesus, who said that He came to serve rather than be served. He gave Himself completely to his disciples; He even washed their feet. When our children imitate Him as a servant leader, they will find others drawn to respect them and consequently, if they serve well, to follow them.

Another socialization skill, related to leadership, is learning how to follow—thoughtfully, not mindlessly—those God has placed in authority. We must take care not to foster the kind of independent spirit in our children that renders them incapable of being taught or led. (We must guard our own attitudes toward leaders so that our children respond with respect rather than a critical spirit.) At the same time we should give our children principles for evaluating whether or not following a particular person will please God.

Both aspects of socialization in the Church—leading and following—are easily integrated in normal family life. Each child has ample opportunities both to lead and to follow others. What an opportunity we have to provide this vital preparation for whatever is God's mission for each child.

The Vatican II *Declaration on Christian Education* speaks of the importance of parents educating their children, in particular with regard to principles of social development for the benefit of society at large.

> For it devolves on parents to create a family atmosphere so animated with love and reverence for God and others that a well-rounded personal and social development will be fostered among the children. Hence, the family is the first school of those social virtues which every society needs.[10]

Developing social virtues within our families not only will help our families but also will strengthen the whole society. Kari Harrington, home-educating mother of seven, reminds us that socialization includes

> mentoring someone in how to function in society, but our calling as parents goes far beyond creating functioning citizens. We are called to train our children to model Jesus Christ in their words and actions as a testimony to society. This mentoring is done in a natural way as we live it out before our children throughout the day.

By instruction and example, we guide our children's daily interaction within the family, preparing them for relationships beyond the family circle that will honor God.

Social Opportunities beyond the Family

Friendships

When parents send their children to school, their biggest social concern is: Who are the children with whom my children are forming close relationships? Are these friendships good ones that

---

[10] *Declaration on Christian Education*, no. 3.

will help my children grow closer to God, or are they divisive relationships that will erect barriers between them and God and us?

All of us are eager for our children to develop solid, lasting friendships. Through hospitality, we extend friendship to a variety of good people, demonstrating for our children the relationship between friendship and service. Family social gatherings often yield fruitful friendships for our children.

The Scriptures contain much wisdom about good and poor friendships. In general, we should encourage friendships for our children with others who are growing in wisdom and grace. If our young ones are watchful, they can discern which children will make good friends, for "Even a child makes himself known by his acts, whether what he does is pure and right" (Prov 20:11).

Begin with Proverbs. You will find many foundational principles for friendships: If others want you to sin, don't consent (1:10); don't withhold good when you have the power to do it (3:27); hatred causes conflict, but love forgives offenses (10:12); don't belittle others (11:12); be faithful when others share secrets rather than break confidence (11:13); wise friends will help you grow in wisdom, but foolish friends will bring you harm (13:20); if you repeat a forgiven situation, you can alienate a friend (17:9); a true friend always loves (17:17); a real friendship isn't built on money (19:4); be loyal (19:22); keep out of quarrels (20:3); don't take gossip from a friend (20:19); don't choose a friend who gets angry easily, lest you become like him (22:24); a true friend will tell you the truth even when it hurts to hear it (27:6).

Our oversight of peer relationships is essential, so that, in wisdom, our children can learn how to be and to have good friends. They need discernment and development of character. "There are friends who pretend to be friends, but there is a friend who sticks closer than a brother" (Prov 18:24). Once again, the family provides the best environment for oversight and encouragement of solid Christian friendships.

Group Experiences

The local home-education support group can provide academic, spiritual, and "pure fun" social events for our children. There are classes in various hobbies, parties throughout the year, and various academic and social clubs. In addition, there are opportunities for a variety of performances, spelling and geography bees, and science fairs.

The possibilities for social opportunities are limited only by our imaginations. One of our guiding principles has been that whatever is fun in an institutional school, if it is worthwhile, we can do. This does not mean that the institutional schools set the agenda for the activities we offer, but neither will we let them "corner the market" on fun.

Though all the students attending these events are home-educated children, that does not mean that each one is a model Christian. It is still essential that we exercise our parental oversight to achieve social interaction that is pleasing to God even at home-education events. This is the kind of social interaction that strengthens us as individuals and families. This is what we want for our children's well-being.

Potential Problems with Socialization at Home

Many of us began considering educating our children at home precisely because we were concerned about the kind of socialization occurring in typical institutional school settings. While we avoid particular social problems associated with institutional schools, we must also avoid various pitfalls in home education if we want to educate our children with a right heart toward God and others.

The dangers in socialization at home find a common root in pride. We must model the right attitudes toward our home-education enterprise and toward others who do not home educate; our children most likely will imitate us.

First, we must avoid the attitude of superiority toward others who do not home educate. We do not home educate because we are all-sufficient or totally capable of doing this in our own strength. Rather, we home educate because we are willing to serve God in this vital formation of our children, and we trust He will make up for what we lack.

Second, we must guard our children's hearts against becoming puffed up with pride or with the self-righteous attitude that they are better than children in typical classrooms, who follow poor peer leadership just to be accepted. It is only by the grace of God that any of us is preserved from falling into sin.

Third, we must be careful that we do not form in our children a basic mistrust of other people so that they want to turn their backs on the world, refusing to serve the Lord as apostles of love. If we end up creating independent mavericks who are not capable of being thoughtful followers, then we have missocialized them; for this kind of attitude will tear down rather than build up the Church.

Fourth, we are not home educating because we fear the world. We are not building an impenetrable fortress within which we will shield our children from the onslaught of the enemy. Rather, our goal as Catholics is to nurture our children, like young plants in a nursery, so that they will stand tall for Christ and help the Church conquer the world for Him. There is a kind of separation from the worldliness of the world for a time, but it is not isolation. God knows how much sin we all face daily among ourselves in our own homes!

Finally, as parents we must maintain a clear authority relationship with our children. Some parents become lax in administering discipline. This translates into a pattern of overfamiliarity, disrespect, an argumentative spirit, and rudeness toward parents and then other adults. Undisciplined children, for instance, on home-schooling field trips are a discredit to the home-school support group and a poor witness to others regarding home education.

We must take care that familiarity in the parent–child relationship does not lead to a shift in the child's heart from a parent–child relationship to a peer relationship. We certainly want to count our children among our friends, but that will occur in adulthood, not when they are children.

Socialization Is a Process

Socialization within the family is part of the process of becoming a civilization of love. It can be a struggle—one day we see our children making progress; the next day we see old habits of disrespect or lack of service emerge again. We want to raise our children to be all that they can for God, yet we are hampered by our own lack of perfection in our parenting skills.

To complicate things further, we are aware others are viewing us in the middle of this process. Consequently, when we are in the public eye, we feel scrutinized and, at times, criticized on the basis of how disciplined our children seem. Sometimes we get more praise than is warranted, because our children appear angelic; other times we feel condemned, because our children act like candidates for reform school!

If we keep our eyes on the Lord, we will be able to put others' concerns for the social well-being of our children in perspective—some concerns are legitimate, and others are not. The task of parenting requires much of us—asking for and receiving God's grace daily for our sins and faults; extending that same grace to our children for their own sins and faults; growing in fortitude so that we persist in the discipline and instruction that will yield the peaceful fruit of righteousness; and maintaining a sense of the vision that held our imagination when we saw marriage and family life as our vocation.

We must take care not to succumb to peer pressure ourselves, worrying too much about how our children are perceived. Socially, our beloved offspring will commit errors of judgment, not always demonstrate maturity, and, in short, sin in front of others, no matter how we choose to educate them. In our earnest desire to "prove" that home education does not stunt our children socially, we may overreact to their faults. Or we may choose not to home educate for fear of what others will say.

Let's have the mind of Christ on this matter. Our own sense of worth is based on the fact that we have been created and redeemed by God. Our children need the same basis of self-worth. The key issue is not how others view us (or our children) but rather how Christ sees us (and our children). The critical issue is not whether we (or our children) climb the social ladder; rather, it is whether we establish and maintain friendships with a variety of people, all within the context of who we are in Christ.

This kind of generosity does not flow naturally from any of us, but it can flow through our families supernaturally with guidance, prayer, and the grace of the sacraments. For us to provide the kind of Christian home in which the best socialization can occur— preparing our children as faithful brothers and sisters in Christ— we need to draw on the grace of the sacraments. The sacrament of Matrimony enables us to be channels of grace to each other and, through us, to our children. The sacrament of Reconciliation cleanses us from our sins and empowers us to live holier lives than before. And the sacrament of the Eucharist—the very Body and Blood of our Lord Jesus Christ—strengthens us with Christ Himself so that we will be faithful examples to our children. (Please see Chapter 15 for more details.)

Remember: we can approach the throne of mercy and find grace in time of need (Heb 4:16). If we ask God for the grace we need to be faithful parents, He will grant it. Philippians 4:6–7 says, "Have no anxiety about anything, but in everything, by prayer and supplication, with thanksgiving, let your requests be made known unto God. And the peace of God which passes all understanding will keep your hearts and minds in Christ Jesus."

Socialization through Home Education Works!

In sum, here are the benefits of home education in the area of socialization.

1. It is in the home first and foremost that the child is better prepared to learn social skills in an age-integrated environment that

will prepare him for the real world. Remember that the real world is rich with environments that mix ages: the neighborhood, the church, and the workplace.

2. Socialization is more than the ability to get along with others. It is the ability to give ourselves in sacrificial love to God, our family members, the Church, and the world. Home education makes it possible, in terms of time, to train our children in this kind of sacrificial love.

3. Children who are educated at home demonstrate a strong self-concept that is the basis for healthy socialization. A strong self-concept leads to self-respect and self-control, which are the foundation for self-discipline and sociability.

4. Home-educating parents can spend more time training their children to make decisions based on Christian values. Consequently, the children are better able to respond well to peer-determined values and to provide good leadership to peers.

5. Home education allows for fewer opportunities for negative socialization. Family members spend more time together developing mixed-age friendships. These friendships are monitored carefully for accountability.

6. Through a variety of field trips, support-group activities, and family ministries, children who are taught at home can have a greater exposure to people in different professions and life circumstances than if they attended an institutional school. This leads to a well-rounded socialization for life.

PART TWO

DECISION MAKING

6

Managing Teacher In-Service Daze

Can I Home Educate?

"My husband would like us to home school our daughter, but I'm not so sure", sighed the young, articulate mother of two. Unsure of what home education would entail, and intimidated by her own lack of teaching credentials, she worried that her children would be shortchanged academically. "I guess I'm just not confident I could do it."

Another mom, a mother of four and a veteran of many late-night tutorials over homework, expressed the same hesitation but for a different reason. "I know I could teach them, but if I had them with me all the time, I think I'd go crazy!"

"Can I do it and do it well?" Most parents considering home education almost inevitably wonder if they *really* are capable of teaching their children themselves. This question actually reflects two very different concerns: educational competence and the fear of being overwhelmed.

On the one hand, you may question your ability to explain math and teach reading or to respond to your child's academic questions. You want to feel confident that you can teach your child well enough so that he truly will learn and retain the information he needs—in spite of your lack of teacher certification or your own academic weaknesses.

On the other hand, you may fear that taking on the education of your children will be the proverbial "straw that breaks the camel's back". Your husband may worry that you will be overburdened, the house will always be a mess, and dinner will be reduced to a hurried plate of hot dogs. As a mother, you may worry that the stress of babies, toddlers, schedules, car pools, and housework will become overwhelming when you add your children's education to the list.

Both areas of concern raise issues that will be addressed differently by each family. However, this chapter and the ones following will help you understand the most important factors for successful home education. We will tell you what it requires from you in terms of time, money, and commitment, as well as temperament and educational background. Most important, however, you will learn the tools available to make it work. (Curriculum materials, for example, list detailed steps for you to follow in explaining each lesson.) In addition, you will find that motherhood has trained you far better for teaching your children than you ever imagined. Finally, you will discover that many of your initial concerns about home education were based on false assumptions—both about schools and about home education. So . . . let's consider what it *really* takes to teach your child!

Love—The Key Factor

The most important ingredient in successful teaching is *love*. Love motivates us constantly to strive harder to give the best to each of our children. Parents possess this love in abundance and in a way no other teacher can equal. That love impels us to discover what our child needs to know, to learn it first if need be, and to find the best way to help him soak up this knowledge.

The best student–teacher relationship is built on that natural bond of love and trust between parent and child. Because we know our children intimately—both their strengths and their weaknesses —and love them unconditionally, we can challenge them to reach their full potential and yet to see their real limitations. As parents, we show love, acceptance, and unflagging belief in their abilities, especially over the years. Our loving support gives our children exactly the confidence they need to reject mediocrity and strive for the best in everything they do. In contrast, a teacher's encouragement, though sincere and well intentioned, is based on specific but limited knowledge of the child's talents. The teacher's judgment of a child's limitations often is unintentionally discouraging, as it rarely is rooted in a constant and supportive love proven over the years.

While teachers are admonished not to play favorites, parents, on the other hand, can lavish love all around but especially toward one child or another who may need an extra dose of love at a particular time. In our dual role, we can be cheerleaders for each one of our children, not just a head coach who must act impartially toward each member of the team.

Finally, the student–teacher relationship in the home school benefits from the natural authority relationship already established between parent and child. Discipline and respect for authority simply are indispensable prerequisites to effective learning. While it is true that all children naturally and periodically test their limits, parents already enjoy the position of authority and respect (unless they have abdicated it!) that allows them to reaffirm those limits. Each teacher, in contrast, when presented with a new class for the year, must assert and establish an authority relationship all over again. No wonder it is so difficult to be a classroom teacher!

Remember Your Goals

While it may be tempting to think that the real goal of home education is to produce academic superstars, it is not. As Catholic parents, our first goal is for our child to know and experience God's love. This means helping him to develop a deep and loving personal relationship with Jesus Christ and to live according to his Creator's plan. All of our family and education-related decisions must be consistent with this goal. Thus, the question we must ask ourselves in every choice is: Will this bring my child closer to, or farther from, Jesus Christ?

Similarly, our next goal is for our child to develop respectful, affectionate, and loving relationships with his parents and siblings.

We want him to know and experience the love of family members and to return that love without measure. Cultivating good relationships within the family takes priority even over academic concerns.

The third goal is to form a strong moral character in our child. Like developing strong family relationships, building character takes time, consistency, and concrete action. Its fruits will last a lifetime.

Fourth, we want each of our children to have a healthy personality, maturing appropriately for his age. We need to keep in mind all the different gifts and talents that God has given each of our children and our responsibility to develop them according to God's plan. Each child's personality, as well, needs to be nurtured differently in order for it to unfold according to God's design. What a delicate task to bring our children to maturity!

Finally, we want each of our children to develop his academic potential to the highest level possible—not to prove to our families and friends that home education is a superior way of educating, but so that he can become the person God wants him to be and can do what God made him to do.

An Asset You Didn't Know You Had: Motherhood!

Before you look at your assets simply in terms of the strength of your own educational background and the time, commitment, and money you have to offer, consider the training that motherhood has given and will continue to give you.

Some educators perpetuate the fallacy that only certified "experts" or fully credentialed specialists are qualified to teach your children. You didn't need to be a speech pathologist in order to teach your toddler to talk; you don't need an early-childhood education degree in order to prepare your preschooler for elementary education.

Keep in mind the specific goals for your child. Considering the specifics of what your child needs to learn helps take some of the mystery out of the "educational process". The preschooler, for example, needs to learn colors, to follow directions, to draw or write with a crayon and pencil, to associate written words with spoken words, etc. Broken down into parts, these academic goals seem far less intimidating than the nebulous task of achieving "kindergarten readiness". Similarly, you may hesitate at the thought of teaching an older child to "write well", until you realize that writing well is a skill mastered one step at a time and that the steps are small and well defined. (Later on we will describe ways for you to find out exactly what to teach your child.)

Even after you realize that you don't have to be "certified" in order to teach your child successfully, you may still wonder if you have the basic skills to teach. Remember, first of all, that you have been teaching your child all sorts of information gradually from infancy through the preschool years without anyone questioning your competency to do so. The skills that you have drawn upon countless times since your child's birth and that have enabled you to teach your son or daughter so far are the identical skills you will need to teach academic courses. The basic methodology remains the same—only the content is different. These skills include: the ability to demonstrate and to explain, patience, understanding, and a genuine appreciation of your child's individuality.

In his "Letter to Families", Pope John Paul II points out that a mother begins educating her child in the womb.

> The first months of the child's presence in the mother's womb bring about a particular bond which already possesses an educational significance of its own. The *mother*, even before giving birth, *does not only give shape to the child's body, but also, in an indirect way, to the child's whole personality* [emphasis in original].[1]

The Pope emphasizes the importance of the "feminine genius" in developing all the dimensions of our children.

> How can we fail to understand the importance of the "feminine genius"? It is . . . indispensable for the initial education in the

[1] Pope John Paul II, "Letter to Families", February 2, 1994, no. 16.

family. Its *"educational" effect* on the child begins when he is still in his mother's womb.

But woman's role in the rest of the formational process is just as important. She has a unique capacity to see the person as an individual, to understand his aspirations and needs with special insight, and she is able to face up to problems with deep involvement. The universal values themselves, which any sound education must always present, are offered by feminine sensitivity in a tone complementary to that of man.[2]

As a mother, you are in the unique circumstance of having observed your child's temperament, personality, and learning patterns for years. Reflect for a minute on your own child. Does he plunge right into a new venture or hang back until he's got the lay of the land? Does he get discouraged easily, or is he stubbornly persistent? Does he learn best by observing, by participating, or by following step-by-step instructions? Is he intuitive or methodical?

Children have a natural desire to learn and a delightful curiosity about the ordinary things around us. Effective teaching really is a matter of channeling this desire to learn into the necessary subject areas and choosing the most efficient method to get the point across. As you continually learn more about your child's abilities and what approaches work best for him, you naturally adjust your methods to suit him. Thus, he learns more easily and absorbs information better as you come to know and understand him better.

What Kind of Educational Background Do I Need?

A teaching degree does not necessarily help you teach your children any better than the mom who teaches without it. At least one study reports "no significant difference" in achievement when first

---

[2] Pope John Paul II, Sunday Angelus reflection, July 30, 1995.

and second graders were grouped "according to whether the parent-teacher was or had ever been a state-certified teacher".[3]

According to Patricia Lines, policy analyst for the Department of Education, "For a determined [home-schooling] family, there's really nothing they can't accomplish. We certify [public-school] teachers to learn how to establish discipline and how to teach to a group. I've seen no evidence that a teaching certificate would enhance a one-on-one situation."[4]

Although parents in home-educating families tend to be better educated than the average American family,[5] even children whose parents only finished high school still score higher than the national norms for their peers.[6] Parents with no more than a high-school diploma still home educate successfully. The loving attention of the parents is the key. A good support group and strong curriculum provide essential help as well. (As we'll show later on in Chapter 10, there are many creative ways to overcome your own shortcomings and educational deficiencies and ensure the best academic preparation for your children.)

Research shows home-educated children outscoring public-school counterparts regardless of the educational level attained by their parents. It's a good bet, no matter what your background, that your children will do better under your tutelage than they would in school. Be aware of your own particular weaknesses, though,

[3] Brian D. Ray and Jon Wartes, "The Academic Achievement and Affective Development of Home-Schooled Children", in *Home Schooling: Political, Historical, and Pedagogical Perspectives*, edited by Jane Van Galen and Mary Anne Pitman (Norwood, NJ: Ablex Publishing Corporation, 1991), p. 47.

[4] John W. Kennedy, "Home Schooling Grows Up", *Christianity Today*, July 17, 1995, p. 51.

[5] The average educational level for fathers in home-schooling families is about fifteen years of formal education (about three years of college). Mothers averaged just over fourteen years of formal education (about two years of college). "For comparative purposes, note that in 1988, 20.3% of those at least 25 years in age in the United States had four or more years of college. In this study of home education, 42.7% of the parents had 4 or more years of college." Source: "A Nationwide Study of Home Education: Family Characteristics, Legal Matters, and Student Achievement", National Home Education Research Institute, Seattle, Washington, and Home School Legal Defense Association (1990).

[6] Ray and Wartes, p. 46.

and be prepared to seek advice and help from others. Home tutoring doesn't imply that you have to teach everything yourself, especially as your children get older. It means being home-based and choosing the best academic approaches for your children. For example, if you don't know the foreign language that your child is going to study, and you have neither the time nor the inclination to study it along with your child, you might want to enroll an older child in a language course—either through the community colleges or through a language course such as Berlitz. (Younger children can pick up much of a foreign language from children's language tapes.)

Finally, don't be afraid to learn along with your children. Most of us have gaps in our educational backgrounds or subjects that we wish we understood better. This is especially true for parents who desire to provide a strong classical education for their children but who themselves were raised and educated in the sixties and seventies when everything "new" was "in" and everything "old" was "out". One of the wonderful joys of home educating is the chance for everyone in the family to continue learning—together.

But How Will I Know What to Teach and How to Teach It?

"Okay", you say. "It's true that I know and understand my child better than any teacher ever will. And that counts for something. But I still haven't a clue what to teach or how to begin teaching it!"

Teachers aren't born; they're trained. Fortunately, knowing what to teach and how to teach it is not genetic. For this aspect of home education, having the right tools makes all the difference. State standards of learning, "packaged" or complete curricula, and simply grade-appropriate textbooks themselves will show you what the typical student is expected to learn at each grade level. (These should provide a starting point for you, although you should not limit yourself to what everyone else is doing.) Teacher guides and detailed curricula typically tell you exactly how to teach each lesson, and most offer enriching activities to reinforce or introduce a lesson.

State Standards

Most states have some sort of standards ("learning objectives") published by the state education department or, occasionally, by the local school superintendent's office. These standards typically give very specific guidelines for what must be covered at each grade level in each subject. For most subjects, each grade level's objectives are summarized in a page or two. For example, one of the Virginia math standards for first grade specifies that a student should be able to recognize and write the numbers from one to ninety-nine.

For the most part, state standards have been keyed to the major standardized tests so that the tests measure what are generally considered to be "first-grade skills" everywhere, regardless of minor differences from state to state. Most states will gladly, either upon request or when you declare your intent to home school, send you the standards for the major subject areas. Stick to the major subject areas, or you might be buried under the blizzard of paper coming in your direction.

Also, don't be confused or intimidated by the educational jargon and the long, convoluted sentences that education bureaucrats often use to describe their objectives. Boil it down: What is the objective? What is the specific thing that my child needs to learn? For example, one Virginia first-grade learning standard specifies that: "The student will determine by counting the value of a collection of pennies, nickels, and dimes whose total value is $.50 or less." What's the real objective? That your child be able to count his change up to fifty cents, using dimes, nickels, and pennies. Like most of the elementary educational objectives, this is not an intimidating concept to teach.

If, however, you don't have the time or energy to plow through the state standards, one shortcut is to look through the public- or parochial-school textbooks, in the major subjects, for the grade your child will be entering. Borrow a playmate's math book, scan the table of contents, and get a general idea of what needs to be covered. (Most schools choose their textbooks to satisfy the state standards.) Or call your local public school and ask what texts they use in the major subjects. However, *do not* go out and buy the text that the public schools use simply because that is the one they use. Chances are that you can do better than that— or find one that covers the same ground but perhaps with an approach more suited to your child. The public school system can show you the minimum acceptable skill level; don't let it set your goals for you.

One easy way to be sure you are covering everything your child needs to learn for each grade level is to buy a preset or "complete" curriculum. Distributors of complete curricula do the research for you. Their texts and teacher guides cover the material that most states require. However, you lose much of the flexibility of tailoring your child's curriculum when you choose this approach. (The benefits and disadvantages of different types of curriculum options are discussed in Chapter 10.) Some curriculum providers offer an advisory service (and often for a fee) as well as the packaged curriculum. Other programs offer on-call reading and math specialists or veteran moms to counsel you on the practical steps to make it work.

Grade-Appropriate Textbooks

Knowing what to teach your child is often as simple as looking in the book. Most textbooks, and even some workbooks, contain at least a table of contents and often a more detailed scope-and-sequence chart. These pages map out what topics are covered in each text and in what order. When planning the year's curriculum, compare the tables of contents in the texts with the state standards for each child's particular grade level. This preparation ensures that you cover the material your child will probably be tested on later in the year. In reality, though, most home educators consider this to be a minimum level of learning.

But I've Never Followed a Curriculum Before . . .

Curriculum is your basic guide of *what* to teach. There is a wealth of curricular materials available, so you don't need to put it all together yourself (although later on you may want to). Most curricula are self-explanatory.

Even though you may never have seen a curriculum or a teacher guide before you decided to home educate, don't worry! Most would-be teachers in education school spend very little time learning substantive areas of study. They rarely train with a specific curriculum, either. Instead, they spend time on methodology courses, learning classroom management, and things like "cooperative learning strategies".[7] Their courses often are very "politically correct", detailing ways to build the students' self-esteem and to be more multiculturally sensitive.[8]

After all, when a teacher takes a job, she will have little or no control over what curriculum or textbooks she will be required to use. Chances are that when she walks into a new classroom, she will be as unfamiliar with the curriculum as you will be the first day you look at it. The curriculum companies and textbook distributors know this, too; that's why teacher guides and step-by-step curricula were "invented".

Both teacher guides (or manuals) and detailed curricula tend to walk you through your explanation of a topic. Typically, the teacher guide resembles a step-by-step instruction manual, often including a list of needed materials, activities or games to reinforce the day's lesson, and review questions from the previous day's lesson. The teacher manuals and curricula really teach you what to

[7] See generally: Rita Kramer, *Ed School Follies: The Miseducation of America's Teachers* (New York: The Free Press, 1991). In a devastating critique of the teacher-training system in the U.S., Kramer details the rarity with which any academic content is covered in education courses. In one example, typical of the prevailing situation, she describes sitting in education classes at the State University of New York: "It has been a long morning, and not once have I heard any mention of content in the curriculum. Instead, they are talking about 'building self-esteem through assertive role playing in peer situations'" (p. 36).

[8] Ibid.

teach. They also can help you compensate for your own weaknesses. For example, if you are not very creative, you may want to choose a curriculum that offers many imaginative multisensory activities to introduce or reinforce the topics you will study. Or, you may look for a teacher guide that provides many examples of in–depth projects with themes that correlate to the rest of the curriculum. Institutional school teachers rely on curricula and teacher texts for the same purpose.

Finally, unlike a classroom teacher, you will have the flexibility to discontinue using a particular text or curriculum if it doesn't work. You can make changes *whenever* it will benefit your children, even if it is already November or mid-March. The curriculum and books are your tools, not your bosses.

Other Resources

In addition to basic curricular materials, there is a wealth of other resources available to enrich your child's education—and to offer support and fresh ideas for you. You may want to subscribe to a home-education national magazine or newsletter. Typically, these feature articles on a particular aspect of home education (for example, socialization) or on teaching a specific subject. They often include teaching tips, updates on new approaches, curricula, or teaching aids, and announcements of major conventions, workshops, and curriculum fairs. Local support-group newsletters may also contain some of these items in addition to local calendars of events. (See Bibliography: Home Education, General, for a listing of newsletters.)

For those who enjoy different forms of media, educational TV and the wide variety of materials available at public libraries offer still another option. Most libraries have expanded their collections beyond books to include audio tapes, video tapes, educational video games, and computer programs.

How Much Time Does Home Education Take?

Comparatively little! Home education takes much less time than the typical institutional school day. The actual amount of time depends on what you include in your school day. Many home-educating families strive to finish academic work and basic chores by noon in order to set aside time for outside lessons, Mom's quiet time, home business, and play time. Others spread out academic lessons throughout the day, intermingled with chores, lessons, and play time. Some families work four days a week and reserve one day for field trips or special projects. The variety of schedule options is endless. The choice is yours. (In Chapter 8 we have included a sampling of different schedules actually used by home-educating families.)

Anecdotal evidence suggests that moms who teach pre-kindergarten- and kindergarten-age children spend less than an hour a day teaching. Mothers of early elementary students spend approximately two hours a day on academics. Late elementary school requires more time, averaging two to three and a half hours. Junior-high and high-school students generally spend more time on their studies, ranging from two and a half to four hours each day. As a child gets older, he usually spends a greater percentage of his time working independently. Interestingly enough, achievement scores remain fairly consistent among home-educated students, regardless of how structured their days are or the number of hours they spend on academics.[9]

Does it sound incredible to you that a mom teaching at home can accomplish in two hours what it takes the school system six hours to teach? Consider this. The National Education Commission on Time and Learning issued a report in 1994 entitled "Prisoners of Time". In this report the Commission faults schools for spending, on average, only three hours per day on what are considered "core" academic subjects.[10] And the attention that each child

[9] Ray and Wartes, p. 46.
[10] "Core Studies Shunted Aside in U.S. High Schools", The Washington Times, May 5, 1994, p. A11.

receives in learning these core subjects is diluted by the sheer numbers of children demanding attention.

Much of the time spent in school is wasted by disciplinary distractions, administrative details, busywork, waiting in lines for drinks or the bathroom, passing out or collecting papers, or waiting for others to finish their work. Hours a day are devoted to nonacademic courses such as sex education, driver's education, environmental studies, and study hall. The Commission's recommendation, not surprisingly, was to lengthen the time spent on core academic instruction by lengthening the school day rather than by cutting the "extras".

In contrast, when you set your curriculum, you begin with the basics and proceed from there. Instead of death education or drug education, you can add tremendous "extras", such as art history or classical music. And your curriculum will still take less time than it would in a classroom.

A mom giving individual attention for two hours, or even dividing her attention between several children, covers a lot of material—certainly more than a teacher who cannot move forward until twenty-six children have caught on. At home, we tutor well-behaved children (most of the time, anyway!), and "classroom administration" takes little time. Our children get to focus on their real task—learning.

Because schoolwork takes less time, we can be better stewards of our child's time—ensuring that it is not all high-pressured, structured time or time wasted (on a tedious bus ride, for example). Children have more free time to play, read, pursue hobbies, or just "hang around" with you or their brothers and sisters. Unstructured time is often when real conversations happen. ("Mom, do you know what I just realized. . . ?")

In addition, children who learn at home can and should help you with the household chores. Oftentimes when children spend so many hours in the classroom and come home facing another hour or two of homework, their parents are reluctant to have them use their little remaining time to help out around the house. Yet these children then are cheated of the opportunity to assume essential responsibility and to achieve personal growth.

Family responsibilities give your children practical living skills and a certain amount of self-sufficiency. And, they are crucial to their character formation. As they help, your children will have the chance to develop self-discipline, willingness, cheerfulness, perseverance, and attention to detail. These traits are not only integral to character formation, they will pay off in both the short and the long term. Their help makes your home more efficient (allowing *you* more time) and gives them the tools to become independent adults.

In order to find two or three hours in your day to devote to your child's education, you need to prioritize your time commitments. Perhaps this will initially mean cutting back on outside commitments. Block out your educational time in much the same way that someone who runs a home business does. A regular schedule is essential. Let others know your schedule in order to minimize interruptions. Phone calls don't have to be answered right away. Use an answering machine to screen calls for true emergencies, and return the other calls when your children don't need your focused attention. Make teaching time a priority and stick to it.

One great advantage of home education is the great flexibility it gives you to find "family time". Parents are free to set their "school time" according to what works best for the family's schedule. For example, one father of five arrives home from work after 7:30 each night. Rather than give up on ever having a family dinner, the family simply eats later than most families. The children stay up until almost 11:00 P.M. in order to spend time with their dad—a chance they would lose if they had to be in school the next morning by 7:30. Flexible time scheduling allows your family to accommodate swing shifts, illness, and new babies, for example, through evening or afternoon classes, year-round schooling, and periodic vacations.

How Much Does It Cost?

Home education, while not free, offers the promise of a private-school education at a fraction of the cost. Unlike public education, curriculum, books, and materials will cost you something. But these costs can be minimized through diligent use of the library, buying used books, or borrowing from friends.

Families who do not have a high disposable income need not worry that their child's education at home will be affected by lack of money.[11] According to the most recent study, home-educating families "averaged a $488 per student expenditure per year".[12] While electronic learning tools, science kits, and math manipulatives may be attractive, they are not necessary. Basic texts, workbooks, pencils, and paper, on the other hand, do not cost much and can be just as effective in getting the concepts across.

But I Know I'd Go Crazy!

Your first reaction to home education may be, "I couldn't do that, I'm not patient enough." In fact, *few* of us are born "patient enough". The most important personal qualities for teaching your children are the same ones that make you a successful parent: unconditional love, respect for your children, a desire to serve them, the ability to listen and to explain, and humility in the face of your own limitations.

For Regis and Roseanne Martin, the parents of eight children, home education helped them to see their own need to depend completely on God in all things.

> Home schooling has brought us face-to-face with our weaknesses and brought us to an awareness of the necessity to abandon our-selves ever more completely to God's providence—to allow His

[11] Ray and Wartes, p. 46. See also: "A Nationwide Study of Home Education Achievement", by the National Home Education Research Institute and the Home School Legal Defense Association (1990), *Home School Court Report*, December 1990, p. 7.

[12] "A Nationwide Study of Home Education Achievement", p. 3.

work to be made manifest through us, to become ever more trusting and confident, and to live only in the present moment, not relying on our own strength to get us through.

Patience grows out of love, self-control, and a supernatural perspective on daily life. If we can recognize the opportunities in life where God is calling us to perfect ourselves, and to grow, then we can overcome the obstacles that inevitably block our way.

A home-schooling mother of four in Ohio shares these words of encouragement with other home-schooling mothers:

> I chuckle when other moms say they couldn't home school be-cause they have no patience. I was and still am the most impatient of mothers. . . . It is fascinating to work on faults with God's grace and help. Home schooling forced me to try to conquer my anger and impatience, to acknowledge the infinite love and patience of our heavenly Father, and to try to . . . grow to be like Jesus. God's ways are truly mysterious!

Just because you are having a real struggle trying to be patient doesn't mean that you never will be.

The particular circumstances in your life that are trying your patience might be precisely the means through which our Lord will teach you to be patient and to rely on *Him* more instead of on your own will power. One mother puts it this way,

> How else . . . will you learn a skill if you don't practice it? God knows what it takes for you to learn patience. Perhaps it's a clingy child, perhaps it's a high-demand child, perhaps it's three very active children, perhaps a very slow child, or perhaps, for an aver-age mom, it's average children. Patience is a fruit of the Holy Spirit, and as I yield my life to Him, I can see the fruit beginning to bear. So, does it take patience to home school? Well, yes, but you don't wait until you have it to begin home schooling; you learn it along the way.[13]

As Scripture tells us in Philippians 4:13, "I can do all things in Him who strengthens me." It's true!

[13] Karen Weber, "What Does It Take to Homeschool?", in *Agnus Dei* newsletter, Woodbridge, VA, March 1994, p. 5.

Patience and self-control are fruits of the Holy Spirit. "But the fruit of the Spirit is love, joy, peace, patience, kindness, goodness, faithfulness, gentleness, self-control" (Gal 5:22). And the Spirit can give them to us in greater and greater measure. The way we see ourselves now, today, is not necessarily how we'll be a year from now. Growth in Christ accomplishes amazing things in us!

Even if you are pretty sure your patience will hold out (most of the time, anyway), you may anticipate feeling trapped—fearing that home schooling would mean you would never again have time for yourself. Without a doubt, home education *does* require more of your time. But it is precisely this active involvement in your child's life that is the key to raising him successfully. Careful scheduling, monitoring outside commitments, and relying on your husband's support will help you get the breaks you need and keep you from becoming overburdened.

Support from your husband is crucial in making home education work. His perspective may help you relate better to a child whose temperament or personality is at odds with your own. His advice may help you find concrete solutions to the problems you encounter. When you have his support and encouragement, it is easier to tell him if you are frustrated, overwhelmed, or just plain need a change of scenery. Genuine agreement between both of you that this is the best decision for your family will make it easier for the wife to say, "I need a break", and for her husband to say, "Let's find a way for you to get the 'time off' you need." Otherwise, you may feel reluctant to share your difficulties, for fear that he will react with, "That's it. The kids go back into school tomorrow!" (We will talk more about this in Chapter 9.)

Yet, it is important to have some time to yourself on a regular basis. Much like a mini-vacation, predictable free time renews your enthusiasm and sharpens your perspective. Time spent on adult interests helps you retain balance in your life. In addition, your children need to see you as a man or a woman, and a husband or a wife, not solely as "Mom" and "Dad".

One way of providing fruitful time for yourself is to take the opportunity for annual retreats and monthly days of recollection provided through parishes, religious orders, and movements within the Church. You not only will have time alone but time alone with God. Time spent in prayer and reflection is vitally necessary. Spiritual refreshment not only gives us a spiritual boost of energy, it also keeps us open to new inspirations so that we can discern the next step in God's plan for our lives.

Another option for time off may be as close as your neighbor or other support-group moms. Many home-schooling moms trade off with each other, either regularly or as needed, to give each other some "child-free" hours. This allows time for doctor visits, shopping, reading, or exercise without interruptions and a hundred questions. Other moms rely on their husbands to give them a few hours a week of completely discretionary time. One mother commented that, since she began home schooling, "My children don't seem to mind as much when I have a baby-sitter come in. . . . They're with me all the rest of the time." When you know that, on a daily basis, you are giving your children the time and attention they need, you're less likely to feel guilty or neglectful when you do need to rely on a baby-sitter or trusted relative.

Our attitudes toward our children are key, even for those who do not choose to educate full time at home. Do we dread the time we need to spend with our children? Do unexpected losses of our own time make us resentful, when, for example, school is canceled for the tenth day in a row due to snow? "I can't wait to get these kids back in school", mothers frequently exclaim by the time August rolls around.

Attitudes like these often hint at two underlying problems: one, our own lack of willingness to put others first and to serve them in love; and, two, our inability to raise our children to be polite, self-disciplined, and aware of others' needs. We should reflect on our own attitudes when we are with our children. Even when we are with them, are our minds preoccupied with "more important" things? Do we feel frustrated, and perhaps communicate resentment toward them, because we can't be doing our own projects when we are with them?

When we give our children sustained time and attention in a

way that shows them how important they are to us, they usually are more willing to relinquish us when we need to focus our energies elsewhere. It's true, our children need to respect our own need for time, including time to accomplish other kinds of work, whether that is housework, apostolic work, or something else. We don't need to give our children our undivided attention twenty-four hours a day. But we do need to give our time freely and without resentment when they need us.

On the other hand, many of us shrink from the sometimes difficult task of training and disciplining our children well. We need to help them grow emotionally, spiritually, and socially, so that if we are surrounded by them constantly, it will not only be bearable but enjoyable. Karen Weber, a mother of five, states it clearly: "If you have trained a child that is not a joy to you, what makes you think he will be a joy to others?"[14] Another mother, Laura Berquist, who has been teaching her children at home for over ten years, makes the same point but from a different perspective. "I like my children, I enjoy doing things with my children, and I enjoy having them around. If you have them there all the time, they become the types of people you like to be with."

Can I Really Make It Fun?

Parents often wonder, "If I teach my children at home, won't they miss out on all of the little but fun things that school offers?" A friend of one home-educating mom was raving one day about her daughter's fabulous preschool, saying that she was already learning her colors and that the classroom offered a good mix of ages. Isn't this exactly what home education can offer? Indeed, much more.

Some of those little but important things, things that can matter to and may be missed by a child, are the fun of riding in the bus, taking music and art lessons, eating out of a lunch box, school pictures, sports teams, and clubs. In reality, each of these fun things *is* something you can provide. Most of the things kids enjoy in

[14] Ibid.

school are extracurricular to the institutional system of education. The challenge is to discover the fun things your children will enjoy and then provide them. Many of these fun experiences can be provided either through family outings or support-group field trips.

Let's take bus rides as an example. A few mothers have commented to us that they would never home educate because they couldn't imagine depriving their children of the fun of riding the bus every day to school. These women obviously enjoyed riding the bus with their friends! Yet, today's school buses are often filled with obscenities, chaos, and ridicule. In addition, riding the bus can have a bad impact on a child's ability to learn when he finally does arrive at school.[15]

Even more important, organizing educational decisions around the need to make sure your child rides the school bus every day puts impossible restrictions on your life. Does it make sense to say you'll never buy a house near your child's school because you want to make sure he can ride the bus every morning? If you want to give your children a bus ride, it's better to buy them tickets and ride the bus with them than to let their educational opportunities be determined by that consideration!

School photos are another popular aspect of conventional education. In response, support groups across the country have engaged school photographers to take individual photos of their children and a group picture for the support group at discounted school rates.

Another idea to consider is this: If your child wants the fun of eating out of a lunch box, let him! He can pack his lunch in the morning or the night before and pop it open when you break for lunch. You can also use lunch boxes whenever you go on field trips or get together for support-group activities.

---

[15] According to research compiled by Raymond and Dorothy Moore, and The Moore Foundation in Camas, Washington, some children suffer from subtle motion sickness that knocks their equilibrium off balance for several hours after riding the bus. This disorder causes difficulty in learning (particularly reading). A lesser but real problem is that in some areas children with long bus rides arrive at school too sleepy to concentrate fully.

Some children earnestly desire a recess period, probably because their school-attending friends usually cite this as their favorite "subject". One mother commented, "It seems ridiculous when our school day only takes two hours to put aside twenty minutes for recess halfway through. But when I lengthened the day by twenty minutes and gave the boys that twenty-minute "recess" in the middle, they loved it."

For some children, playing team sports is the best part about going to school. Yet team sports often are available through community-based programs or the local parish CYO teams. Generally, these teams are open to members of the community or parish regardless of where the child attends school. Several states now allow home-schooled children "dual enrollment" in both their home school and their local public school.[16] This innovation lets home-taught children play on school athletic teams or participate in after-school clubs and specialized classes. In other states, the Home School Legal Defense Association is considering legal action to require public schools to open their teams to home-taught students who live within their boundaries. In an increasing number of locales, teams made up of home-educated children compete against other local teams. Other popular sports (for example, karate and skating) are not organized around school teams and are equally available to your children.

Studying music and art definitely can be a rich part of home education. Because these subjects require more expertise to teach, you may want to see what classes are offered through your area support groups or community resources. One mother found an art student from the local community college to conduct a two-hour studio art class once every other week for her children. The children, all except the preschooler, were introduced to all the major art media. They loved having a substantial block of time in which to learn and perfect their skills. If you live in a university community or have a community college nearby, you can probably find a

[16] "Why Your School Should Cooperate with Home Schoolers", in *Ideas and Perspectives*, July 24, 1995, p. 34. See also: "Hostility Fades As Home Schooling Grows", *Harvard Education Letter*, May/June 1993, p. 6.

qualified art or music instructor pretty easily. Another alternative would be to see if the parish music minister would be willing to train a children's choir or chorus.

The guiding principle for us is that home education should always offer more, not less, than what the schools provide. Find out what is important to your children. Ask them what they think would be fun to add to their school day. Find out what works. In many cases, these little things are easy to provide and can make the day more interesting and enjoyable for your children.

Oftentimes, too, the novelty wears off—those lunch boxes might not get packed as frequently, but your child won't feel he's missed out on something his school-bound friends experience. He may just decide after experiencing it for himself that it's not *that* important. It may help him realize that opening a lunch box in a lunchroom is not so wonderful as to make him want to give up the fun and freedom of learning at home. When parents accommodate the fun things that a child desires, they help him become aware of the greater flexibility that home education provides. He won't feel he's missing out on something—he will know he's got the better deal!

Will I Be Alone?

In 1991, the U.S. Department of Education estimated that 300,000 to 500,000 children were being home educated.[17] In 1993, the Home School Legal Defense Association estimated between 750,000 and one million children were being home educated.[18] Numbers continue to swell each year as more and more parents discover this option. The typical family that home educates has

[17] Home-education experts generally think the true number of home-schooled children is underestimated by the U.S. Department of Education. Discovering the actual number of home-educated children is difficult because some homeschoolers are "underground", and Education Department estimates based on curriculum sales can be self-selecting and fail to account for used or borrowed curricula.

[18] HSLDA "estimates that there are 750,000 to 1 million children being educated at home in the United States". "More Parents Choose to Be Their Child's Teachers", *The Washington Post*, May 23, 1993, pp. B1, B5.

three or more children and parents who are slightly better educated than the national average. The average family income is slightly above the national median. While almost all home-educating families are intact families,[19] "[a]bout 11% of the mothers reported that they work outside of the home, and they do so for an average of 14.6 hours per week."[20] Catholics constitute a small but growing percentage of home-educating families. In general, the number of converts to home education is doubling every three or four years.[21]

In practical terms, what significance do these statistics have for you? First, the number of Catholics who are choosing to home educate, in spite of the nationwide network of Catholic schools, is exploding. Attendance at Catholic home-education conventions all across the country has been doubling in size each year for the past several years. Similarly, participation in Catholic home-education support groups has also doubled or even tripled in some areas since 1990. Ten to fifteen years ago, most home-education support groups and home-education resources were secular or Protestant. Now, however, Catholics are becoming a force in their own right within the home-education movement.

In almost any area of the country, chances are good that you will find other Catholics who are teaching their children at home. New support groups are constantly springing up in order to provide practical support for mothers and peer support and friendships for home-taught children. So, you will not be alone out there!

Even if you live in an area with few home-educating Catholic families, you can stay in touch and find support through newsletters, magazines, and journals. Several new publications specifi-

[19] "A Nationwide Study of Home Education Achievement", p. 3, reporting that "only 1.6% of the families were headed by a single parent, and all of them were mothers."

[20] Ibid.

[21] "Learning from Their Parents, More Students Start School Year without Leaving Home", *The Washington Times*, September 14, 1993, p. A5. In Virginia, for example, "since homeschooling became legal in the state in 1984, the number of children being taught outside schools has grown by about 25% each year." In the last year (1992) for which statistics were available in Virginia, home education grew by 28 percent. "More Parents Choose to Be Their Children's Teachers", p. B1.

cally address the practical and inspirational needs of Catholic home-educating families. (See Bibliography: Home Education, General.) Some even offer help in arranging pen pals for your children with other children who learn at home.

The Variety of Options

While we believe that full-time home education is a wonderful way to live family life and to educate our children, you can achieve many of the same benefits even if you are unable to make a full-time commitment to their education. The essential commitment for every parent is to accept the responsibility for directing, shaping, and evaluating your child's education.

Supplementary Education

A "supplementary" approach to home education is what *every* parent should consider if the full-time approach is not workable or desirable right now. In this approach, your child remains in the school setting. As parents, however, you monitor the information your child receives in school and supplement this instruction at home. At a minimum, parents need to review and reinforce the academics taught at school. But in fact you may need to reteach some subjects or introduce others that otherwise would be skipped. As the Pope expressed in his 1994 "Letter to Families", even when children are in a formal school setting, their parents' "educational presence ought to continue to be constant and active."[22]

One father of ten explained why he and his wife chose to begin teaching their children at home in addition to sending them to school.

> Our parish school taught reading by the sight method. Yet, we felt phonics instruction was crucial for our children to become fluent

---

[22] "Letter to Families", no. 16.

readers quickly. So we taught each of our children how to read, using the phonics method, before kindergarten. Over the years, we continued to supplement the school's instruction in math, history, and religion—wherever we thought it was necessary.

The challenge with the "supplementary approach", however, is the burden it places on your child. Problems can arise when a child is not home based but is in school all day, and the parents have to teach subjects while school is still in session. A parent who is determined to teach history, for example, won't find it easy to convince her child's school to exempt her child from the school's history class.

In religious and moral formation, you should not only review concepts but help your children see practical ways of living the principles taught. In matters of faith, especially, it is key not only that you make sure your child is being taught correctly but also that faith is not seen as "just another subject". Family prayer times, Bible reflections, reading saints' lives, discussing what you believe and why—all these are not ideas just for the home school. They need to be an everyday part of every family's life.

Part-Time Home Education

Some parents choose a "part-time" option, especially for younger children. In this type of education, the child does attend a traditional school at least part-time, or is taught by other parents as part of a cooperative effort, but is home based the rest of the time. This can be ideal for some people, but for many it causes difficulty in establishing a set routine.

One mom, for example, sent her child to preschool three mornings a week and taught him at home on Tuesday and Thursday. What the mom thought was the ideal situation soon turned out to be a headache, as her child had two completely different types of "school days" to adjust to. It also worried her that her child was beginning to bring home certain attitudes and habits from her classmates. Fading fast were the attitudes of respect, discipline, and love. Growing in their place were defiance, disrespect, and distance between parent and child. The next year the mom moved to full-time home education.

Full-Time Home Education

In the full-time option, the mom (typically) is the one who teaches all or most of the subjects. A slightly different approach would be the family that is home based but also uses cooperative teaching, clubs, and outside classes or tutors to help in the actual teaching. These two options are very similar in that the parents are clearly the ones who choose the curriculum, oversee the progress, and are directly involved in at least some of the teaching. The children in these kinds of families would not attend institutional schools. Most of the information in this book pertains directly to full-time home education but can certainly be applied to the part-time and supplementary options as well.

What Kind of Commitment Do I Need to Make?

Your children need stability in their education. You need time to work through the inevitable difficulties and discouragements that this venture (like any new undertaking) will bring. So, in order to give home education a real try, you should commit yourself to it for a reasonable period, such as an entire school year.

This does *not* mean that in order to try home education you must plan to teach at home for the next twelve years. Take it one year at a time. When and for how long you home educate may depend on each child, family circumstances, your health, etc.—in short, on events in the future that you can't foresee now. But, especially with younger children, there is little at risk and much to gain by experiencing a year of family-centered education.

To decide whether you *really* are capable of home schooling your child, don't ask yourself: Am I so talented and so independent that only I should teach my children? Instead, ask yourself: Am I willing to be available—with God's grace—to teach my children with love the best I can? The Blessed Mother is a great example to us—she didn't say that she was sufficient for the task of raising the Son of God but only that she was available. Likewise, we must be available to serve the Lord. We know He will give us the needed grace to teach and form our children to be the persons He wants them to be.

The Reasons You *Can* Do It

1. Love is the most important credential needed to teach your child successfully. The love and trust that underlie your relationship with your child allow you to understand, motivate, and challenge him beyond what a classroom teacher can do.

2. Motherhood has trained you well for teaching: you have been explaining, teaching, and demonstrating countless things to your child over the years. You know his temperament, personality, and learning patterns better than any teacher ever will.

3. State standards, textbooks, and complete curricula give you the step-by-step knowledge of what to teach in each subject.

4. Teacher guides tell you the most effective ways to convey the material as well as how to review and reinforce it.

5. Home education takes as little as two hours per day for younger children and up to four hours a day for older children.

6. You don't need to be the most patient or organized person in order to home educate. God will provide plenty of opportunities to grow in these areas as you teach. Depend on Him!

7. You can make home education fun for your children—there is nothing attractive offered by schools that you cannot find a way to duplicate or even surpass.

8. Those families that are not able to home educate on a full-time basis should at least monitor and supplement the basic educa-

tion provided by the schools. Parents *need* to be involved in their child's education.

9. Remember—your decision to home educate is made one year at a time. Try it for a year. You'll be glad you did!

7

Should Homeroom Be a Study Hall?

Should I Home Educate?

Decision time.

Deciding to home educate is a family decision—one that depends on the unique circumstances of each family. Yet, at times, even we "grown-ups" can find ourselves vulnerable to peer pressure. What will my friends think? How will my neighbors and coworkers react? What if my parents think we're crazy? Subtle (and not so subtle) pressure comes from every corner.

In some Catholic communities, home education is becoming increasingly popular among young, faithful Catholic families. This can become pressure if you worry that others will think you less committed to your Faith or to your children if you do not choose to home educate. Or you might have siblings who are teaching their own children at home and are totally convinced that you *have* to do the same for your children. Pressure might come from the other direction if you are the first in your circle of friends, or in your parish, to consider it. Negative reactions from your parish priests and families in particular can be hard to ignore.

A Family Decision

The freedom of all parents to choose what is best for their child's education must be respected. Regardless of whether a family decides to embark on full-time home education or not, it is a decision that rests squarely with the parents, not third parties. Instead of allowing others' personal opinions to weigh heavily in your decision, try to ground your decision in a realistic appraisal of your family situation and an expectant faith that God will show you the best way for your family.

Because education is an important part of the family's mission, both spouses should agree in their judgment of how best to accomplish it. For home education, this means both husband and wife should be united in their willingness to try it—at least agreeing that a trial run for a year is the best course for their family. Unity not only makes things work on a practical level, it also prevents one spouse from having a "secret agenda" of getting the kids back into school. Of course, a husband and wife might not share the same level of enthusiasm or knowledge! But an attitude of openness helps a more knowledgeable spouse, for example, to educate the other. Home education probably isn't for you if one spouse is adamantly opposed to it or only grudgingly capitulates to the other's badgering and manipulation.

What Does God Want for Our Family?

How, then, do you make the right decision? The central question in deciding whether to home educate is: "What does God want for our family?" If God's plan for your family includes home education, then trust that He will give you everything you need to accomplish His will. Of course, just because it is God's plan for you to teach your children doesn't mean that it is necessarily His plan for it to be easy, or for your children to score 99.9 on all their achievement tests! Lots of people are called to do things that in fact are very difficult for them or entail some suffering. But, if it really is His will, then you can trust Him to bring good out of difficulty—even if the good fruit isn't immediately apparent. "You did not choose me, but I chose you and appointed you that you should go and bear fruit and that your fruit should abide" (Jn 15:16).

The first step, then, in discerning if home education is the right choice for your family is to pray. In faith, simply ask God if this is what He desires for your family. Pray with the confidence and trust that He will show you the best path. Besides making this part of your personal prayer, pray together with your spouse that God will show you His will clearly.

Many families take advantage of retreats, spiritual directors, and the Ignatian Spiritual Exercises to help them discern God's will for their children's education. Sometimes God's will is experienced through a heartfelt conviction that this is the right decision. Other times it is expressed through the husband's leadership in the family. For some, God makes His will known by closing all the other doors—leaving you with only one viable option. Or He may lead you to see His will by suddenly smoothing the way for you, removing what had seemed like an insurmountable objection (such as time, money, or state approval).

Short of a direct inspiration from God, you can rely on what St. Ignatius calls "consolations" and "desolations" in prayer. These are really the inclinations of your soul when you pray about something in particular. For example, do you feel peaceful or in turmoil when you pray about home educating? This is where a spiritual director can help you sort it all out.

If your prayer yields no clear sense of what God might be asking, then St. Ignatius encourages a matter-of-fact weighing of all the pros and cons of the situation in order to discover God's will. But all the pros and cons need to be evaluated, not just for their practical significance, but from the perspective of "What brings the greatest glory to God?" and "What effect will this have on the salvation of my soul (and the souls of others entrusted to my care)?"

Evaluate Your Motives

If you are going to try to sort out, on a very practical level, the risks, benefits, and feasibility of home education, it can be helpful first to look at your own motives. Ask yourself why you are considering home education. Or ask yourself why you have been unwilling to consider home education for your children. Are you sincerely open to doing the Lord's will, no matter what the cost?

Keep in mind that people often begin with one primary motivation for home educating (for example, a desire to help your child achieve academic excellence) and later discover other deeper, over-arching motivations (such as building stronger family relation-ships). In reality, the best motivation is spiritual: you are choosing home education because you really believe that this is God's plan for your family right now.

Most people actually have many interconnected reasons for con-sidering home education the best option. Be wary, however, about letting inadequate motives carry the greatest weight in your deci-sion. For example, peer or family pressure can lead to a decision you may regret later on. Similarly, don't choose home education out of a need to withdraw, because you feel that "the world is a terrible place." Although there are problems in the world, our attitudes as Christians must not be to hide but rather to nurture children who will be apostles and eventually change men's hearts and the world.

Another improper motive in choosing home education is to punish your children for discipline or educational problems. ("If you don't shape up and show some respect, I'll take you out of school and teach you myself!") Your efforts will be doomed to failure before you begin.

Also, keep in mind that choosing home education doesn't mean you have to accept every reason home education makes sense. Nor do you need to accept every ideological position of other home schoolers you know. Similarly, you might agree intellectually with all the reasons home education works yet know in your heart that it is not God's choice for you. Your decision can be made only by focusing on the specific situation of your family.

Look at Your Life Realistically

Now . . . down to the nitty-gritty! Examine your life circum-stances realistically. Weigh the time and commitment you are will-ing to make. Think about your temperament and your own educational background. Consider your child's special needs and the stresses already present in your family life. Can home education help meet these needs and lessen the stresses? Assess how much support your spouse will give you as well as your child's receptiveness to the idea of home education. (An unreceptive child does not mean home education is not for you. However, in making the decision for your family, be aware that a negative attitude is an additional problem to be overcome. See the next chapter for more information). Mull over the practical things that need to get done every day in your life and how you can make them go more smoothly if you choose to home educate.

Check Out Support-Group Opportunities

If you are unsure whether or not to try home education, make some calls and find out what local home-education support groups are in your area. Support groups provide inestimable help—moral support, encouragement, friends for your children and yourself, ideas about curriculum, books, teaching strategies, field trips, household organization—more than you would expect. Support groups often make the difference in whether you will weather the first "storms" that darken the sky after your switch to a home-based routine. If you have been somewhat unsure about choosing home education, knowing that a support group is available can give you the confidence to try it.

Be Confident in Your Decision

Once you have decided, be confident in that decision. After ten years of home education, Susan Waldstein maintains that "the first thing is to be convinced. I'm convinced that this is the best thing for my children, and so I'm sure God will give me the grace to do it." Others will pick up on your positive attitude (or on your lack of confidence) and reflect it in their comments to you.

Many home-schooling moms say that when they confidently tell people about the benefits they have reaped from teaching their children at home, the reaction is positive. More often than not, sharing positively elicits supportive and encouraging comments. At the very least it encourages others to be curious about why you are so content in what you have chosen.

It is especially important for your children to see that you are firm and sure of your decision—even if you have a few fears and reservations lurking in the background. If they perceive you are waffling, and *they* want to be back in school, your children will find your weak point and lean on it. In contrast, if both parents present a united front communicating their confidence in the wisdom of their choice, children accept it much more easily.

As one mother realized halfway through their first year of home education, "We were putting too much responsibility on the children for our decision to home school. We kept asking our daughter if this was a good idea, until we realized this was a ridiculous burden to put on a little girl." The parents adjusted their own attitudes, and, instead of being tentative about this decision, they freely spoke about home education as the *best* thing for the whole family. The children responded receptively and enthusiastically. Nine years later, they are still home educating with great success.

Trust in God!

The words of Psalm 127 offer a fruitful reflection on being faithful to God's plan and on the blessings of trusting in His plan for your family.

> Unless the Lord builds the house,
> those who build it labor in vain.
> Unless the Lord watches over the city,
> the watchman stays awake in vain.
>
> It is in vain that you rise up early
> and go late to rest,
> eating the bread of anxious toil;
> for he gives to his beloved sleep.
>
> Lo, sons are a heritage from the Lord,
> the fruit of the womb a reward.

Like arrows in the hand of a warrior
are the sons of one's youth.

Happy is the man who has
his quiver full of them!
He shall not be put to shame
when he speaks with his enemies in the gate.

If, indeed, home education is what you are being called to, we hope that a few years from now you will share the perspective of Laura Berquist from California. After ten years of home education, she tells us that there is "no question life is better. . . . I wouldn't go back for anything!"

The Deciding Factors

1. The decision whether to home educate is one that rests squarely with both parents. Though one may do more research than the other, both spouses should agree.

2. The big question is: "What does God want for our family?"

3. The first step in discerning whether you should home educate is to pray about it.

4. Beyond prayer, you will need to evaluate your motives and look at your life circumstances realistically.

5. Once you have decided, be confident in your decision and project that assurance to your children.

6. Finally, trust in God! If home education is His will for your family, He will give you everything you need to accomplish it.

8

How to Make Home Education
a Class Act

How Do I Home Educate?

Now we are ready for the nuts and bolts of formulating our plan for Catholic home education. At each step of the process, both spouses' involvement is critical, though one spouse may do more of the research or planning than the other. Remember this is not *mom* education but *home* education, which means it requires a full family effort.

Educate Yourself—Get the Facts

Resources

Get the facts on home education from books and magazines (see Bibliography: Home Education, General). Situations vary for each family, so the more reading you do, the more likely you will find people who have a situation similar to yours. Then you can "try on" the idea of home education through their experience. You will find many practical tips for developing your own strategy for the new school year.

Talk to the Experts

The next step toward your overall plan is to become familiar with the particulars involved. Families who are home educating in your area are an important resource. These people are the experts in home education because they have done it. And they will be happy to tell you what has worked and what has not. They, in turn, can put you in touch with a support group in your area and perhaps with one of the national Catholic home-education support networks.

Visit several families during their school time, so that you get an idea of different ways home education can be done. Otherwise, if you visit only one family and the mom's style is radically different from your own, you may find yourself discouraged even before you begin.

If you do not know how to find home educators in your area, contact your local public library for information. Sometimes support groups will leave the name and number of a family who is currently home educating with the librarian. Also, check with the local paper to see if an article was done recently on home educators in the area.

Reporting Requirements

Next, get the facts on the reporting requirements in your state. Laws do vary from state to state. You can check with the Home School Legal Defense Association[1] for the particulars. For a reasonable fee, HSLDA will be your legal representative, which may be very valuable in the event you have conflicts with local officials.

Support groups for home educators can provide copies of state regulations; however, double-check the information for accuracy with your superintendent of schools. Do not rely on someone's oral description of the requirements. Get it in writing.

Many states require standardized testing at the end of the year. Seton Home Study Institute provides the Comprehensive Test of Basic Skills; Bob Jones University Press offers home educators both the Stanford Achievement Test and the Iowa Test of Basic Skills.[2]

[1] Home School Legal Defense Association, P.O. Box 159, Paoenian Springs, VA 22129; telephone (540) 882–3838.

[2] The *Comprehensive Test of Basic Skills* (CTBS) is available from Seton Home Study Institute, 1350 Progress Dr., Front Royal, VA 22630; telephone (540) 636–9990 or (540) 636–9996. The *Stanford Achievement Test* and the *Iowa Basic Skills Test* are available from Bob Jones University Press, Testing and Educational Service, Greenville, SC 29614; telephone (800) 451–2402.

(However, there are some restrictions limiting who may use the Stanford test.)

Subject Requirements

A number of states publish goals a student should have mastered by the end of a particular grade. For example, the Virginia standards for fourth-grade math list specific math skills that fourth graders should be able to do by the end of the year. (They should know multiplication tables through the nines and should add fractions with common denominators.) If these standards are available to you, then obtain copies for your child's grade level in all subjects that you will teach. Perusing them will help you choose a curriculum that will cover items likely to be on standardized tests. Also, if you must submit a curriculum for approval to the state, you can make sure it covers the most important items in the standards.

Discover Your Philosophy of Education—
Get the Focus

Before you spend the time and money for specific curricular choices, you should clarify (as best you can at this point) your philosophy of education. There are a number of questions to consider. Below you will find brief discussions of these questions, which we hope will help your decision-making process. This process is more than choosing one philosophical approach over another; it is a discovery of the basis of your prior inclinations (what you liked growing up or found worked well with your children already) and whether or not an approach discussed below will better suit your family. For more information, you can read the books listed in the Bibliography: Home Education, General.

What is the basis for selecting curricula for Catholic education?

Since what is authentically Catholic includes anything that is true, good, and beautiful, materials that reflect excellence in these areas should be used, regardless of who the author or publisher is. Part of the beauty of the Church is her ability to take that which is "secular" and, in many but not all ways, to Christianize it.

Catholic education does not mean, however, that religion is a theme in every subject. St. Thomas Aquinas is an example of someone who took a secular philosopher, Aristotle, and utilized his insights about truth to construct the framework of his philosophy and theology. Today, Pope John Paul II has encouraged the pursuit of excellence through the establishment of various academies of the sciences. In doing so he has said, in essence, that the sciences are valid and make a contribution in and of themselves, because they are pursuing truth.

Likewise, we strive for excellence in educational materials. In the sciences, we want material that presents the best information gathered thus far, well illustrated and in readable format. In mathematics, we want texts that best explain foundational principles in a clear and systematic way. In the area of literature, we appreciate great books that are written and illustrated well. In the study of the fine arts, we expose our children to what is beautiful and discuss why it is so. In all subject areas, we want material that is presented with excellence to challenge minds and nourish souls with what is true.

When should you begin formal education?

There are three responses to the question of when to begin formal schooling, whether in or out of your home: first, "the earlier the better"; second, "better late than early"; and third, "whenever the child seems ready". Each of these positions has particular advocates who have written on the subject. They all have some valid points.

The "earlier the better" approach has been set forth in the last few decades by child development experts. They present a case for early education of children, saying that a delay in children's education could greatly limit their intellectual achievement down the road. This approach has been applied in different ways with varying degrees of success.

Maria Montessori was an Italian doctor who altered the learning environment of a group of Italian slum children in such a way that they demonstrated dramatic academic improvement and intellectual development. Then she taught teachers to create a classroom in which children could accomplish adult tasks with kid-sized materials (e.g., pots, pans, gardening tools). The teachers did not teach directly; they helped children learn to use the materials, and then they observed the children learn.

> The data was there—hands-on experiences by the roomful. The framework was there—carefully graduated exercises led the children almost imperceptibly to reading, writing, and figuring. The children learned.[3]

Montessori wrote a number of books, which are available in local libraries. In addition, many companies sell Montessori materials, and you can even join the International Montessori Society.

In the field of music, Dr. Shinichi Suzuki has created a method of formal music training that can begin at very young ages on down-sized musical instruments. His method demonstrates that young children are capable of playing musical instruments with mastery when adult-sized instruments are modified to accommodate children as young as even two or three.

The Suzuki method has met with great success in a variety of countries for very young children. Many parents have enjoyed seeing their children succeed so early in music. Yet the drawback can be that some families might spend a lot of time and money on very young children's lessons when older children can acquire greater mastery in much less time.

One advocate of early formal education is Glenn Doman, author of *Teaching Babies to Read*, *How to Give Your Baby an Encyclopedic Mind*, and other similar books. Doman illustrates his theory by documenting babies and young children who perform challenging feats (for their ages) in basic math and reading skills. He demonstrates his techniques on television talk shows, amazing audiences.

---

[3] Mary Pride, *The Big Book of Home Learning*, vol. 1 (Wheaton, IL: Crossway Books, 1990): 100.

Parents are captivated by the idea that their young children can get a jump start on the educational process and prove their brilliance to others at an early age. This can present a challenge for parents: Are they motivated to teach their child for his own good or for the sake of their pride?

The concern is this: Is the child, in fact, learning intellectually, or is he just following the steps of a process (such as reading) without the necessary comprehension skills? Many educators of second and third graders have reported difficulties in those children who demonstrated reading at an early age: though they could decode words, they were not really reading, because they had poorly comprehended the words they had just read. This is only one of the difficulties spoken about by those who believe that early formal education is not best for children.[4]

Dr. and Mrs. Raymond Moore have written a book entitled *Better Late Than Early*. They document more than eight thousand studies of children's social, emotional, and physical development that challenge the philosophy of early formal education. In fact, the Moores say, "A number of research studies by brain specialists and by psychologists had suggested that the normal child's brain is not ready for sustained learning programs—until he is 8 to 10 years of age."[5] In contrast, "we know of no such studies that clearly support the idea of early entrance to school, or that demonstrate that early entrants make significant continuing gains in attitudes, motivation, achievement and social and emotional growth."[6]

The Moores challenge parents to "Look at the facts, not at the neighbors"[7] to lessen our pressure on the child to perform. "Premature teaching often results not only in damage to the child, but also in an enormous amount of wasted effort by parents and teachers who feel compelled to teach skills or facts too early."[8] The Moores' substantial research can be a helpful tool for us when

[4] Raymond and Dorothy Moore, *Better Late than Early* (New York: Reader's Digest Press, 1975), p. 86.

[5] Ibid., p. xv.

[6] Ibid., p. 90.

[7] Ibid., p. 7.

[8] Ibid., p. 78.

answering others' concerns about our delay in nursery school or preschool enrollment for our children. What children gain academically is minimal at best; what they lose developmentally and emotionally by not being at home is great.

The Moores' research is helpful in analyzing the ability of children to function in a typical classroom; however, some of the stress on delaying formal education may not be applicable in the home setting. Rose Grimm from Ojai, California, reassessed her approach to formal education.

> In the beginning, maybe we were too casual. We wanted our children to learn about the things they're deeply interested in. But we realized they may never be deeply interested in math, yet they still had to learn it. So we're seeking a balance between those things they're deeply interested in and some things that they just need to know whether they're interested in them or not.

We must strike the balance between disciplined study and the joy of learning. Both are needed.

An approach that modifies the one presented by the Moores and can apply even to some techniques of earlier education is this: *Teach when the child is ready.* As parents, we sense when a child is sincerely interested in more formal education and when he is simply inquisitive. Since we proceed at the child's pace, we take the time he needs to learn the appropriate skills.

Mary Pride, a noted curriculum expert, recommends teaching children to read as early as they are ready, since it is so foundational to all other areas of study. On the one hand, she is not advocating teaching babies to read; on the other hand, she is encouraging parents to teach reading without waiting until the children can do all of the language-arts skills.

When our child does not seem ready for a particular skill, we wait for a better time to teach it. We open the doors of learning when our children are ready to walk through them; if they are unable, then we wait patiently at the threshhold and reintroduce the skills at a later time. For example, one child may have a particular aptitude for math and can be guided through a year's program in just a few months or weeks; but the same child may not have the developmental skills to put the individual sounds of letters together for reading yet. We can take into account his real abilities and natural rate of progression by tailoring the curriculum to suit him. It is possible—but more difficult—to accommodate his pace and developmental readiness when we feel pressured to follow a curriculum provider's schedule.

To go at your child's pace, being sensitive to his skill-maturity level, is not the same as *child-directed education*. In some institutions, educators have applied to their classes the nondirective approach of counseling therapy developed by Dr. Carl Rogers, Dr. William Coulson, and others. In nondirective education the focus is not objective truth but the subjective thoughts and feelings of the children. Dr. Coulson now openly regrets encouraging this trend and strongly cautions parents to be aware of it.[9] Thankfully, most home-educating parents do not flounder in this kind of subjective mire. Rather we are motivated to instruct our children in objective truth at the appropriate levels for their comprehension.

How much structure should you have?

We offer mixed advice about structure: you need some; you probably need less than you think. Whether you are a person who was born organized or a go-with-the-flow type, begin your school day with structure. Include free time for children to investigate their own interests. If you strike the balance between scheduled and unscheduled times, you will avoid the problems of burnout from too rigid a structure at one extreme and failure to meet goals from a lack of direction on the other.

On the one hand, disciplined use of a schedule is not the same as a rigid schedule. When we provide our children with a plan for school time, they know what is expected and can often anticipate the course work required, getting started on the day by themselves.

---

[9] Dr. Coulson, "Repentant Psychologist: How I Wrecked the I.H.M. Nuns", *The Latin Mass*, special issue. Additional copies are available for free on request: *The Latin Mass*, 1331 Red Cedar Circle, Ft. Collins, CO 80524.

In addition, we can avoid a major pitfall (one of the few, in fact) of many home educators—lack of disciplined drill in math or grammar facts—by putting the drills into our schedule. (Many creative curricula diminish the boredom of drill.) Cathy Gualandri saw the positive effect on her children when she scheduled the day.

> Looking back I realize how important it was to have a written schedule for the children as well as the teacher. The children know what is expected, and it helps things run more smoothly. It assures that you get formation and family prayer time in as well as academics.

At the same time, our schedule can include flex time for projects that require time for free exploration of materials or ideas.

If you withdraw your child from an institutional school, he may initially need structure more than flexibility. Your child may be accustomed to structured learning and will feel more at ease having a plan for the day.

Other parents echo the home educator who said,

> We started off with a lot of structure because I didn't know if we could achieve our goals. The second year was less structured because the children themselves knew what was required of them, and they knew how hard they needed to work to complete their course requirements.

The more you reach your goals, the more confidence you gain in the whole process of home education.

Avoid the temptation we all face to reproduce the inflexible classroom experience we had growing up. Judy Bratton has been a pioneer in the area of home education in the Ohio Valley over the last twenty years.

> It has taken me over ten years to break out of the traditional classroom routine, to get the focus off grades, and to allow my children to learn according to their own style, without abandoning high standards. I now spend less time on formal deskwork and have taught my children that learning is always.

Mary Madden echoes Judy's sentiment. "Some days, we hit the

books, and some days we don't. Some days we have home chores to do, and some days we don't. We intermingle educational excursions in our schedule also."

Home education is not transporting an institutional experience into the home. Consequently, some parents want a radically different experience from the regimented structure of a typical school day. They see home education as part of family life and do not think that structure for education is necessary for intellectual growth. These people are not lazy—they just prefer not to feel locked into a set schedule with textbooks and workbooks. This view in particular has been encouraged by John Holt and his associates in what they call the "unschooling" approach.

Most of us find ourselves temperamentally between these two approaches. We need enough structure so we can accomplish measurable academic goals with each child and enough flexibility so we enjoy the educational process rather than simply check off assignments. Our choices of curricula and schedule will depend on our approach to structure. It is important that we not become critical of others who have different personalities and therefore different approaches—there is no one way to home educate.

We train our children in self-discipline through designated times for study and chores, all the while allowing flexibility for the inevitable and necessary interruptions inherent in family life. Long term, a certain amount of structure—not too rigid and yet not absent—enables our children's growth in self-motivated education. One hopes that, as a consequence, they will develop into life-long, self-motivated learners.

What method will best enable us to home school?

Most of us were educated with a *traditional method*. The teachers taught subject by subject using workbooks and textbooks. Then they evaluated what was learned through regular testing. Children met goals for one grade level before proceeding to the next. The classroom and the schedule were, out of necessity, highly structured.

In home education, a number of families opt for this method with some modifications (since there is not as much necessity for regimentation). They find workbooks and textbooks readily available, including tests. This approach eases their concerns regarding satisfying state requirements for curricula. One of the dangers of this method is that it can sap the joy for learning if children sit for long periods of time over poor quality materials. However, good quality materials exist, if parents look for them.

Another method that is similar in structure but quite different in the presentation of material is a classical style of education. The *classical method of education*, which was the method of the medieval era, is otherwise known as the trivium. The trivium begins with a stage in which grammar and the rudiments of various subjects are learned, with an emphasis on memory. The next stage involves the study of formal logic. The last stage develops effective rhetorical skill. Depending on the age of the children, these stages are tools for tackling various subjects of study rather than simply a study of the subjects themselves.

An article by Dorothy Sayers entitled "The Lost Tools of Learning"[10] has been instrumental in inspiring many home educators to desire a more classical method of instruction. Very little work has been done thus far in putting together specific curricula to assist parents in this endeavor. One resource worth noting is a book by Laura Berquist entitled *Designing Your Own Classical Curriculum*.

The *unit study method* is another option for parents, either by itself or in conjunction with other methods already mentioned. Rather than studying subject by subject, parents select an interest of the child and then teach a variety of subjects in relationship to that topic. For instance, if children are interested in hot air balloons, they might apply science in understanding how they work, read the history of how they were invented and who set records flying them, build a replica hot air balloon as both a science and art project, and write a report for oral presentation to the rest of the family. This kind of "delight-directed" learning can produce amazing results in

[10] Dorothy Sayers, "The Lost Tools of Learning", in *A Matter of Eternity* (1947; reprint, Grand Rapids, MI: Eerdmans Pub. Co., 1973).

terms of the energy given the project, the amount of spare time children spend on it, and the joy in learning together.

Unit study can be particularly helpful in teaching science and history when our children vary in age. The number of lesson plans per subject area decrease, and the opportunities for enjoyment in learning something together increase. Everyone can be challenged at his own particular level; everyone can contribute something. This works especially well with children from kindergarten through sixth grade. For older children, unit study can have its limitations, especially as the number of subject areas in their schedule grows.

Who will teach?

Typically, mom is the primary teacher, with dad either team teaching a subject or taking responsibility for one or more subjects. As we talk about our strengths and weaknesses, often we see the complementarity of interest that helps determine who teaches what. For example, if dad really enjoys math and mom does not, the math classes can take place in the early morning before dad leaves for work or after supper when he is free.

Some home educators employ tutors for help in a given subject area or with a particular age level. (If the tutor is a man, he can be an important role model for boys who, at a certain age, greatly benefit from male teachers.) Another option that is inexpensive is the idea of "swap tutoring" among home-educating parents. One parent might offer a math class, and another parent might teach science. Particularly in the upper grades, the use of tutors can lighten the load in the subject areas in which the parents feel weakest. Regis and Roseanne Martin have had great success with assistance from tutors.

> We try to find as much human help as we can afford, preferring that to expensive programs. We have been blessed with some excellent tutors, who are not only a help but have been good influences on the children, reinforcing those same values we hold.

Tutors can strengthen our home-education programs.

Some home educators live near a college campus. They tap into the rich resource of college students interested in earning money and of professors who tutor children in the upper grades in subjects more difficult for parents, such as literature, history, science, or math.

If this seems like a viable option for you, confirm this as a legal option with your local officials. In areas where local school administrations have responded unfavorably to the idea of tutors, some families have established various clubs (e.g., history, literature). These clubs do not substitute for classes taught at home; however, they do provide some group interaction for older students, who benefit from forming and sharing their own opinions and hearing the rationale behind the ideas of others. This is especially helpful when the clubs are led by experts in the field, who select materials used and guide the discussions.

Choose a Curriculum—
Get the First-Rate Formula for Your Family

Unlike a typical classroom teacher who has curricula preselected by committees, we have a tremendous selection of materials from which to draw. Publishers, whether they be secular, Protestant, or Catholic, will sell to those who will buy. The key is figuring out what curricula will best suit us and our children. (For a much more thorough explanation, please see Chapter 10 on curricula.)

First, see what others have used. Undoubtedly, in the local support group, you will find a variety of choices: some people use a program from a curriculum provider, some people use materials all of which come from one company, and others use a variety of resources as they tailor-make their program.

Get the opinions of those you respect in your area, and, in particular, see if you can examine the materials they are using. When you browse through borrowed curricula, compare the effectiveness of the teacher guides, the clarity of the explanations and illustrations for the children, the quality of material used (style, attractiveness, and durability so it can last through more than one child), and the overall goals of the curriculum.

Consider companies that sell or rent curriculum packages and offer support services. Find out the reasons behind their selection of materials, and see if those reasons fit your own philosophy of education. For example, find out why some curricula are Catholic and others are secular. Look at the subject areas they have added to those required by your state—are they necessary or even helpful?

Find out if these companies allow flexibility in substituting curriculum in a particular subject area. Inquire about the quality of support services offered and whether or not that is a benefit you must pay for in case you decide you do not need that service. Finally, see whether or not there is a certain time frame in which your child must demonstrate his knowledge to the provider's satisfaction—is this a reasonable requirement for your family situation?

Next, look into the curriculum packages that are produced by one publisher. There are strengths and weaknesses with this approach, but it could make the selection process easier, at least for the first year, with just one curriculum provider. Unlike companies in which you enroll your children and pay to rent books, you would be purchasing them. The more children you have who use the nonconsumable materials, the lower the cost per child per class. This is irrelevant, however, if you discover you dislike the materials.

Do you know people who have decided to mix and match from a variety of curricula? Ask them for the particular pros and cons of materials they have examined. It can be challenging to put your own program together, especially if it is your first year. However, selecting the particular materials that fit your goals for each child and both your style of teaching and their style of learning can be very rewarding. (See Appendix B for Kimberly's and Mary's choices of curriculum.)

You also have the option of altering your choice midyear, if necessary, which might not be an option with a program provider. The flexibility in choices and also in time frame for accomplishing the goals you set can be a real asset. After all, you will feel a certain amount of pressure to accomplish your goals, and you may not want the added pressure of performing on someone else's schedule.

Finally, do not forget the free resources available, especially through the public and school libraries. You can borrow books, audiotapes, videotapes, films, and computer programs. In addition, some government agencies regularly make free resources available, such as maps, posters, and even seeds.

Based on your curricular choices, you will need certain additional books, research materials, and school supplies. After looking through the curriculum for specifics, you might check out your local library for the availability of books and research references. There are numerous catalogues that sell everything from notebooks to magnifying glasses to globes. Back-to-school specials throughout August and September may provide better deals for most basic equipment at local stores than through catalogues. Again, check with local families who are home educating for lists of school supplies that have been most helpful before purchasing the items. This could save you both time and money.

Make a Plan—Get the Framework

For the Year

With next year's curriculum in one hand and all of the creative ideas you have for Catholic family life in the other, you are eager to find the right blend for accomplishing your goals for each child. We all know the number of inevitable interruptions that can occur at home and the challenge of thinking creatively late at night. Could you make arrangements for the children for a day and have your own teacher in-service day, either at home or in some secluded place? Time for prayer and careful reflection to set the course of the school year is invaluable.

First, begin with prayer. You need the serenity of the Spirit to establish a plan for the year that will have as its goal honoring the Lord, first and foremost. This will help you guard your heart from making secondary goals primary: making your kids brilliant (there

are brilliant atheists, after all), or showing the disbelieving neighbors you have not lost your mind (we have to resist peer pressure,
too!).

Second, with your spouse, set goals for each child for the new
year. One couple, Mark and Kari Harrington, share how they have
developed this part of planning the new school year:

> At the beginning of each school year, we agree on five goals for
> each of our children: spiritual, physical, academic, character qual-
> ity, and hobby. We pray over these goals, share them with our
> children and periodically reread them to see how we are meeting
> them throughout the year.

Discuss with your child what steps are needed for meeting those
goals. Plan an evaluation time for each child in January—are the
goals reasonable? And mark a date for an end-of-school-year celebration in May or June when the goals have been accomplished.

Third, figure out how many days you will designate as "school"
days. (Your particular state may require a number of days for
school, but not all do.) Decide what feast days, holy days, and
holidays will be vacation days for you. In your year-long plan,
include family celebrations. For instance, will you have "school"
on birthdays, baptism anniversaries, or each person's saint's feast
day?

Factor in some fun days when field trips will substitute for
regularly scheduled study. (Depending on the support group, field
trips or group classes may have a regular schedule that will enable
more specific planning.) In addition, allow time for inevitable
sicknesses (yours or the kids), family upheaval (new baby, moving),
and adjustments to home schooling (especially if your children
have been in institutional schools for any length of time).

Some families follow a schedule similar to the local institutional
schools: they begin in late August or early September and end in
May or June. Other families opt for a regular school schedule plus
a lighter load of schoolwork in the summer—a small amount of
time daily in the summer helps children maintain their skill level in
math and reading so that time is not wasted catching up in the fall.

And some families plan "school time" three weeks out of every month, taking the fourth week off, rather than taking off the entire summer.

The planning of school time may be tedious, but it brings with it the blessing of days that run smoothly, of mothers who success-fully juggle myriad children and tasks, and of children who accom-plish their year-end goals. Different programs and curricula require different amounts of planning. Whatever the amount of planning necessary, make it a priority to do it regularly. Included in that is time for correcting your child's work in a timely fashion so he can learn quickly from his errors.

As a result of long-range planning, one family made a major decision regarding out-of-the-home activities.

> The biggest change we made was to cut out outside activities from the first to the second year. We have a good support group, but sometimes at 7 p.m. after a day of school, carpooling, dinner preparation, etc., staying home to read and chat with my husband was more appealing.

This might be more radical than most families want, but even cutting back on outside activities for the first year of home educa-tion might ease your transition.

Another mother, Lorri McCaffrey, who is expecting her eighth child, shared this:

> The key I have found to "keeping everything together", including my sanity, is to limit myself to only essential outside activities or responsibilities. I always ask myself before taking on additional activities, "Is this going to benefit my children spiritually?" "Is this going to be good socialization for my children?" "Is this going to broaden my children's horizons in a positive way?" I have chosen to limit my personal activities dramatically during this season of life in order to make time for my children's schooling, realizing that this is only one season in my life, and the next season of life will have more personal freedoms accompanying it.

Once you have a plan, you can be flexible; without a plan, you cannot possibly know whether or not you have accomplished your goals. This could be an optimal time to fill out whatever forms are required by your state, without the stress of waiting till the last minute. Within your overall plan, set realistic goals. Begin with modest expectations on which both spouses agree. You can always add more goals later.

Monthly Goals

Now take the yearly goals for the family and for individual children and break them into measurable goals for each month. For instance, in your goals for living the liturgical calendar more fully, designate the special feasts and times of fasting that will occur monthly. In addition, mark which days are planning days so those events can be the meaningful experiences you desire. (For example, mark days in late November for preparing for Advent.)

If you are covering curricula from September to May, divide the number of chapters (or number of pages) by nine months for a workable goal per subject area per month. Sometimes the curricula have helpful suggestions in this regard. Write an overall plan for each child in this way. Where you cannot be guided by curricula that are designated by grade, look for another helpful way of setting a goal. For instance, if you want the children to learn a foreign language but have no idea what is a reasonable pace, designate a certain amount of time you want them working on the language per month.

Since you may not know in advance what is the best pace per subject area, plan on evaluating your progress and make needed adjustments sometime within the first month. Math may take longer than planned, so you would then either decrease the number of pages required or allow more time. You might study a foreign language more consistently if you allot ten minutes each day rather than two half-hour sessions a week, or vice versa.

Life circumstances can certainly change between September and January, and this might necessitate an adjustment in your goals for the remainder of the school year as well. Plan a day in early January for evaluating progress toward your year-end goals so you can adjust the rate of learning the material in any one or all of the subject areas. This could be a good time for ordering next year's texts—if progress has been much quicker than expected in an area, your child may need the new text sooner than next year.

You might want to alter your class schedule based on the other commitments your children have regularly, such as musical lessons, knitting club, art class, or history club. Factor these activities into your monthly goals for completing assignments. Are there some days you should plan fewer studies for one child? Perhaps a child could skip a subject one day or do double another day. Or if there is a trip coming up, plan some studies that easily go "on the road" in your goals for the month. For example, you could save the workbook on map skills for car travel to Grandma's.

Finally, if you can, designate a cooking day for the month. This may sound a little radical, but *Once-a-Month Cooking*, by Mimi Wilson and Mary Beth Lagerborg,[11] lays out the plan, step by step, to cook meals for your family that will last for a month or longer in your freezer. It's difficult to overestimate the vital difference this book has made in our lives. Since most time in meal preparation is spent in set up and clean up, most of the work for thirty meals is already done for you because you have cooked all day once that month. You can even plan it as a school day, since there are so many things your children can learn while helping you. Or you can challenge your children to accomplish five days' schoolwork in four, so they can cook with you.

Not only does once-a-month cooking help you save money and *lots* of time, but the peace of mind it gives you (and the compliments you'll receive) can hardly be measured! After teaching all morning (and possibly some in the afternoon), you'll be able to rest or focus on other projects, all the while knowing you have a great meal ready for your family with almost no preparation needed.

With your month-by-month plan in hand, you can see how doable your year will be. Rather than rummaging through stacks

[11] Mimi Wilson and Mary Beth Lagerborg, *Once-a-Month Cooking* (Colorado Springs, CO: Focus on the Family, 1986). Another option is *Dinner's in the Freezer* by Jill Bond (Lake Hamilton, FL: Reed Bond Books, 1993).

of resources each week, feeling at loose ends, you have the big picture before you.

Weekly and Daily Schedule

Break down monthly goals into measurable weekly and then daily goals. Decide whether you will teach five weekdays or teach four days and reserve one day for testing, special projects, service projects, or support-group activities. Get good ideas from others, but customize your schedule for your own family's goals and needs. Be flexible so you can depart from your schedule for good reason and great opportunities! But start with a plan.

What are the spiritual disciplines around which you will plan your academic goals, such as Mass, Confession, and family prayer time? We want to encourage good spiritual habits for life in our children. Mary Anne Greene from Hopedale, Ohio, helps her children develop their spiritual disciplines throughout the day.

> Living our faith with the children is the most enjoyable and re-warding part. We start with the assumption that we want to be saints and then "take the next good step forward". Daily exercises of piety include morning and evening prayers, rosary, Mass, Ange-lus, and just talking about God. Weekly Confession, occasional novenas, saint and feast-day celebrations, and the liturgical-year observances help keep us going.

Select the time of day you will begin formal education—this may depend on whether or not you intend to complete the book work by noon. Are there times one child can be with a toddler so that you can tutor another child? Can you capitalize on nap times by teaching particular subjects during those times? How much work do you want accomplished as independent work by older children, perhaps in another room? Are there subjects you must accomplish in the morning so you are sure they are done?

Include opportunities for older children to teach some skills to the younger. This helps the older child learn the material well so he or she can teach it. It also builds self-esteem and leadership skills in the older one and strengthens the ability to follow and be teachable in the younger ones.

Prioritize free time outside of "school time" for the peace and well-being of the entire family. It is an ongoing challenge to do those things that are most important rather than constantly responding to what is urgent. Let's keep our priorities straight: first, we are children of God; second, we are spouses; third, we are parents responsible for many things, one of which is teaching our children.

We need daily intimate time with God; personal prayer time, as well as family prayer, is essential. In addition, time alone with our spouse will help us nurture our love, improve our communication, and keep open the channels of sanctifying grace for each other. This relationship is the fount of sacramental grace from which we draw strength for the rest of our family tasks. We must structure our time appropriately so that we keep our priorities straight. Such a schedule need not be rigid; but without a plan, we cannot accomplish the goals God desires for us apart from school.

The children also must be aware of God's priorities for their lives. Since it takes much less time to cover studies at home, make a general plan for each child's free time that includes time alone with God and time for chores. One potential home educator saw this plan in action:

> The summer before I began home educating, I went to visit a home-schooling mother of five children to chat and pick up tips on curriculum, organization, etc. What I came away with, however, was the realization that my first priority for the next six months would not be implementing the right phonics program but would be training my children better—character formation that starts early.
>
> Her wise words to me in response to my question of "How do you do it all?" were "I train my children to help me and teach them to obey." The results showed in her children and her house: happy, helpful, respectful, bright children whose lives were in order because they knew what was expected of them and their parents were lovingly consistent in requiring it of them. And her house was

immaculate, because it's true—children can be taught to pick up after themselves.

Besides scheduling chore time, plan time for the children to assist you with a family business or a family ministry. A weekly schedule helps you set measurable goals so that you can accomplish your family goals for the year.

Many moms plan a full schedule of academics in the morning so afternoons are free for housework or rest time for mom, and chores, play, sports, or hobbies for the children. Other moms plan lecture-type classes for the afternoons during nap time so that distractions for the older children are minimized. Taking your family's needs into account, decide on a daily plan. Since needs can change, do not feel bound to the schedule you have established if it no longer seems as helpful as another schedule would be.

Here are a few sample schedules to give you some ideas.

1. 7 to 10 A.M.   breakfast, Mass, household tasks
   10 A.M. to 1 P.M.   classes with older kids sometimes
                                     continuing into the afternoon
   afternoon   sports, music, reading

2. 6:30 to 8:15 A.M.   Mass, breakfast (kids make it)
   8:30 to 10 A.M.   begin with youngest on basics; older
                                     kids do independent work
   10 A.M. to 2 P.M.   work with older kids on basics
                                     around lunch
   2 to 4 P.M.   work with eldest child while others
                                     play

3. 7 to 8:20 A.M.   breakfast, morning prayer
   8:20 to 11 A.M.   schoolwork scheduled
   11 A.M. to 1:30 P.M.   Mass, lunch
   1:30 P.M. on   work until finished with day's goals;
                                     music; art

4. 7–8:30 A.M.   breakfast, chores, family devotions,
                                     music practice

8:30 to 9:45 A.M.	language arts, unit study (recess for 3-year-old)
9:45 to 10 A.M.	read history together while eating a snack
10 to 11 A.M.	math, logic, art
11 to 11:40 A.M.	typing, Church history, catechism
11:40 A.M. to 1:30 P.M.	Mass, lunch
1:30 to 3 P.M.	fine arts for all; science or Latin on alternate days for the older kids

5.
8:30 to 11:30 A.M.	studies for all—the younger children finish
11:30 A.M. to 1:30 P.M.	Mass, lunch
1:30 to 3:30 P.M.	music lessons for all; older kids do schoolwork
3:30 to 5:30 P.M.	time for sports, friends
early evening	older kids continue studies or practice

6.
6 A.M.	Papa gets boys up for hot chocolate and history
7 A.M.	Papa wakes Mom with coffee; takes older ones to Mass
8 A.M.	breakfast, music, chores
9 A.M.	tutor arrives for the 6-, 8-, and 10-year-olds; Mom is with baby, 2½-, and 4-year-olds
11:30 A.M.	lunch and recess
12:30 P.M.	Mom reads to everyone (saints, Bible stories)
1 P.M.	rest break; older ones work on history or read
2 P.M.	formal school is finished; time for activities

7.
6:30 A.M.	Mom gets ready and prays, cleans bedroom, starts laundry

7 A.M.	children up, prayers, chores, clean rooms, laundry
8 A.M.	breakfast; clean-up chores; home straightened
8:30 A.M.	school runs on half-hour segments per subject until noon with a half-hour break; 13 subject areas covered per week
noon	lunch, afternoon chores
1:30 to 3 P.M.	finish schoolwork; naps for little ones

It seems helpful to vary activities. If the children have been using small motor skills with a good bit of writing, you might next schedule time for listening to history or science books. If younger ones finish faster and begin distracting the older ones, you might send them out for recess. Midmorning can be a good time for a break with a snack and a drink—it keeps up their energy and changes the pace and location of activity. Enjoy the flexibility you have with home education for an adjustable plan that can best meet the needs of everyone (including you!).

Plan Record Keeping—Get the Form

Once you know the requirements of your state, you can comply in a timely fashion. Notify the authorities with the proper forms and choose the best method for record keeping that fits your state's requirements. If you think the local authorities may be overstepping legal bounds in their requirements, check with the Home School Legal Defense Association.

Teacher-planning books can be a simple and efficient way for keeping track of assignments and grades. (They are available through curriculum-supply companies and teacher-supply stores.) Some moms use two books—one marked in pencil with the planned assignments and one in ink with the achieved schedule, because plans sometimes change. Other moms keep track of the work actually done each day by recording it on computer.

Another method of record keeping is the folder method. Each child has a folder for each subject area. Throughout the year dated items are placed in the folder as a sample of work accomplished. It is not necessary to keep all of the assignments; a sample showing progress is what is needed.

At the high-school level, it is essential to keep careful track of materials used, assignments accomplished, and grades recorded. Thus far, colleges do not require a certificate from an "accredited" high-school program for considering student applications. However, they need a transcript of some kind listing the courses taken, texts used, and grades earned. For some examples of forms that may assist your record keeping, see Appendix D.

Location—Get the Furniture

Decide where you will teach. If you can, designate a particular room as your schoolroom for several reasons: it sets the tone for the activities of studying; it helps everyone—including mom—stay on task rather than being distracted by TV, toys, or housework; and it can increase safety for toddlers by limiting their wandering ways. However, some families do not have the space for an entire room for home education. Instead, they use the dining room or kitchen table or some other part of a room. Wherever you teach, be sure the children have comfortable seating (preferably desks or low tables) with good lighting so they can do their best work.

Clutter is the enemy of efficiency. Find an accessible place to store student books and materials, as well as your own. Designate a place for schoolwork you need to check—the work won't get lost, and you will correct it in a more timely fashion because you can find it.

With the other expenses in setting up your school, it may be hard to part with hard-earned cash for bookshelves and a file cabinet; but these organizing tools will help you maintain order. Yard sales can be an inexpensive way to acquire desks, tables, and cabinets for your school. Some people advertise them for sale in the want ads of the local paper. And some home-educating families will either sell or give away their extra school furniture after they no longer need it. A clean and orderly work space helps children do their best.

Take the Plunge! Decide the Future

Your family can talk about the possibility of home education, but the decision to home educate must be made by you and your spouse. Once you believe this is the best direction for your family, communicate it to your children.

Think through your strategy for respectful consideration of your children's desires and concerns relative to home education. If they are unsure about the new idea, find out why. How can you address their needs? fears? hopes for the future? What are the advantages of home education for each one of them? Can you flex your schedule to meet their needs?

Either a family discussion or a one-on-one time with each child over these legitimate questions will produce rich fruit in the future. It may also yield some delightful suggestions you had not yet considered for successful implementation of home education in your family.

Sometimes children balk at the suggestion of home education, especially when they are teenagers who are used to a traditional education. If you are convinced home education is the best decision for your family, however, follow through on your decision even if it is not a popular idea with your children.

Teen rebellion can occur whether a child is learning at home or taking classes at school. However, through home education parents and teens can deal with rebellion in a constructive way. Laura Berquist describes her struggle.

> I realized that this was a battle of wills here [with her daughter] and I was going to win. And I did. Once you make up your mind, the children feel that change in your own conviction. When

you're ambivalent, your tone, body, attitude changes. But once you decide, it's [the decision] not going to change. It [the approach] worked. My daughter became convinced that I meant business and she conformed. . . . If I were sending her away to school, I couldn't win this. When she was angry, she'd turn away and there'd be somebody else there and I'd lose her; here it's only me.

Resolving conflicts of this nature is not easy—the solutions are not simple; however, resolution of problems and restoration of relationships are worth the time and effort they take for the sake of the child and for the sake of the family.

Begin with Fun and Fanfare

In the Beginning . . .

You might want to "phase in" your schedule at the beginning of every year. The week before school begins, make sure your household routine works. For example, if your plan calls for kids dressed, beds made, dishes done, and morning prayers said before lessons begin, then spend a week seeing if you can complete these by your target time for schoolwork. If you consistently miss, adjust your schedule accordingly. Then you will not be making schedule adjustments and academic adjustments at the same time.

When you are ready, phase in the academics: first week, do math and spelling reviews; second week, add language arts and phonics; third week, add history, science, and extra courses.

Regardless of how your schedule is established, make sure opening day is a fun day. Some suggestions for this special day include the following: Have the children select special clothes (perhaps even new ones) for the first day of school. Put up a big banner declaring it the first day of school and take your pictures in front of it. It might be fun to begin a video-yearbook as a keepsake for the year. Offer the children new supplies (pencils, paper, crayons, or scissors) as well as new books. Make predictions about the new school year in a time capsule to be opened at the end of the school year. Have a shortened school day—it's a nice surprise to "get out early". Plan on attending Mass as a family to commit the new year to the Lord. And finally, top off the day with a special dessert at supper to celebrate the start of the new year—a fun end to a great beginning.

Throughout the Year . . .

Frequently people ask us how we maintain a sense of order and discipline in the midst of the challenges of home education. Our response has two answers: *B.C.* and *A.D. B.C.* means that order and discipline began *Before the Challenge* of formal education was seriously entertained. *A.D.* means that *Additional Discipline* both for our children and us is necessary for home education to succeed.

In reality, it is the early training in discipline you have already done with your children that has been the beginning of your home education—now you are making it more formal. Build on the discipline you have already taught. When you say it's time for school (just like mealtime or bedtime), it's time for school. If you are calm and firm, there will be little resistance.

Some mothers tolerate disrespect from their children because they want to appease them—peace at any price, which is not real peace. They confuse motherhood with friendship, or they get overwhelmed by a child's strong will when they themselves are more compliant in nature.

If you have neglected discipline, or have not insisted that children accept your authority and respond obediently, then be prepared for some battles. We must teach our children to respect our authority not only for the true peace it brings our homes but also in preparation for their response to God's authority. We do not look for their approval in how we run our school days, though we should be sensitive to their needs and aware of their desires. Likewise, we do not respond to their whining or complaining by placating them, but rather we require obedience with a pleasant attitude.

You and your spouse must set the ground rules. Be consistent, firm, and loving. Discipline and correction are not the products of anger and resentment but rather the result of love and forgiveness.

On the flip side, sometimes mothers, through their impatience and quick tempers, show less respect for their children than a regular schoolteacher would. For our part, it is necessary that we be respectful toward our children. Typically, a good teacher does not yell at the students, call names, or glare. We have even more of a responsibility than a regular teacher to have self-control when we are disappointed or angry with our children's behavior or performance. If only we could remember St. James' words: "Let every man be quick to hear, slow to speak and slow to anger, for the anger of man does not work the righteousness of God" (James 1:19–20).

Instilling good habits is easier if begun when children are young. And lessons in forgiveness and humility abound when any of us blows it, which will happen. As they get older, we want them to demonstrate self-discipline and self-control. Home education provides many opportunities for us to model these virtues as we teach them. We, in turn, can challenge our children to grow in these virtues as well.

To a Successful End!

Flexibility is the name of the game for successful negotiation of your home-school year without crashing on the jagged edge of burnout. Unexpected situations arise, and you may find the will of God for that day is other than what you have scheduled. For instance, sometimes children need unhurried conversation without feeling as if they are interrupting your plan. Other times illness can mean juggling the class schedule of the others from the sick child's room or taking a bag of books along to a doctor appointment.

Fortunately, flexibility is a strength we have been exercising from the ever-changing schedule of our first newborn right up to the present day's demands of our children's needs, desires, and activities. It is no different with home education. Diane Aquila, home-educating mother of seven, encourages first-time home educators to "realize everyone does it differently. Each person or family has to find out what works best. Also, each year may change. Usually, the first year is the hardest."

Not only do our needs and the children's change from year to year, but so do the opportunities for assistance. Roseanne Martin, home-educating mother of eight, says, "A home-schooling family should remain open to help whenever it is offered as coming from the hand of God and to have fun—enjoy these brief days with your children."

If we begin home education with a well-thought-out plan, maintain good order and discipline throughout the year, and keep a flexible grip on our expectations, we will be able to end one year of home education looking forward to the next!

One Step at a Time

1. Collect information and resources from friends who home educate and from official Church and state sources.

2. Decide with your spouse what your philosophy of education is. Discussions include the basis for selecting curricula for Catholic education, when you will begin formal education, how much structure you will have in your schedule, what method you will use, and who will be the primary instructor.

3. Choose your curriculum after examining friends' recommendations, home-education providers' packages, and companies' curriculum lines.

4. Build the framework of your year-long schedule by constructing long-term and short-term objectives broken down into monthly, weekly, and daily goals.

5. Take care of practical details—legal forms and appropriate school furniture in a suitable place.

6. Begin formal home education with a good balance of discipline (respectful obedience) and flexibility (with a schedule that serves the family rather than one that enslaves it).

9

Principals of Home Education

The Father's Role

Often one spouse—usually, but not always, the wife—hears about home education and looks into it before the other. Sometimes a lack of information or meeting a home-educating family that fits someone's negative stereotype (such as a leftover from the Woodstock generation or someone who seems more Catholic than the Pope) can cloud the issue for the husband. Clarify for your spouse what roles you envision him playing if together you decide to home educate your family.

The Roles

The role of the father in home education varies from time to time and from family to family. Alternately, he may be a coach, a teacher, or a principal; he is always a team player. No matter how convinced a mom is about home education, it takes the support, encouragement, and effort of both parents to make it work.

Team Player

Help your husband understand the facts. You can share this book or others like it (listed in the back), pointing out helpful information so he does not have to read it from cover to cover. A few specific statistics on the academic success of home-educated children or a few quotes from papal encyclicals on the fundamental responsibility of parents as educators can reassure your husband that home education can be good Catholic education. His questions about the legality or costs of home education can also be addressed.

Look for a meeting of your local support group that will include husbands—it's a real boost to meet normal-looking Catholic men and women who are also involved in home education. Likewise, attend one of the home-education conventions in your area together. You will hear speakers address topics of concern, such as socialization, making your way through curricular choices, principles of time management, etc. In addition, you will meet others, like yourselves, who are investigating home education. Rather than seeing this as a fringe movement of people who are trying something completely new, your husband can perceive this movement as one of parents returning to quality education in the home, which was long the norm.

Concerns about socialization are often at the top of a husband's list of concerns. Look over the chapter on socialization (Chapter 5) so you can share the facts about the purpose of developing your children's social skills. In addition, let him know when your children will interact with other children through support-group social events and community clubs (such as Boy Scouts, Girl Scouts, or 4–H Club).

It's important to contrast the popular notion of socialization as getting along in a crowd of peers with true socialization, which forms the character of our children both as capable leaders and as thoughtful followers. Address the concerns you have about peer-dominated situations. Show how the home is the more natural environment, because of the mixture of ages, for learning social skills for the "real" world.

Many dads wonder how their children can be involved in sports, something they themselves may have enjoyed a great deal as part of their own educational experience. Find out what is available through your town or city. Often there are first- through eighth-grade teams in baseball, softball, volleyball, street hockey, basketball, soccer, and swimming. Some communities have opportunities for wrestling and tag football teams as well. There are even support groups with teams of their own, coached by home-educating dads, that compete with local school teams.

Another option in the area of sports is developing individual sports such as karate, judo, ballet, ice skating, roller blading, golf, tennis, or gymnastics. On the one hand, we do not want home education to limit what our children can do. So in the area of sports we encourage participation in the sports of their choice. On the other hand, whether a child will play high-school football is not determined by where he is taught during his elementary-school grades. In other words, cross one bridge at a time. Unless your child is already high-school age, the issue of sports may not be relevant yet. (This year, home-educated children in our area played on public-school flag football and basketball teams. Whether this is a desirable option for your family is another question.)

Your husband may be sensitive to criticism from family members, clergy, or friends. It is important that you give him solid answers to questions he raises so that he in turn can share that information with the critics. Some people do not want to hear the facts—they have already decided against home education. But others are curious enough to hear your reasons and might become cautiously supportive once they hear the facts, especially from your husband. Whether or not you convince the critics, your husband will have more information on which to base his thoughts about home education.

Nothing succeeds like success. Your critics may become your biggest fans once they see how well your children learn and how well mannered they are in attitude, speech, and actions. It is not easy to ignore the pressure their negativity can add to your desire to perform well. But if you can focus on the task of home education, the results will speak for themselves. Here again you can see the necessity of being of one heart and mind with your spouse on the decision to home educate. You need support—not pressure to perform—under your own roof.

Pray about your desire to home educate. Assume both you and your spouse want the best for your children. Keep your conversations respectful, responding to the concerns your spouse expresses. Trust God—He will work through your husband as the spiritual leader of your home. Do not manipulate your spouse into doing what you want. If it is God's will, there will be a harmony of desires and interests—a real sense of being team players.

Coach

As a coach from the sidelines, your husband plays a critical role for both you and your children. Judy Bratten shares the important role her husband has played in their home education over the past twenty years.

> My husband is encourager, supporter, and, if necessary, disciplinarian. Although he is not a teacher, he sets the tone of our home by the books and magazines he reads, the time he spends in prayer and Bible study, and the kinds of family discussions we have. Since he is always at home, he is available to them when they need him.

It is not necessary for your husband to be involved in the day-in and day-out activities of the home school to encourage everyone involved. But how can your husband coach throughout the day?

First, your husband fortifies the whole family through daily prayer for your family—and, preferably, with your family—at the start of the day. If there are difficulties during the day, he can be available (via phone if he is not home) with words of encouragement or suggestions to deal with a difficulty. He can also speak to the children to reinforce discipline.

Next, your husband can express interest in what the children are learning. What a difference it makes to have dad let a child, who is just learning to read, read to him! When dad looks over work accomplished and jots comments on book reports, stories, or tests, he provides additional incentives to his children to do well. This anticipated review, in turn, helps hold the children accountable to finish their assignments.

Sometimes your husband may underestimate the power of his praise. You and your children thrive when your efforts are appreciated, even when the results are less than perfect. Throughout the year there are opportunities to highlight academic, spiritual, physical, and skill growth in each family member. Your husband should take advantage of those times by strengthening each person's self-esteem and calling each one on to greater achievement.

It can be very helpful at critical times throughout the year for your husband to share with your children about the sacrifices you are making in order to home educate them. Children can easily lose sight of the challenge that home education is for you. One mother recounted this story:

> After a difficult morning when it seemed that the children were not responding respectfully, I marched them in to their father and said, "Please tell these children how grateful they should be that I teach them at home! I'm going for a walk." When I returned, I found a group of chastened children, thankful for my sacrifices. My husband gave me the support I needed.

Both you and your spouse must discipline your children, even if one is with them more than the other. Your teamwork is evident when support like that just mentioned occurs.

One area of discipline in which both you and your husband play a critical role is practice of the Faith. Religion is *not* a woman's thing; it is for all those who take seriously their relationship to God.

Your husband's involvement in family prayers, going to Mass (daily, if possible), and getting the family to Confession on a regular basis is essential in order to communicate to your children (especially your sons) their own need to know, love, and serve God. A home-education schedule flexes more easily than most other school options. Take advantage of this by including your husband in daily religious practices.

Lastly, as a coach, your husband can offer practical help by offering you some much-needed breaks. Sometimes this means being with the children so you can go on errands to the grocery store, hardware store, or post office. Or perhaps you could plan a fun break alone or with a friend, or even possibly attend a retreat.

Other times it may mean lending a hand with the laundry or pitching in, rather than complaining about cleaning that is not always done on time. Finally, it might mean agreeing to pay for help with housework or baby-sitting. These kinds of practical help might be just the thing to ease tension over unfinished tasks and provide you with the refreshment you need so you can focus on what is most important.

Teacher

One of the more important roles of the father is teacher of the Faith, as has been mentioned in previous chapters. According to Deuteronomy 6:7, teaching the Faith is a daily task: "And you shall teach them diligently to your children, and shall talk of them when you sit in your house, and when you walk by the way, and when you lie down, and when you rise." Clyde Gualandri, father of four sons, is the primary instructor of the Faith in their home. Cathy writes,

> He teaches a large part of the religion or catechesis. His example, guidance, and support are invaluable. He backs up and enforces the discipline and helps motivate the children in our home schooling. He is there for the children to share their experiences, pray with them, or help with extra tutoring they may need.

It is through the sacrament of Matrimony that your husband receives the grace to teach your children the Faith.

Your husband probably has strengths in academic areas that are weak points in your own training or interest. Your husband may enjoy teaching those subjects. Everyone benefits. Your husband benefits when he teaches the children about an area of interest, such as science, and sees them share that interest. The children benefit by getting to know their dad better and spending time learning something together. And you benefit by having a shared teaching load, knowing that the children are learning the subject area from someone who genuinely enjoys it (and them).

How can your family best utilize what your husband can offer to the children in the limited time he may have? First, you and your husband should think through his primary areas of interest in both the academic and life-skill areas. Second, given the ages and skill levels of the children, what could he offer in the coming year? Finally, what days and for how long would he teach the children? It is important to schedule the time to be sure it happens, especially if it involves the critical areas of math, science, history, or language arts.

For many families, husbands take on greater responsibility as the children get older. Kari and Mark Harrington's oldest child just became a teenager. "As our children are moving into the teen years, we feel that the father's role is becoming more accentuated. It's important for our children to get his feedback on their work." This is particularly helpful on the junior-high and high-school levels, according to Susan Waldstein. "My husband gives our older son an article from a magazine and has him read it on his own and prepare to discuss it with him. My son takes this very seriously." This could be done regularly or periodically.

Not only might your husband assist the family by offering to teach the children a subject—say, science—but he might want to make it available to one or more other home-educating families. This might open the possibility of "swap tutoring" with other families, who in turn could offer other subjects to assist your family.

If time does not allow for a regular class, perhaps your husband could occasionally train the children in certain life skills or hobbies. For instance, if he is an artist, he could take one evening to demonstrate drawing faces. Later in the month he could review the work the children have done, pointing out how to improve their work. Then he could teach them how to use an art medium, such as water colors, and give them the tools with which they could work for the next month.

In the areas of yard work or car care, it might be as simple as your husband handing the children yard tools or taking the children into the garage when work needs to be done. He may not schedule time on a regular basis, but he can impart knowledge and skills while the children work alongside him. And there is the added benefit of time spent together while learning something important.

Foreign languages are not always included as part of the class schedule. If your husband is fluent in another language, he could initiate a time during dinner every night when that is the only language spoken. He could introduce new words and phrases and lead conversation in that language for a short period. This is an especially meaningful experience when the foreign language is part of the cultural heritage of the family.

Another way your husband might teach the children regularly is by reading to them in the evening, either during dinner cleanup or before bed. Together they might read in a particular subject area, such as the Civil War, or perhaps just share best-loved stories from your husband's youth.

Besides teaching certain classes as part of the home school, your husband could teach alongside you on field trips. The field trips would be easier physically for you because there would be another adult along. And the children would benefit from hearing their dad's perspective, whether they were going to the zoo, a museum, a concert, or just picking apples.

Perhaps your husband could take your family along on one or more of his business trips with field trips scheduled on the side. (This kind of flexible schedule for the children is possible only with home education.) Besides giving the children opportunities to travel, it also limits the number of times your husband is separated from your family. The Saxton family of State College, Pennsylvania, frequently travels together as part of Bill's ministry. Barb shares how a recent trip enabled their family to apply what they had been learning at home.

> When we travel as a family, we are exposed to opinions that vary from our own. For instance, when hiking through the Grand Canyon, we had a guide who explained the making of the gorge, from an evolutionary perspective. That gave us an opportunity to evaluate with our children what we were hearing in the light of what we had studied. Rather than giving pat answers, we are

training them to think critically and then to articulate well-reasoned opinions. They are learning to think through issues thoroughly and respond rather than react to others.

Home education enables dads, like Bill, to take the home school on the road.

Your husband might invite your children periodically to join him at work so he can show them what he does, introduce them to coworkers, and share lunch. Fathers who work at home can do this, too. Children learn from their dads by watching them work. Jesus spoke of this in relationship to His heavenly Father in John 5:19–20,

> Truly, truly I say to you, the Son can do nothing of his own accord, but only what he sees the Father doing; for whatever he does, that the Son does likewise. For the Father loves the Son, and shows him all that he himself is doing.

In addition, home businesses can be great opportunities for teaching children all kinds of practical skills.

Finally, in the area of living the Faith, your husband can teach your children the curriculum for Calvary (2 Macc 7). As he takes up his crosses each day, in faithfulness to the Lord and to the covenant of marriage, he instructs the children in how to take up their own crosses. Your husband does not need to be perfect—he can't be—but he can be faithful. As he teaches the children, he must follow St. Paul's admonition in Ephesians 6:4, "Fathers, do not provoke your children to anger, but bring them up in the discipline and instruction of the Lord."

Principal

As principal of the home school, your husband oversees the whole operation. He may delegate responsibilities, but he is still the primary person accountable to God for stewardship of funds and the time involved in home education.

Together you and your husband need to establish a budget for your home school. Your husband helps you think through essential purchases, what is available secondhand through yard sales and used curriculum sales, and what can be borrowed from the library, public schools, or parent-teacher resource centers in the community. Here is a good example of where two heads are better than one: you can explain the results of your research—why a certain curriculum looks good—and either he will agree with your choices or temper your enthusiasm with thoughtful comments that add balance to your assessment. This kind of interaction limits the amount of money wasted on curriculum that is less helpful for your family.

In addition to assisting your curriculum choices, your husband can help you decide what are reasonable expectations for the new year. If you are attempting too much, he can caution you to adjust your goals. If you are missing an area of study he thinks is critical, you can add it. And when you decide on mutually agreed upon goals for your new home-education year, he can hold you accountable to follow through with them—again, not as an outside critic who is adding pressure, but as an inside encourager who wants to make it a great year in home education.

Another role for your husband as principal is disciplinarian and advisor when needed. Mary Madden, mother of five, says, "I use John as a sounding board for any difficulties I may be having in the education of the children, and he will advise me." It helps a mom so much to know that dad will listen carefully and respond with suggestions.

The Difference Dad Makes

Children benefit from a father's involvement in the enterprise of home education at many levels.

1. They have more opportunities to see his faith in action through more time together, especially as he teaches them the Faith and leads them in practicing the Faith.

2. They get to know him better as they spend time with him, learning the subject areas, hobbies, and skills in which he takes the

greatest interest. In a way not possible given other educational options, they can share these interests with him.

3. Their own sense of self-worth is strengthened regularly as their father specifically encourages them in their academic efforts. They thrive as a result of his support, suggestions for improvement, and praise. The children have opportunities to grow in their love and respect for their father as their relationship is strengthened through home education.

4. Children sense the mutual support between Mom and Dad for their education. And they mature through consistent discipline from both parents.

5. The whole enterprise of home education strengthens the relationships within the family, especially the husband–wife relationship as partners in their vocation of marriage.

Eliminating the Bored of Education

Curriculum Choices

Throughout this book, we have used the word "curriculum" in two ways. First, it refers to a particular program for studying a specific subject. For example, a typical first-grade math curriculum teaches such skills as number recognition, counting, grouping, adding, and subtracting. The plan or "curriculum" for teaching math at this level includes problems, drills, games, and hands-on ways for the children to learn each skill. Finally, such a math curriculum includes tests or other ways to check on your child's progress and comprehension.

The second way we have used the word "curriculum" is to refer to the overall plan or program for all of your child's studies for that year. Commonly, an overall curriculum is described by grade level. Two different curricula for the same grade, however, might vary. For example, one publisher's (or family's) fifth-grade curriculum might cover math, geography, U.S. history, biology, and language arts, while another fifth-grade curriculum might include math, world history, earth science, language arts, and Spanish.

Now, since we're talking about Catholic home education, the first curriculum question is . . .

What Makes a Curriculum "Catholic"?

Authentic Catholic education relies on and includes all that is true, good, and beautiful—in short, everything that points the way to God, the source of all truth, goodness, and beauty. Yet not every curriculum source that meets this criterion comes wrapped in paper stamped "Catholic". And, sadly, not everything that proclaims itself "Catholic" truly is. How can we make sure that our children will learn from an authentically Catholic curriculum?

Our own faith, the Catholic atmosphere we create in our homes, the specific resources that we use to teach the Faith, and our ability to weave the Faith into the fabric of our children's lives are really what ensure a Catholic curriculum. (Assuming, of course, that all secular materials we might choose contain truth, not falsehood, and won't undermine our children's faith.)

Creating a Catholic atmosphere doesn't mean adorning our homes with every available holy card, statue, or image of Christ and the saints that we can find. (Although we *should* use images, especially crucifixes, in every part of our homes in order to recall continuously His presence in our homes.) Rather, the atmosphere we seek is created by the way we speak and act and the sincerity with which we include Christ in our lives.

Similarly, Pope Pius XI emphasized how important it is for Catholic schools to "be regulated by the Christian spirit".[1] True Catholic education first and foremost must be grounded in Christian charity at the service of God. Charity requires us to act a certain way toward those in our families (or schools).

> Love is patient and kind; love is not jealous or boastful; it is not arrogant or rude. Love does not insist on its own way; it does not rejoice at wrong, but rejoices in the right. Love bears all things, believes all things, hopes all things, endures all things (1 Cor 13:4–7).

This is the first step in establishing a truly Catholic atmosphere for our children's education.

It is just as important, however, for our children to understand that all we undertake—including education—must be for God's sake. We learn, not simply for the joy of learning (although this is a

---

[1] The subsection entitled "The Catholic School", in Pope Pius XI, encyclical letter *On the Christian Education of Youth*, December 31, 1929.

wonderful thing, too!), but also to learn about our Creator. The more we learn about the world, the more we learn about God and how He works. Finally, we must see everything we learn or master as a tool to help us accomplish God's work, so that we can be better instruments in His hands.

Well, you might wonder, how much of that intangible "Catholic atmosphere" is created by using patently Catholic materials? Does everything we use need to be obviously Catholic? In his encyclical *On the Christian Education of Youth*, Pope Pius XI explained that in Catholic schools every subject must be "permeated with Christian piety".[2] Yet, this principle doesn't mean that a math curriculum, for example, is made Catholic because the workbook problems have the children count pictures of crosses instead of pictures of sticks. Instead, the point is to find a curriculum that teaches the truth as effectively as possible—in this case, one that teaches math principles clearly and completely. At the same time, we need to create the charitable and inspirational "atmosphere . . . [that will] warm the hearts of masters and scholars alike".[3]

Further, it is more imperative that schools provide identifiably Catholic books than it is for Catholic families to do so. The considerations at work in families are entirely different from those at work in schools. A school becomes a Catholic place mostly through artificial devices and methods designed to unite diverse individuals and to create a common sense of Catholic purpose.

Families create such a Catholic environment much more naturally and fluidly. The countless bedtime conversations about who God really is and the power and love He has for us, combined with the rich texture of faith lived together on a daily basis, year after year, are infinitely more effective in creating a Catholic atmosphere than counting holy symbols instead of apples.

You do not need to limit your curriculum choices to those pack-

---

[2] Ibid.

[3] Ibid. The Pope makes clear that he is referring to the atmosphere in a school: "If this sacred atmosphere does not pervade and warm the hearts of masters and scholars alike, little good can be expected from any kind of learning, and considerable harm will often be the consequence", quoting Leo XIII.

ages sold by Catholic suppliers in order to provide your children with a Catholic curriculum. Some home educators find that they *are* most comfortable with a packaged curriculum from a Catholic supplier. Others feel confident enough to pick and choose among the best from both Catholic and secular sources. Ultimately, you must use your own discretion.

When you choose curriculum materials, ask yourself, "What subject will I teach from this book?" This can help you decide how important it is for the materials to be identifiably Catholic. If you are looking for a literature text, you want the best literature you can find—not something that is well crafted but tawdry or inappropriate in its subject. On the other hand, some Catholic readers are full of selections that teach good moral principles and the lives of the saints yet do so at the expense of good writing. They might be fine for devotional or recreational reading but not for teaching literature.

A literature selection that is well written and imbued with Catholic culture would be a great choice. But so also is a secular text that is so well written and so beautifully illustrated that it touches the child's heart and draws him toward what is good—even without preaching or overt religiosity. The best-selling *Book of Virtues* by William Bennett is a great example. Good literature moves the heart but in a way different from materials designed for devotions or simply to get a doctrinal or spiritual point across. Again, the purpose of the materials affects your choice.

Math, geography, and to some extent science are subjects that are only subtly different when taught from within the Catholic vision. Other subjects—penmanship, for example—are not really different at all. Thus, finding good Catholic resources for history or language arts is more important than finding a handwriting text or math workbook that includes "Catholic" examples. If you find good books in *any* subject that include examples of Catholic culture, discuss history from the Christian viewpoint, or relate Catholic teaching to current events, then use them!

What about Materials for Teaching the Faith?

It *is* crucial that you have the best books and resources for teaching the elements of the Faith. A good translation of Scripture (such as the Revised Standard Version, Catholic Edition, which Ignatius Press prints as *The Ignatius Bible*) is essential. A religion text teaching *about* Scripture can supplement but can never substitute for God's Word.

The *Catechism of the Catholic Church* should be an indispensable part of your religion curriculum. As the teacher, familiarize yourself with its layout so that you can look up sections from it that pertain to the topic you are teaching. (Better yet, begin a systematic reading of it yourself—even fifteen minutes a week will increase your own knowledge!) Other catechisms, such as *The New Baltimore Catechism* and *The New St. Joseph First Communion Catechism*,[4] provide for basic memorization of Catholic doctrine.

Some parents look to see if a book has an *imprimatur* or a *nihil obstat*, which means that the bishop has declared that it states Catholic teaching without doctrinal error. Catechisms and religion textbooks typically do have this official Church authorization. Yet, many sound teaching tools are available that do not. Theological books that deal less directly with setting out dogmatic points don't necessarily carry an *imprimatur* (nor are they required to seek one), as these declarations are often difficult and time-consuming to obtain. The lack of an *imprimatur* shouldn't disqualify a book from your consideration. Indeed, there have been a few celebrated cases of books containing false teaching that first obtained and then, in some cases, lost their *imprimaturs*.

Other parents find a treasure in some of the preconciliar texts still available. Many of these books, however, would benefit from up-to-date reprints, with more color and larger print to increase eye appeal. Nor should they be considered complete in and of

---

[4] *The New Saint Joseph Baltimore Catechism* (New York: Catholic Book Publishing Co., 1964); and *The New Saint Joseph First Communion Catechism* (New York: Catholic Book Publishing Co., 1963).

themselves, as they do not contain references to either the Second Vatican Council or the *Catechism of the Catholic Church*.

As we teach our Faith to our children, it is important that we impart not only the unchanging doctrinal truths but also the more fluid "mind of the Church". The Pope indicates the Holy Spirit's direction for the Church in the language and themes he chooses for encyclicals and weekly audiences. (For example, the Pope's unfailing emphasis on the dignity of human life, at all stages, is a starting point for analyzing society's problems.) It is important that we parents stay abreast of the Church's approach to the challenges of the modern world.[5] Read, and encourage your teens to read, every encyclical the Pope issues. "He who has an ear, let him hear what the Spirit says to the churches" (Rev 3:6).

Once you have thought through your approach to making your curriculum Catholic, you can turn your attention to the big question of what kind of curriculum to choose.

Options for Your Overall Curriculum

The kind of overall curriculum you choose depends on your approach to teaching, the amount of research you are willing to do, and what you think will best suit your child's needs. Your basic choices are these: a complete preset curriculum package; a partial package (a fixed curriculum covering some, but not all, of the subjects you intend to teach) combined with your own choices for the rest of the subjects; or a personally tailored curriculum, where you have complete freedom over what to teach.

Most parents of home-educated children choose to create individual curriculum plans for their children. According to the most recent comprehensive statistics, 67.4 percent[6] of home-taught chil-

---

[5] Keep abreast of Vatican trends and papal pronouncements by subscribing to the Vatican newspaper *L'Osservatore Romano* or Catholic magazines such as *Catholic World Report* and *Inside the Vatican*.

[6] "A Nationwide Study of Home Education", sponsored by the National Home Education Research Institute (1990), *Home School Court Report*, December 1990, p. 5.

dren use an overall curriculum put together by their parents. This includes those who draw together the best resources from two or three major curriculum suppliers as well as those who create their own curriculum from innumerable sources.

The second most popular curriculum option is the complete or "package" curriculum. Parents choose a fixed curriculum for 31.4 percent[7] of home-educated children.

The Complete Curriculum

Many curriculum providers offer what are called complete or fixed curriculum packages, organized according to grade level. Typically, a child's grade level is determined by age, although occasionally companies offer pretesting or rely on achievement test scores to determine a child's placement.

With a complete package, every parent who orders the first-grade program, for example, receives the exact same package. Each first grader using that package would study the same subjects and, within each subject area, would study from identical books, take identical tests, etc. Some providers permit you to mix grade levels within a child's curriculum, while other companies do not. In other words, one particular curriculum provider might allow you to substitute a third-grade reading program, for example, for a second grader who already reads at the third-grade level. Another curriculum provider might restrict you to using only second-grade materials if you have purchased the preset second-grade package.

In choosing a fixed curriculum, you are relieved of the responsibility of choosing a particular curriculum for each subject. The curriculum supplier chooses not only what subjects your child will learn at each grade level but also the units of study within each subject and how they are to be taught.

The components of a complete curriculum vary according to the curriculum provider. (See Appendix C for recommendations.)

[7] Ibid.

One of the best programs provides absolutely everything you need for the entire year, right down to the pencils and paper.[8] All of the textbooks, workbooks, literature selections, tests, and projects arrive at your home ready for you to dive into immediately. Other complete curricula provide all the books, workbooks, and tests but rely on you to get all the basic school supplies for the year. In some "complete" packages, you will need to obtain some of the literature selections from your library or bookstore; in addition, you are expected to make extensive use of the library's resources in order to complete all the projects in the program. As you can tell, some "complete" packages are more complete than others.

One of the biggest benefits of a complete curriculum is also its greatest drawback: everything is predetermined for you. On the plus side, this choice is the least complicated way to choose a curriculum. The company has figured everything out for you. When you buy the package curriculum, it tells you exactly what subjects you will study for the year, and, within each subject, it specifies what books, lessons, tests, and projects will be completed. Often, the curriculum will provide time estimates of how long to spend on each unit or project in order to help you stay on track and complete the entire curriculum within the school year.

Newcomers to home education often are attracted by the thoroughness of these packages as well as by the security of knowing that, by using a complete package, their child will be less likely to miss something he should have covered that year.

One mother who has always used a package curriculum commented, "I like it because it is a Catholic curriculum, it is planned out for us, and I feel it is superior academically."

Laura Berquist, who put together her own curriculum for her younger children, chose instead to use a fixed curriculum for her older children. "I wanted reassurance that I was covering everything a good private school would", she explained. The company, in fact, turned out to be very flexible and individualized parts of

---

[8] For a complete curriculum package, including basic supplies, contact Calvert School, Dept. 2CAT, 105 Tuscany Road, Baltimore, MD 21210; telephone (410) 243-6030.

the standard package to accommodate her daughter's academic interests.

When families use complete programs over consecutive years, they are assured some continuity in what is taught from year to year. Younger siblings who will be taught from the same curriculum in later years will reap the benefit of their mother's familiarity with the materials used and the subjects taught.

Some complete curriculum providers also offer other helpful services, usually for an additional fee. These extra services may include record keeping, grading (when the student's work is sent directly to the curriculum provider for grading and evaluation), testing, and transcripts. In addition, some will give advice and consultation on everything from teaching special-needs children or many age levels at once to explaining the base-ten number system. Being accountable to someone else for completing the work on time and correctly can be a good motivator for some parents as well as their children.

One variation of the complete-curriculum package is that offered by regular institutional schools. Home-taught children make up part of a "satellite" school to the institutional school. In effect, the children are enrolled in a correspondence school. One drawback may be that the instructional materials sometimes are designed more for classroom teaching than for one-on-one tutoring. The biggest benefit is continuous enrollment in an existing, usually accredited school that will keep transcripts and offer a diploma.

If you decide at the last minute to home school or if you remove a child from school in the middle of the year, the complete curriculum might be your lifesaver! Under time pressures, you usually don't have the luxury of perusing the wide range of resources available. Packaged programs provide a systematic, organized, and comprehensive way to begin home education on very short notice.

Others who find complete packages appealing are parents who want a lot of structure or those who consider themselves disorganized and need a system that somebody else has already thought through. Parents who believe that education at home should reflect classroom education often prefer a preset curriculum.

The biggest drawback to a complete package, however, is that it can deprive you of one of the greatest advantages of home education: flexibility. Because the subjects and texts are already chosen by someone else (the curriculum provider), you lose the ability to tailor your child's curriculum to accommodate his interests, learning style, and academic strengths and weaknesses. Your child's time is filled with assignments predetermined by someone unfamiliar with either his progress or the most effective way for him to absorb information. With a fixed curriculum, you may not have the option of skipping assignments that your child either has mastered or, alternatively, is not yet capable of mastering.

Maggie Murray of Virginia began home education with a packaged curriculum but soon abandoned it in favor of a less-structured approach. A more flexible curriculum, which she herself pulled together, allowed her to take into account her children's differences in pace and learning style. She says, in retrospect, "I wouldn't push them so hard when they're little."

Another potential difficulty with a fixed curriculum is that your time frame and schedule are often controlled more by the curriculum company's timetable than by your own. For example, some curriculum providers help their customers maintain a pace that will enable them to complete the materials provided by the end of the school year. They require work to be finished and sent in by certain dates. This usually works fine, unless you are expecting a baby at the "wrong" time, your child needs extra time to comprehend a particular concept, you are moving, or someone gets very sick. Some providers adjust to these personal situations by extending deadlines, while other companies are less accommodating.

Parents who use a fixed curriculum often end up feeling harried and pressured. Worse, they can feel overwhelmed when these schedules and deadlines are multiplied by three or four children. Even parents who do not adhere to curriculum deadlines and who have no paperwork to submit for grading sometimes feel pressured and boxed in by an inflexible curriculum. Although nothing should prevent them from exercising their own judgment and skipping, reducing, or expanding certain sections of the curriculum, they often feel compelled to stick with the program no matter what.

A final drawback to complete packages is their cost. They can range in price from two hundred to well over six hundred dollars for each grade level. Especially for kindergarten and early elementary grades, you may find such a large initial investment unnecessary. Also, the fact that you have spent so much money on the curriculum can discourage you from abandoning it even if you feel it has not turned out to be the best curriculum for your child.

Partial Packages Combined with Your Own Selections

Partial packages, combined with your own curriculum selections, afford parents more flexibility all around. A partial package offers a preset curriculum usually within a general subject area, such as math and sciences or language arts. Often the subjects that are part of a package are integrated together, so that the spelling words are taken from the literature selections and the writing assignments are chosen from the literature themes discussed. You can choose the remainder of the overall curriculum from your own sources.

For example, if you bought a curriculum that offered an integrated or coordinated language arts program, all the major language arts subjects (spelling, grammar, creative writing, reading and reading comprehension, reference work, handwriting, and possibly history) would be covered for that grade level. However, you would be on your own for the other major subjects that should be part of your curriculum (math, science, and possibly history).

Some parents stumble upon this method of curriculum planning by accident. They choose a complete curriculum, discover that they love the language-arts components, for instance, but are very dissatisfied with the science and math selections. They jettison the unsatisfactory sections, keep what they like, and find their own replacements for the texts and curricula in the remaining subjects.

Other parents intentionally construct a curriculum using a partial package in order to combine two different educational approaches. For example, they might do "unit studies" (see later paragraphs) in language arts and history and still maintain a drill-oriented "workbook approach" in math or science. Or they might favor a phonics approach to reading, rather than the "whole language approach" offered in a particular package, but stick with the integrated science and history offered by that package.

Some of the benefits and drawbacks of this kind of curriculum—where some of the subjects are preselected for you and others are chosen at your own discretion—are similar to those of a complete package. For those subjects that are part of the package, all of the assignments, textbooks, and projects are chosen by the provider. This can be a real plus when the package covers a subject area about which you feel less confident. For example, you may feel more comfortable teaching science from a program that coordinates textbook lessons and hands-on experiments rather than relying on your own ability to find appropriate experiments to teach the desired concepts.

In addition, some subjects are often learned better when they are taught in conjunction with other subjects. A mother might find that her nine-year-old son has more enthusiasm for spelling and grammar when they are taught in conjunction with creative writing. Or she may find that, because of time constraints, she wants certain subjects laid out in detail for her, while in other subjects, she is more interested in letting her children's interests and creativity direct the specific areas of each subject they will study.

A partial package is generally less restrictive than a complete curriculum. You have greater flexibility to mix grade levels within the curriculum according to your child's ability in each subject. Some partial packages, especially those that are unit studies, are multilevel anyway. Multilevel curricula can be adjusted to a child's actual skill level or can be used to teach more than one child simultaneously from the same material.

An Individually Tailored Program

Constructing an individually tailored curriculum, the most popular option, maximizes the parent's and student's freedom—their ability to make the best choices for each child's education. When it is done right and you hit upon the winning combination, your curriculum will be a powerful tool in shaping your child's mind. His enthusiasm will be higher, and he will learn more easily and effectively. A personal curriculum is designed to build on his strengths and help him shore up his weaknesses. You can strike a balance between catering to his intellectual curiosity and requiring that he study whatever you deem essential to his formation.

Another advantage of hand-picking your curriculum is that it allows you to coordinate the curricula for all your children. Children who are relatively close in age can be taught some subjects together. Instead of having three children learning about different periods of history, for example, you can all study the same period. Assignments can be made more or less difficult according to the children's ages.

Balancing different educational approaches becomes easy when you customize the curriculum. Marsha Jacobeen, home schooler for four years, recommends this approach.

> Home schooling has allowed me to teach each individual child on his particular level. My sixth-grade son started algebra this year and my fourth-grade son is using a sixth-grade math book. I have the flexibility to use the curriculum that best suits my children. If I am using a workbook, I can tailor it to my child's needs. In some subjects, my children have not needed as much practice or repetition as the book gives—we can skip problems or even entire pages if we want to.

The curriculum is at the service of the child, not the other way around.

You are the one making the decisions about which approach will work best. If your daughter, for example, thrives on the routine and order of math workbooks, you can adopt that approach for math without necessarily taking the same approach to grammar or science. In contrast, you might want a science curriculum that is composed mostly of experiments rather than the text-workbook routine. "Mixing and matching" educational approaches helps complement your child's learning style rather than inhibiting it.

The individualized approach to curriculum allows a parent to choose the best books available in each subject. For example, many home educators find that history comes alive for their children when they throw away the standard textbooks. Teresa Cunningham, a home educator from Oakton, Virginia, describes the benefits of this flexibility for her son and daughter.

> One of the benefits for our family has been the discovery of how exciting history can be when using *real* books, such as biographies and historical fiction, rather than typical school textbooks. We noticed an increase in interest, understanding, and retention. History is now one of our favorite subjects!

The freedom of an individualized curriculum creates this kind of enthusiasm.

The disadvantage of a personally tailored curriculum is that it takes work. Sometimes lots of it. You need to research and spend time finding the best resources for each subject. Occasionally it can take a year or two of experimenting with different educational approaches before you really feel you have discovered what works. This risk is inherent in all kinds of home education, but it is also one of the benefits—we are free to keep trying until we find whatever best helps our child learn.

Later sections in this chapter will discuss the many ways of discovering and drawing upon the best curricular materials available—knowledge that is essential if you hope to construct your own curriculum.

Remember, though, that tailoring an overall curriculum to fit your child does not mean you will need to *create* individual curricula for each subject. More commonly, you simply are choosing the most effective curriculum for a particular subject from among the many available to you. For example, you might look at the math texts provided by four different publishers, investigate the best math manipulatives that your friends recommend, and examine several different teaching aids for memorization of math facts. Then, you select the best options for your child.

Unit-Studies Approach

Many parents, whether choosing a packaged curriculum or creating their own, incorporate an integrated approach to learning into their curriculum through "unit studies".

"Unit studies" put into practice the basic elements of many subjects at once by organizing study around one particular topic or "unit". A unit on the American Revolution might include reading and discussing *Johnny Tremain*, mapping the major battles, calculating the distance traveled by the British soldiers in their march on Lexington and Concord, writing essays keyed to various themes from the book, and doing weather-related science experiments. The student learns reading, writing, geography, math, and science through a coordinated approach that links all the subjects in one theme.

One big advantage of unit studies is that they often are multi-level, that is, they include material that is appropriate for a two- or three-grade range. Several children can be taught from the same material, with just a variance in the difficulty of the accompanying assignment. In addition, parents can vary the level of difficulty for each assignment, according to the needs of each particular child. For example, the child's skill level in grammar may call for him to do the second-grade assignment, while his spelling skill may require a third-grade assignment. The parent has greater flexibility in choosing the level of difficulty for each assignment.

Unit studies create the opportunity for increasing family unity when all the children are taught together in a small group setting. Even when each child has a different assignment, all their assignments are related to the same theme and can be shared with other family members for their enrichment. Family creativity often flourishes as the children brainstorm together and come up with interesting joint projects related to the unit. Some families conclude each particular unit with a presentation to dad, grandparents, or friends, displaying or explaining their work.

You can put together your own unit studies (there are books to guide you in creating them) or buy a complete or partial package made up of unit studies, such as the Konos curriculum. (See Appendix C for more recommendations.)

Because unit studies are thematic by nature, your real choice lies in selecting the themes you want to emphasize. Some unit studies curricula—Konos, for example—use the virtues or character traits as their organizing principle. Others use historical events as the basis for the units. Some parents choose topics based on their child's interests. For example, a child who is passionate about airplanes but detests writing essays may be more easily motivated when he writes about what he loves—airplanes.

A final benefit of unit studies is that they often help students retain better the information they have learned. Because all the subjects are interrelated, students are less likely to think they are memorizing disjointed facts. In addition, most unit studies rely strongly on interesting and creative projects to get the points across. The children learn by doing and without the tedium of endless workbook exercises. Besides, the kids have more fun! Finally, your children can delve more deeply into the topic they are studying, instead of reading a cursory paragraph or two about it in a text.

Using unit studies as the sole basis for a curriculum does have some drawbacks. First, it can require quite a bit of time and effort to gather the resources and references yourself if you are using a unit-studies curriculum that does not provide all the materials for you (and most don't). Creating your own unit studies requires even more effort, as you must not only conceive of all the projects for each subject integrated into the unit but also collect all the necessary materials.

A second drawback is that a continuous stream of unit-studies projects, without some connecting thread, can yield an ad hoc assortment of projects. Education undertaken in this fashion is less comprehensive and more liable to leave gaping holes in a child's academic background. This becomes more of a problem as the child becomes older and needs to cover more material.

Drill work and memorization skills may suffer when the parent focuses exclusively on unit studies. As unappealing as it may seem, multiplication tables, spelling words, and vocabulary words are learned best through repetition and memory work. Similarly, children need practice in quickly and succinctly recalling certain information. Some unit-studies curricula focus solely on written or oral essays and projects, to the exclusion of timed or "objective" tests. Neglecting memorization, or omitting the challenge of tests with time or space limitations, deprives them of skills needed for later intellectual growth.

Finally, using unit studies on a regular basis requires a strong commitment from the parent to follow through on all the projects begun. A mother teaching four children may find it more difficult to keep track of and coordinate different projects for each—unless all their work is done as a group project. Projects simply take more time and effort than other academic work.

Unit studies *do* contribute much to a child's creativity, motivation, and in-depth knowledge. The best approach strikes a balance, offering enough unit studies to keep things fun and interesting but enough systematic study in the core subjects to ensure a thorough education.

How to Choose a Curriculum

Think about Your Children

All curricula are *not* created equal. Before plunging in and buying the first curriculum that catches your eye, sit down with a pen and paper and consider a few things.

Think about your child. Write down his academic strengths and weaknesses. If you are bringing him home after a few years in school, was there a subject in which he fared poorly and on which you really want to concentrate? Is there a particular subject that he found "boring" and about which you want to excite his imagination? Are there any areas he is well ahead in and that he need not spend much time studying?

For a kindergarten student, your assessment will be more basic. Ask yourself how her writing skills are. Can she write her name

easily, or is it a chore? Does she know her alphabet? Is she interested yet in learning how to read? Is she comfortable using scissors
and a pencil? What kinds of books interest her?

Next, list personality traits and characteristics that will affect
your child's ability to learn. Does he have a hard time sitting still for
more than twenty minutes? Is she naturally inquisitive and self-
directed or in need of constant encouragement and incentives?
Can she follow directions and work independently, or will you
need to be at her side constantly? Does he like routine, organized
schedules where he does the same thing (for example, workbooks)
day after day? Or does he thrive on a constant stream of "new"
projects?

Think about and try to discern your child's best way of learning—does he retain information best when he hears it, reads it,
writes it, or experiences it some other way? (For a good discussion
of the major learning styles—visual, auditory, and kinesthetic—see
Cathy Duffy's book, *The Home Educator's Curriculum Manual*. She
evaluates home-education materials in light of their effectiveness
for each learning style.)

Know Yourself

Choose a curriculum that compensates for your weaknesses and
builds on your personal strengths. For example, if your weakness is
creativity, and you're afraid you will fall into a rut (and learning will
degenerate into the grind of "getting it done"), choose a curriculum that builds in very interesting, fun projects in almost every
subject at regular intervals. If your weakness is procrastination,
perhaps you need a curriculum with detailed, sequenced lesson
plans so that academics won't suffer if lesson planning is something
you hardly ever "get around to". If your own math skills are not
very strong, choose a curriculum with a detailed teacher's manual
that drills, repeats, and reinforces each skill so you are sure you are
covering the concepts well.

Weigh Your Friends' Recommendations

Talk to your friends and find out what materials they recommend. What have they found most effective and fun, and why? What resources have they tried and disliked, and why?

Always keep in mind that your friends' children, personalities, and backgrounds are different from yours. Your friends may have found the "perfect" curriculum, but it might not be suited to you or your child. If your friend has a quiet child who loves to read and is naturally fascinated by anything to do with nature or science, then factor that in when she raves about her science curriculum and recommends it to you. Your active, hands-on learner may need a quite different curriculum—one that lets him learn by doing and keeps his interest through absorbing activities.

Find out specifically what your friends liked or disliked about the curricula they use or have rejected. What they dislike might be exactly what you are looking for! For example, one woman in a support group shared her dislike for a particular reading program that relied on basal readers; she preferred her children to read real literature almost from day one. Another woman in the same group was looking for a reading program with exactly the approach the first woman disliked so much. She wanted a program that controlled vocabulary in the beginning and limited stories to words that the phonics skills had covered. She would add the literature later when all the skills had been taught. The women had two different approaches: the same reading program that one of them loved would frustrate the other.

Read All about It!

The two best resources for evaluating curricula are *The Big Book of Home Learning,* by Mary Pride, and *The Home Educator's Curriculum Manual,* by Cathy Duffy. Use their evaluations and summaries to narrow your curriculum choices. These sources and others provide extensive descriptions of home-education resources and books. Don't feel bound by the author's preferences. However, the more information you get before you start writing checks, the better.

Other written resources to check are home-education books and magazines. (See Bibliography: Home Education, General.) Many will have curriculum recommendations in addition to teaching tips.

Even when you are still in the researching stage, order catalogues from curriculum publishers and suppliers. Publisher's catalogues are often free (e.g., Modern Curriculum Press and A Beka) and usually contain good descriptions of the materials. Both Mary Pride's and Cathy Duffy's books note which publishers send out free catalogues to aid your search for just the right curriculum. Most publishers who publish specifically for home-educating families have friendly, helpful staffs who are knowledgeable about their materials. Call with your questions. Remember that non-Catholic Christian sources will not alert you to materials that may contain conflicts with our Faith.

Catalogues from suppliers are available, often for a nominal cost, but may or may not provide descriptions of the materials. If you know what you're looking for, the supplier catalogues often have the desired materials available at a discount from the publisher's price. Find out what materials can be returned if you are dissatisfied with them. Many companies will accept returned merchandise if it is unused and in resalable condition, but they sometimes charge a restocking fee that may be as high as 25 percent.

Look before You Buy

Look at as many of your friends' curricula as you can. Support groups come in handy here, as they give you access to many different kinds of curricula and approaches.

Attend home-education curriculum or book fairs, if possible, before you buy. In many places now there are Catholic home-education conventions. (Contact NACHE, listed in the Appendix, for more information.) In almost every state, statewide home-schooling organizations (Christian or secular) sponsor conventions as well.

If possible, attend more than one convention or curriculum fair, with the purpose of the first one being, not to buy, but simply to look and learn. Once you have a sense of what curricula offerings you might be interested in (or at least what type—unit study, specific subjects, package curricula), you will be less likely to over-buy.

Purchasing at curriculum fairs can allow you to take advantage of special discounts, avoid shipping costs, see before you buy, and complete your purchasing efficiently and comprehensively. Some curriculum suppliers (notably Seton) offer their own mini-conferences on home education, which give you a chance to see and evaluate their curriculum offerings.

Making the Choices

Leaving a curriculum fair with an armload of great books or unpacking your first curriculum shipment is exhilarating! Just having the books *there*, in front of you, can have you chafing to begin the new school year!

However, accept the fact that in choosing curriculum materials you *will* make some mistakes (just as school districts do). You may find out that something you ordered just sits on your shelf and is never used. You may realize belatedly that it's not suited for your child's learning style or that it's too easy or too advanced for him.

Keep your mistakes in perspective. The advantage to your child is that you are never stuck with your mistakes. Unlike a school-teacher, you won't need many meetings and many months to obtain permission to discontinue a less-than-successful program. Be judicious about the quantity of materials ordered. For example, if you anticipate covering two grade levels of math in one year but you've never used this particular program before, then don't order the second book before you're sure you like the first.

One mother of four, as she recalled her own mistakes along the way to finding the right curriculum, emphasized the need

[to] start simply. When my oldest was prekindergarten, I ordered countless workbooks and activity books so he could perfect his

printing, counting, and phonics. Now as my third child reaches this age, I've given away most of those materials and use three puzzles (capital letters, small letters, numbers) and one phonics workbook that we use about once or twice a week for ten minutes at a time. In the beginning I was so caught up by all the educational offerings that I overbought and bought the wrong things.

But mistakes are never totally wasted. Your mistake may be someone else's gold mine. Give away or sell what you don't want. Exchange materials with others in your support group. Hold your own local "mini-curriculum fair" where you can sell what you haven't used and buy cheaply what others don't need. Finally, simply pitch some of them out and chalk it up to experience.

If you can, put aside a small part of your curriculum budget for midyear purchases. This will free you to purchase supplementary materials as you need them. As one mother explained, "When my daughter was several months into learning her math facts (addition and subtraction), I realized she needed extra drill work. I ordered a math game ('Math-it') that gave her that extra drill work but also varied the routine so she enjoyed it more. The younger kids were soon clamoring to play 'Math-it' as well."

Final Thoughts about Curriculum

Some research on the achievement-test scores of home-schooled children indicates that they scored highest in science, listening skills, vocabulary, and reading. Students also did well in mathematical reasoning. The weakest area for home-educated children (while still above the norm for institutionally educated children) was in math computation.[9]

[9] Brian D. Ray and Jon Wartes, "The Academic Achievement and Affective Development of Home Schooled Children", in *Home Schooling: Political, Historical, and Pedagogical Perspectives*, edited by Jane Van Galen and Mary Anne Pitman (Norwood, NJ: Ablex Publishing Corporation, 1991), p. 45, discussing results of the Washington State Homeschool Research Project.

While these statistics of course can't be used to predict how your own children will fare on tests, they are a good reminder not to neglect math drill work. Even if your children understand a concept, only repetition and practice will ensure the speedy recall necessary to score well in math computation. So remember to include games or practice activities that will help your children stay sharp in math computation even after they have initially mastered the concepts.

On another note . . . one of the beauties of home education is that it takes into account your family's unique situation. Curriculum choices also reflect the individual preferences and needs of each one of your children. So, while you may think one type of curriculum approach is far superior to another, respect the freedom of another family to decide differently. Curriculum choices are inherently subjective.

Curriculum—It's Your Choice

1. A Catholic curriculum includes all that is true, good, and beautiful. All subjects must be taught within a Catholic atmosphere created, not by the number of obviously Catholic resources, but rather by our successful interweaving of our Faith into the fabric of our lives.

2. Materials for teaching the Faith must communicate the truths of our Faith authentically and consistently. Include Scripture (RSV, Catholic edition), the *Catechism of the Catholic Church*, and sound textbooks, such as the *Faith and Life Series*.

3. A "complete" or "packaged" curriculum provides a fixed course of study in all the subjects for a particular grade level. Its biggest advantage is its structure: the lessons are planned out for you and offer continuity from year to year. The biggest drawback is the lack of flexibility: parents cannot tailor the curriculum in light of their child's real skill levels, his way of learning, his natural interests, and his preferred pace of learning.

4. A partial package combines preselected curricula for some subjects with resources selected on an individual basis to suit a particular child's strengths and weaknesses.

5. An individually tailored program (the most popular curriculum choice) requires more initial effort than a package curriculum but offers the greatest flexibility to accommodate the child's learning needs, pace, and interests.

6. Unit studies coordinate the study of several subjects around a common theme. They promote integrated learning and accommodate different skill levels at one time, allowing you to teach more than one child at once or to teach one child on varying levels. The disadvantage is that it takes more preparation and can result in a series of ad hoc projects, without continuity.

7. Choose a curriculum by deciding your goals, evaluating your and your child's needs for organization, structure, and flexibility. Gather information from books, catalogues, and friends before choosing; remain open to midcourse corrections or new choices if a chosen resource fails to meet your expectations.

PART THREE

EXTRA CONSIDERATIONS

11

Adjusting the Learning Curve

Toddlers and Transition Time

Special situations require thoughtful planning to ensure successful home education. It is worth taking some time to think through your strategy before tackling the new school year. Two special challenges for your home school may be incorporating toddlers or adjusting during the transition time when you bring your children home from institutional schools. Careful consideration should be given to the ways they can contribute to your home-education enterprise.

Toddlers

Toddlers need you. They need to be with you, to see you, and to have access to you. They want to feel included in what the family is doing even if they do not understand what is happening. They also require a safe environment in which to play and do their style of "work". How can we best provide for these needs all the while making steady progress toward our academic goals for our older children?

Your Attitude

Resist the temptation to cage your toddler or attach him to a clothesline on a leash to allow safe roaming—there is a better way! Seriously, decide your toddler is an important part of your school; you will be able to see him as an asset rather than as a liability. Your welcoming attitude opens your child's heart to feel included, rather than excluded, in your activities. Remember: you are a mom first and a teacher second, for each of your children.

Caroline Nelson, mother of six (two of whom are toddlers), says,

> Toddlers fit right in and want to do things along with us. They "absorb" a lot from their older siblings. It's not easy, but it's worth it, to include them as much as possible or let them play beside you.

You can communicate this attitude: Let's enjoy this learning experience together.

A toddler can sit with the older children for opening school prayers, stand for the Pledge of Allegiance, and assist with the weather seals on the calendar. Draw him up onto your lap for reading time, whether it be history, science, or language arts. He may not understand what you are reading, but he will relish the close contact with you, feeling a part of the experience. Your toddler will benefit from hearing material before he is required to learn it, just as he would in a one-room schoolhouse.

Reward a toddler with stickers for small increments of independent play. This encourages a balance between the time he requires for guidance and time he plays by himself. When you designate some time for puzzles, playdough, or water colors for your toddler, he will feel as if he is important enough to have "classes", too. If you offer the same praise to your toddler that he hears you give the others, he will sense your positive attitude toward him.

Lorri McCaffrey, home-educating mother of eight, including three toddlers, offers this advice.

> Home educators and non-home educators alike wonder how a mother can teach older children and have little toddlers at the same time. I struggled in this area as well until, by God's grace, I started looking at my role as schoolteacher a bit differently. I have come to view each of my children, whether two days old or eleven years, as one of my home-schooling pupils. This may sound simplistic. However, I plan the little ones' day and activities as well as the older ones'. I find that my days run much smoother this way. I don't plan the toddlers' schedule as compactly as the

older children's, but I have a very good idea of what activities they will be engaging in for the morning and encourage them in quiet play when I sit right down on the floor with them as school begins.

The older children have schoolwork assigned first thing in the morning that they can accomplish easily on their own. After my little ones are immersed in their own activities, usually within the first half hour, I switch to a subject that requires my time with the older ones for the next half hour. I rotate this way throughout the morning, taking breaks for exercise or singing as I see the need arise. The most important aspect of my day, I have found, is to be prepared. It takes some time on Saturday or Sunday evenings to think through all the children's schedules, but preparation ahead of time has been the key to a smooth-running schoolroom. The children have direction, and I have direction as well.

Your attitude sets the tone for how your other children either respond or react to the toddler in the house. On the one hand, train your older children to place their projects out of the toddler's reach. That may mean you clear off a shelf for those projects in advance. On the other hand, plan time for your children to play with the toddler so that he feels specially included by his siblings as well as by mom.

Sometimes older children resent a toddler's lack of a schedule. "Why does he always get to play?" is a common complaint. We quell discontent by pointing out that a toddler's play *is* his work— his play prepares him for the kind of learning in which the older children are engaged. Lorri McCaffrey capitalizes on her toddlers' curiosity and energy, enhancing the home education for everyone.

> I can use the toddlers' energy to help in the schoolday by letting them help me set up for the older childrens' projects coming up in the next time segment, or use their exuberance to help me . . . pair socks, if that's the activity planned for them. The key I've found is to have activities to keep them busy, but quiet, such as puzzles, coloring, magazine cut-outs, Lego blocks, and quiet stories. (I have even recorded their favorite books on cassette and let them put the headphones on and listen the time away while they turn the pages for themselves.)

Children are so inquisitive in their toddler years, and they enjoy being of help or a part of the action in any way they can. I must confess that I really enjoy the toddler years. Those chubby, angelic little faces are outgrown in such a short time, and I enjoy being right there on the floor for part of my day to enjoy them as much as I can.

Never underestimate the difference your attitude toward your toddler can make in the harmony of your home, particularly in home education. Ask God for the grace to keep your heart tender toward your toddler, through the interruptions, times for discipline, and the ways his actions may alter your schedule. That way you will home educate God's way, with each child knowing how significant he is, including your toddler.

Your Location

Toddlers are, by nature, inquisitive. Due to their short attention spans and your lack of supervision, they may leave a trail of Legos, Lincoln Logs, GI Joes, and costumes. Left to themselves, they create messes in other rooms while you focus on other children. (After all, "Out of sight, out of mind.") Further, they can be dangerous to themselves; their untended curiosity can open the door for injuries. Creating a kid-friendly environment can focus their curiosity, limit safety concerns, and minimize the mess.

Keep your toddler in the same area where most of the teaching is done. You can monitor his play as it develops so that your toddler sees you, hears you, and knows you are near. You save time by not leaving the room to check on him.

When toddlers feel they have access to you, it actually minimizes interruptions. They don't like to feel excluded (understandably!). Roseanne Martin, mother of eight (two of whom are toddlers), gives this advice:

Teach in a place where you can have snacks, diapers, bottles, and activities at hand to cut down on trips to get these things. Have a drawer or box of learning toys that can only be used during school time and then put them away. Then they will look forward to using these special things.

One family chose a special ark with many animals as the toddler toy for school time only. Another family purchased a Playmobil pirate ship with the same idea in mind. When school is over, the toy is put away until the next day.

Some families employ the electronic baby-sitter—the TV—to manage the toddler. Is this a good idea? The TV is an impersonal, mindless machine. It takes the child away from the prelearning he could acquire in your one-room school. It substitutes entertainment for learning. (Down the road, that could be a difficult thing with which to compete, as many other teachers have found.) And, for the most part, it dulls your toddler's imagination. Popping a video into the machine may seem like the easiest way to "take care of" the toddler, but be sure it is genuinely in the best interests of your child.

Your Plan

Include your toddler as much as possible. Even if your child cannot understand what you are reading to another child, cuddling on your lap can satisfy his need to be with you. Perhaps he can "work" in a workbook (one purchased at a yard sale or partially used by a sibling) while others are doing seat work. Or he may want to color alongside a child who is drawing.

Routine helps them know expectations. A toddler learns he will get a drink and a snack midmorning, following the science lesson. So he interrupts less. He looks forward to outside play that will happen during a sister's recess time. He discovers that one-on-one time with you each day helps him to be less demanding at other times.

Rules, clearly stated and consistently enforced, set necessary boundaries for toddlers. There may be an occasional battle over what can and cannot be touched, especially at the beginning of your school year. If you explain the behavior you require, and work to be consistent, your toddler will understand what you expect of him. This is excellent preparation for later instruction you will give him. Just be sure to have realistic rules with which a toddler can comply.

For older toddlers, daily structured activities can prepare them for the discipline needed for schooling: putting blocks in order, stacking boxes, sorting by color or shape. A few minutes of focused time with a toddler can often satisfy his need for attention.

Some unit-study projects can include the toddler. For example, if the older children have made a large-scale replica of an ear, the toddler can crawl through it just like his siblings. Or if they have made musical instruments, the toddler can have a turn playing them as well. Nature walks are a favorite, even if the toddler is not the one looking for seeds, insects, or leaves. Certainly any toddler can be included easily at snack time or recess.

Place materials they can use at their level. Designate a desk or place at a table as their place for coloring or drawing. Give them a supply of crayons, paper, pencils, markers (perhaps scissors, depending on the age) for their desk or in a special tub just for them. Give them access to the blackboard when other children are not using it. (If they are trained to use chalk, they will not ruin the board with crayons or markers.)

You might want to structure the time with your toddler more than this. Some suggestions for different kinds of development are as follows: auditory learning—listen to tapes, speak and sing into a tape recorder, make musical instruments and play them; motor skill development—large motor skill development through running, jumping, and outdoor play, and small motor skill development through sorting small objects (such as keys or buttons) according to various patterns; visual stimulation and eye-hand coordination—classify by color, drop clothespins into a bottle, use pegboards, Legos, felt shapes, or lace-up cards; and verbal skills—share and dramatize Bible stories and fables, memorize nursery rhymes, listen to stories and talk about them.

Finally, there are preschool curricula available. This may or may not be a helpful way to structure your time with your toddler, depending on your personality and your child's. Having specific tasks might give the older children an opportunity to "teach" the younger ones. For helpful critiques of preschool curricula, see volume two of Mary Pride's *Big Book of Home Learning*.[1]

Toddlerhood is a special time in your child's life and in the life of your family. Your toddler is an asset, not a liability, in your home-education experience. With proper planning, your toddler will make a sparkling contribution to your overall home-education venture.

Toddlers Belong in a Home School

1. Toddlers have special needs: to be with you, to feel included, and to play in a safe environment.

2. Your attitude sets the tone for how your toddler feels and how the other children either react or respond to the toddler in the house.

3. Your teaching area should welcome the toddler with age-appropriate toys, accessible materials, and a special place just for him. Be careful about using the TV as an electronic baby-sitter.

4. Include the toddler in your daily plan. Established routines and consistent rules help toddlers understand your expectations.

5. Depending on your toddler's age, you might want to structure some learning time for him especially geared to his learning style.

Transition Time—Adjustments from Institutional School to Home Education

There are several areas of concern for a child who has experienced education in an institutional school. He might be struggling with his own burnout from poor teaching methods or unnecessary stress

---

[1] Mary Pride, *Big Book of Home Learning*, vol. 2 (Wheaton, IL: Crossway Books, 1990): 13–15, 37–52, 69–77, 260–64.

on performance for grades. He might be concerned that home education is not "real" education because his mom is not a "real" teacher and the structure of the day is so different from what he has experienced. He might be unsure about adjusting to so much time with siblings and fear that he will lose his friends from school. These legitimate concerns need to be addressed.

Before dealing with the specific adjustments, know that it is worth the effort. Barb Hoyt of New Lenox, Illinois, shares her perspective after pulling her children from a local Catholic school.

> Uprooting children from a current school system to a home-school setting reminds me of gardening—transplanting to a more wholesome environment produces sturdier plants. As their personal gardeners, parents can oversee and nurture their growth and development, where the soil is richest and cultivated with love. ("If the root is holy, so are the branches"—Ps 127.) Some people would contend that a home-school setting is too sheltered, yet we as parents are preparing our children to face conditions in the world that will demand a strong sense of character. Only young men and women deeply rooted in their Faith can weather these conditions and survive spiritually.

Home education is a greenhouse in which we nurture our young ones *so that* they can be transplanted in the harsher environment and flourish!

Adjustment: Method of Learning

If a child resists home education because he is discouraged or burned out, he might need a period of refreshment with a focus on "delight-directed" learning. Perhaps some time without textbooks and workbooks is just the thing to reroute a child's interest in learning. Some children are so burned out by school, pressure, and peer competition that they need informality and flexibility in order to regain their enthusiasm and mental energy.

Other children enjoy their experiences in school. In fact, some children might be quite dependent upon a very scheduled routine and may feel lost or disoriented by having too little structure or direction in the home-education daily plan. A preset curriculum that reflects the format of classroom study may be a good start for the older child who needs more structure initially.

Though some children feel overwhelmed when competing in school, others thrive on it. If your child really enjoyed rising to the challenge of competition, you might need additional incentives for motivation. It might take a while to shift the child's focus from learning the material for the best grade to learning the material for the inherent rewards of knowledge.

Allow for a reasonable adjustment period. Even if the child is eager about home education, this is a major change in his life. The child who is apprehensive about or resists home education might require a longer time to settle into a new routine wholeheartedly. Realize there are many changes for the child with this new academic structure: new curriculum, greater demands, more independent work, more intensive work, and possibly new subjects.

Adjustment: New Teacher

Your child might need to reestablish a proper respect for your authority. He might struggle in accepting you as a competent teacher, especially if he has been in school for many years and if parental involvement in his education was limited to asking if he had completed his homework before he went out or turned on the TV.

Here your husband is the key. His show of support and respect for your role as teacher, especially in the children's presence, sets the tone for their support and respect. In addition, he might need to talk specifically about what is expected of your children in terms of proper attitudes and demeanor.

Adjustment: Family Rather Than Peer Dependence

Your child will have emotional and social adjustments as he shifts from an institutional setting to home for the bulk of his day. Sometimes a child is relieved to get out of the school environment where he was, at best, unsure of himself in relation to his peer group or, at worst, traumatized by his peers. In the secure environment of home, he is now free to explore his talents (such as music or art) without facing criticism. Or he can regain a confidence once lost in certain subject areas such as math or reading because there is no peer mocking his failure.

Another child might genuinely miss the comraderie of friends and be unsure how he will get time with them. Let him know your willingness to help him get together with friends and then make the effort to follow through. At the same time, help him enjoy and appreciate the family more and more. Be aware he might need time for weaning from peer dependence to a healthier dependence on parents and God.

If friends from school don't seem as interested in him, he might have to make new friends (if the children in your home-education support group were not acquainted with him already). Encourage him to foster good friendships with siblings and peers alike.

Adjustment: More Time with Siblings

It can be quite an adjustment for your older child to spend most of the day with siblings. It might be difficult for the very peer-dependent child. Sometimes it takes a whole year for the child to make the change. But persevere—especially for the sake of the siblings. Rebuilding those relationships takes time, but it is worth it—both for the future relationship between older and younger children and also for the older child's ability to make independent decisions without undue influence from friends.

If he is sure that being around "little kids" (siblings) all day will be boring or drive him crazy, then you need to deal with this concern on two fronts. On the one hand, help him rebuild good sibling relationships. On the other hand, take his concerns seriously when he shares his real need for some private space and time without younger ones around. For example, if he is in the living room, engrossed in a good book, then make sure your six-year-old does not play the piano at the same time.

Adjustment: New Free Time

It might take a while for him to know how he can best spend his newfound free time. Here your proper planning will ease the transition. You can provide outside lessons in music or art, encourage hobbies, and teach him some new skills. Point out that since he is home educated, he now has time to pursue those things he has always wanted to do but never had enough time for before.

Be creative. Ask your child what he enjoyed most about school and what he is most apprehensive about in the switch to home education. Try to meet his real needs. Instead of saying, "You're home, so get used to it", understand what his fears and needs are. For example, if he's most afraid that a special friendship will be lost, make a special effort to keep up contacts with that friend. Provide fun opportunities for them to strengthen their friendship (assuming it is a friendship that is good for your child).

If he is afraid of being bored, come up with a list together of the interesting things he would like to do, try, read, think about, or visit. Prioritize and work these into your school calendar. Or keep the list for him to look at on a day when he seems particularly restless. If he enjoyed team sports, find teams on which he can play through the home-school support group, community-based programs, or the CYO.

Adjustment: Personality Conflicts

There are times when parents and children struggle with personality conflicts. Often this is true when they share the same trait they do not care for in the other. Is this an insurmountable difficulty in home education? No. This represents a real difficulty, but there are solutions.

It is important to work through the struggle rather than to dodge the problem by sending the child off to school in order to avoid him. Rather than sidestep this conflict, moms and children can deal with it so that the whole family benefits. Through discipline, training, prayer, and example, parents and children can grow in character development and in respect for one another. We must demonstrate respect for them just as we want their respect.

Another attitude challenge is this: How do I mix my roles of mother and teacher? It is essential that we see ourselves as mothers who teach rather than teachers who add mothering. We must lead with nurturing love. After all, that is our strength—we love them like no teacher could. We must keep our perspective: the child, not the lesson plan, is most important.

Sometimes our problem is sin. We become impatient, raising our voices in anger. We lock wills with one of our children. We do not show them the same respect an ordinary schoolteacher would show them.

We should take the time necessary to respond rather than react to them. We could leave the room for a minute and pray for peace and wisdom. Or the child could sit apart (perhaps on the stairs) and ask the Lord to help him take concrete steps toward changing his behavior.

Adjustment: New Motivations Needed

For some children grades and report cards have been their incentive for good performance. You may want to give your child grades if this is such a strong motivator. However, many parents do not grade their children, since tutoring eliminates most of the need for it, at least at the elementary-school level.

Other children have been encouraged to do well by peer approval or teacher responses. In some cases, celebrations within the family—perhaps performing for grandparents or another family—can be helpful motivators in the home school as well.

Encouraging children to tackle and complete their weekly work successfully is a challenge. Some mothers make a list of the assignments for the week for each child. Depending on the age of your child, some assignments might be obligatory each day, and the rest could be done when he feels ready. Your child soon learns not to leave all of the undesirable work to the end of the week. It encourages independence, allowing the child to make some of the choices, which in turn helps create a good attitude.

Another successful idea has been offering extra-credit incentives. It works like this: the child must do the expected day's work without reward; but every day he can do future assignments and get an extra-credit marble in a glass. The parent figures out the value of each marble (say, ten cents) and purchases an item the child might like (a doll, a model airplane, baseball cards). She tells the child how many marbles it will cost.

With older children you may need to think of time, rather than money, as the extra-credit incentive. Children in the twelve-to-eighteen age bracket seem to have discretionary money to purchase the clothes, movie tickets, books, or videos they want. However, they often have difficulty getting to the shops, theater, or bookstore. Perhaps your incentive can be marbles for trips to the various places they want to go. Or they may want to exchange marbles for an outing with you or your husband. You will keep motivation high if you select extra-credit incentives they really want.

Extra-credit work does not replace daily assignments; the next day's assignment will pick up where your child left off. For instance, if one page of math is required every day, instead of your child doing five pages in a week, he might do eight pages. Now he is three pages ahead of your original goal, and he has three marbles toward his prize. The advantage of the extra-credit system is that, as your child goes ahead in a subject, you feel less and less pressure about finishing the curriculum. The incentive system has worked extremely well and enabled children to accomplish more work in less time and with less pressure on them (and mom) each year.

Adjustment: New Schedule for Mom

One of the concerns frequently expressed by moms looking into home education is this: How will I accomplish all my housework if my mornings are consumed with teaching? Good question. Here are a few ideas: Make housework part of your planning. Since life skills are part of the education of your children, teach them the skills. Some moms schedule chores before school; others utilize their children's help after school and before playtime. (See Bibliography: Family Life, for a brief bibliography of books with helpful suggestions for organizing housework and for what children can do best at what ages.)

The husband's support is crucial. Hopefully he can express his desire for a clean and orderly home while giving you time to work out how to accomplish this. A "mother's helper" might be a solution: a young girl watches the children while you are at home, freeing you to do housework, rest, or make something creative. It is cheaper than baby-sitting or paying others for cleaning.

One "solution" to avoid generally is doing housework while teaching. Though a few moms can juggle housework and schoolwork, few do it well. Children need focused attention, and when mom's attention is divided, they tend to wander. Then schoolwork takes longer and eventually eats into time that could have been used for housework. Eliminate the distractions of housework during school hours with a plan for housework later.

Along the same lines, decide how to deal with interruptions by the telephone or visitors. Make a plan and stick to it. Many families find it helpful to alert relatives and friends that calls or visits in the morning will not work since school will be in session. A telephone answering machine can be a strategic tool as well.

Adjustment: New Pressures

Regardless of how much support you may have to home educate, you will have internal pressure to be successful. If your family and close friends are wary of this venture for you, you may feel additional pressure to prove home education works.

Roseanne Martin attests to the fact that there's a difference between feeling concerned about whether you will do a good job as a home educator and feeling gripped by anxiety about your success.

> When we first began home schooling I didn't have much confidence and was losing energy in being anxious about whether we could manage and if the children would learn everything they

should, according to the school-system criteria. I am much more relaxed now, more organized. I set reasonable goals and have pared down to real basics that I actually teach. I trust the children's own ability to learn. And every day I pray that they will learn what God wants and that He will provide the means, people, and materials we should use.

Pray that the Lord will help you not be anxious, because anxiety will not produce the good fruit you desire in yourself or your children. At the same time, your concerns are valid. Take them to the Lord in prayer, and see how abundantly He answers you with His supernatural strength for the task at hand.

> Have no anxiety about anything, but in everything, by prayer and supplication, *with thanksgiving*, let your requests be made known unto God. And the peace of God, which passes all understanding, will keep your hearts and minds in Christ Jesus (Phil 4:6–7).

Remind yourself that your children need not fit someone else's model of what a "perfect" kid is like or reach certain academic milestones others select. What matters is what you and your spouse think God wants you to do for the good of your children. After all, God—not others—will be the judge.

Establish realistic expectations. Nothing sets the stage faster for burnout than unrealistic goals. Evaluate the curriculum as you go along and feel free to change it if it is contributing unnecessary stress in your home. Talk to friends in your support group for ideas on flexibility if you feel overwhelmed by the task.

Making Choices—Making Changes

1. There are a number of academic, social, and personal adjustments when children are brought into home education from an institutional-school setting.

2. In academic structure, your children will have changes due to tutoring, more independent or intensive work, and possibly new subjects.

3. Your child may need to reestablish a proper respect for your authority. Your husband is the key in his support and respect for you as a teacher.

4. Your child will have emotional and social adjustments as he shifts from an institutional setting primarily spent with peers to home with siblings for the bulk of his day. Take his needs seriously both in helping him rebuild relationships with siblings and in fostering solid peer friendships.

5. It may take a while for your child to know best how he can spend his newfound free time. Be creative in exploring with him music lessons, hobbies, sports, or new skills.

6. If there are personality conflicts, deal with them. Through discipline, training, prayer, and example, parents and children can grow in character development and in respect for one another.

7. Provide new motivations for accomplishing work, replacing grades, performances, and teacher approval with mutually agreed upon incentives.

8. It *is* possible to accomplish housework and home educate. Planning ahead and recruiting your "students" helps you get it all done and trains your children in life skills.

9. You may feel pressure from family or friends who want you to prove home education works. Keep your focus on the Lord and pray for help. Be faithful and in due season your home education efforts *will* bear good fruit for all to see.

12

Home: A School of Choice

Teens

Some people dread the teen years right from the time they cuddle their firstborn; this dread is inspired both by their culture and by their own experiences as teens. But these can be wonderful years, when your relationship to your teen grows and matures, especially when you home educate. In fact, while the teen years pose new challenges and promise more complex relationships with your children, both you *and* your teens can really enjoy them. Even if your children are years away from this critical stage, the relationships you build now will help them climb over the inevitable obstacles in the road to maturity. Here is where home schooling gives you a definite advantage: you really will know and understand your children better.

Successful teen-parent relationships are sown with the seeds of love, respect, and understanding—all of which are cultivated more easily when you spend time together talking about things that matter. Susan and Michael Waldstein from Notre Dame, Indiana, have cherished the opportunity to grow closer to their teens through home education. As Susan points out, "It's exciting to have teenagers and see them growing into beautiful young men and women. I don't see that kind of relationship with some of our friends whose kids are in high school." Home education gives you the time and opportunity for the in-depth discussions that enrich your teen's intellectual and emotional development and cement your relationship with him. It allows you to work out the inevitable conflicts away from the overshadowing, dominant peer culture of most high schools.

As your teens round the bend of childhood and stare down the long path to adulthood, the way may seem rocky indeed. That is not surprising. Our children experience amazing changes—emotionally, physically, and intellectually—in uneven bursts and at unpredictable times. And just as in other stages of development, each one will grow according to a unique timetable—one that home education will not only accommodate but take advantage of as well.

The Bratten family from Ohio, for example, discovered that the flexibility of home education gave them the freedom to adjust to their teens' needs. As Mrs. Bratten explained,

> During the stressful years, I did not put quite as much emphasis on the academics, realizing that a lot of energy was going into growing and learning emotionally. By the later high-school years, things went more easily, and they caught up with their academics.

Home education allows both parents and teens to keep a long-term perspective when measuring progress.

It is important to remember that our teens, while approaching adulthood, are still children. And for many years, they will straddle the imaginary line between childhood and adulthood, until at last they are ready to cross the line into adulthood.

> Teenagers are children in transition. They are not young adults. Their needs, including their emotional needs, are those of children. One of the most common mistakes parents, teachers, and others make regarding adolescents is to consider them junior adults. Many people in authority over teenagers overlook their childlike needs for feeling love and acceptance, for being taken care of, and for knowing that someone really cares for them.[1]

Teenage children still need moms and dads to meet their needs and help them grow into independent, mature, secure, and holy adults.

Don't be surprised if your child's intellectual and emotional progress sometimes looks more like a seismograph reading during

---

[1] Ross Campbell, M.D., *How to Really Love Your Teenager* (Wheaton, IL: Victor Books, 1993), p. 16.

an earthquake than a steady upward curve. That's to be expected; after all, teens are human beings, not machines!

Set Concrete Goals with Your Teen

The best way you and your teen can keep perspective and make balanced progress is to set concrete goals in all areas of his life—not just academics. It's not enough to ask, "What subjects do I want to teach him during high school?" or "What is the best academic preparation I can give him for college?" These years provide us with the last chance to shape our children and to prepare them to use their freedom well when they are out on their own.

Together, you and your teen should chart milestones for his spiritual formation, human formation (which includes personal maturity and character development as well as large doses of fun), and intellectual formation. Set out your own expectations for your teen in these areas and find out what his expectations are, both for the coming year and for the next few years. Let him express his fears, hesitations, and aspirations, as well as the changes he would like to see in himself over the course of the year. Help him to see that you, too, desire his independence, but at a pace compatible with his ability to assume responsibility and demonstrate good judgment.

Spiritual Formation

Your teen's spiritual formation should focus on establishing a more mature prayer life of intimate, personal conversation with God, increasing his familiarity with Scripture, deepening his participation in the sacramental life of the Church, and developing an attitude of serving others through the Church.

The more concrete your goals are in this area, the more easily you will find the specific ways to reach them. For example, if your mutual goal is for your teen to develop a personal prayer life, help him pick a specific fifteen-minute time slot every day for private prayer. "Praying with them and scheduling in times for this, with

them involved in the planning, helps them form good habits",
notes Cathy Gualandri.

Encouraging our children to develop their own prayer life is a
must for their spiritual growth. We want our children to experience their own personal need for and love for God. Their relationship with Him, and consequently their willingness to be open to
His will for their lives, is built the same way as any other relationship—by spending time together. Time spent together in family
prayer or liturgical celebrations helps to develop this relationship as
well. For most teens, however, the challenge is to put aside time for
God alone. They need to perceive God's personal invitation to
them and to exercise their *own* wills to build a relationship with
Him—not praying just because Mom and Dad "say so" or because
it is "the right thing to do".

In his address to the world's young people at World Youth Day,
1993, Pope John Paul II urged teens and young adults to make a
personal commitment to Christ.

> I ask you to have the courage to commit yourselves *to the truth*.
> Have the courage *to believe the Good News about Life* which Jesus
> teaches in the Gospel. Open your minds and hearts to the beauty
> of all that God has made and to his special personal love for each
> one of you [emphasis in the original].[2]

Help your teen to make an "appointment" with God. Pinpoint
the time of day most conducive to quiet reflection and prayer so
that he can respond to God's personal invitation. Talk about the
various forms of prayer (petition, intercession, praise, and thanksgiving). Respect the privacy of your teen's prayer—don't interrupt
to ask him to take out the garbage or to tell him that a friend is on
the phone. Nor should you ask at the end of every prayer time,
"How was your prayer today?" or "What did you pray about?" Be
open to talking about it, but don't pry.

In addition to prayer, an essential aspect of spiritual formation is
a deeper participation in the sacramental life of the Church. The

---

[2] *Vigil*, August 14, 1993, no. 4.

Eucharist and Confession are just as essential to teens as they are to us. Daily Mass and frequent Confession will fortify our teens for the times ahead when they will likely face moral challenges on a daily basis.

Cultivate a love for the Eucharist by attending holy hours or Eucharistic Adoration with your teen. Make it a special "adult" time with you and take him out for pizza and one-on-one conversation (but not a cross-examination) afterward. Although you will probably want to insist that your younger teens attend daily Mass when the entire family does, you might encourage Mass attendance for your older teens by tying it into their desire for greater independence. (Sunday Mass, of course, should never be optional.) For example, one mom allows her young teens to ride their bikes alone to an earlier Mass, rather than waiting for the 5 P.M. Mass, which is more convenient for her. Another gave her new driver permission to take the car to daily Mass.

During the teen years, your child needs to deepen his sense of what the sacrament of Reconciliation is all about. Confessions should become less of a childish "I disobeyed my mother five times" and more of a reflective examination of the vices, weaknesses, and occasions that led into the specific sins, as well as a confession of those sins themselves.

In spite of your teen's reluctance or seeming indifference to the need for frequent Confession, these are not the years for parents to back down or stop insisting that their children receive the sacrament. Even if we are free from serious sins, we still need frequent Confession in order to retain the clarity of conscience and sensitivity of soul that help us recognize and respond to God's will in our lives. Think of the grimy film that accumulates on our car's windshield during a long car trip—it goes unnoticed (and we assume our vision is just as good as before) until the day we clean the windshield and realize how poor our visibility really was. Our teens especially need the grace of the sacrament to keep their consciences from becoming dulled by repeated sin, even when that sin is "only" venial sin not requiring Confession.

Emphasis on God's mercy and the completeness of His forgiveness, relief from guilt feelings (which teens often find so over-whelming), and the practical advice a confessor can give help teens find additional incentives to take advantage of this sacrament. (As we discuss later in Chapter 15 on sacraments, it is essential to teach your children how to recognize different types of temptations and what to do about them.)

Give your teens some flexibility about when they attend Confession and to whom they confess. Encourage your child to find a regular confessor. A younger priest may be easier for your teen to talk with than the older, fatherly priest you prefer. While the personality of the priest does not affect the validity of the sacrament, it can have a great influence on a young person's attitude toward Penance—whether he approaches it as an opportunity for repentance and healing or with reluctance and even dread. Make an effort to accommodate your teen's preference.

Give your teen incentives to take advantage of this sacrament. One mom, for example, encourages her teenage daughter to go to Confession with her friends and follow it with a special outing (tennis or shopping). Make it a priority to instill in your teens an appreciation and love for this sacrament.

A third area of spiritual formation concerns Scripture. Our teens need to increase their knowledge and love for Scripture as God's Word. Intellectually, a good Bible study course yields a greater understanding of God's Word. (*The Word among Us* monthly magazine[3] offers biblical commentary and insights that are helpful for teens as well as adults.) More important, daily reading from Scripture builds a familiarity with and dependence on His Word for inspiration and guidance in daily life. As with prayer, a family time of reading and discussing Scripture is helpful. But teens still need encouragement to spend a few minutes alone reflecting on how God, through His Word, is speaking to them about their own lives.

The fourth major component of your teen's spiritual life is developing a more mature understanding of the doctrinal underpinnings of our Faith. This is not simply a matter of intellectual

[3] *The Word among Us*, Box 6003, Gaithersburg, MD 20897–8403.

study but rather a matter of relating what the Church teaches to the challenges of daily life—including the many moral challenges they must face. Teenagers are old enough to understand *why* the Church teaches as she does. They need to know what the Church teaches, how to spread this teaching, and how to defend it.

Play "the devil's advocate" with your teens, challenging them on what they believe: "How do you know that?" "Why do you believe that?" "But what about this objection?" Of course, you need to find the answer yourself first[4] so that if they fall short in their understanding or defense of what they believe, you can provide the full answer. Parents who feel their own doctrinal training is inadequate might prevail upon a better-trained parent or a sympathetic priest to hold apologetics classes for a group of home-educated teens once a week. But it is incumbent on the parents either to sit in on the classes or to do independent reading and thus continue their own growth in understanding.

Training our children not only to understand their Faith but also to explain, defend, and spread it is crucial. As they grow and step out into the world, our teens will encounter more and more people who do *not* believe as we do, including many who are "Catholics" in name only. We must help our children think through and understand their Faith so that they can not only withstand challenges to it but become apostles in every sense of the word.

Finally, a teen's spiritual formation should include fostering a desire to serve others through the Church. The self-absorption of the teen years can be balanced beautifully by taking advantage of a teen's natural altruism and idealism. Help your teen find some service project where he can make a practical contribution (for example, caring for an elderly person's lawn without expecting to be paid). Encourage him, in addition to some individual charitable work, to become involved in the ongoing service projects of the Church. Let him see that making a united effort with others in the Church has a real impact on others' lives.

---

[4] We suggest parents acquire a good reference book on doctrinal questions, such as the *Handbook of Christian Apologetics*, by Peter Kreeft and Ronald K. Tacelli, S.J. (Downers Grove, IL: InterVarsity Press, 1994).

Human Formation—"Be All That You Can Be"

Human formation concentrates on developing all our human qualities and talents. It includes acquiring personal and physical maturity, making responsible, mature decisions, developing the personality and talents each of us has been blessed with, and growing in strong character and virtues.

On the physical side, our teens' bodies typically mature into men's and women's bodies before their minds acquire a complete understanding of the dimensions of manhood and womanhood. Recognize your teen's awkwardness and uncertainty about what it means to "be grown up". Gentleness and understanding are as important as firmness in correcting the inevitable mistakes of judgment they will make. Many objectionable choices or desires that teens express are often more a matter of erroneous judgment than malice or rebellion.

The physical changes in our teens contribute to the stress of these years emotionally, both for the parents and for the teen. One mother described her son's entry into the teen years in this way: "I noticed a huge change—suddenly emotional, volatile, incredible testing. It was very exhausting. . . . My husband was very, very important at this time, not only to spend a lot of time with my son, but to be a rock. He [our son] knew he couldn't get anything past his father."

Some parents find their home-schooled teens, especially boys, benefit from slightly older role models of the same sex. For example, one mom found male college students to tutor her adolescent and teenage sons in some subjects. "They need that male influence, and it's easier for them to work with a strong male. One of my sons said to me, 'Mom, I'm just not embarrassed enough to work hard for you.'"

Many parents use tutors or swap tutoring with another home-schooling family so their teen can cultivate friendships or mentor relationships with other adults. Judy Bratten was blessed to find a great role model for her two teenage daughters.

I knew that what they needed at that time was a younger adult role model, someone who was more "cool" than Mom, but who held the same values. The Lord sent a youth minister our way who became that for my girls and who was able to provide some of the "fun" activities that I couldn't or wouldn't offer.

Tutors, coaches, youth-group leaders, other parents, and older students are all potential mentors for your teens.

Human Formation: Acquiring Self-Mastery

One of the most important aspects of human formation in these years is to help our children grow in self-mastery. We need to teach (and model in our own lives) self-control of all our faculties, including temperate use of food and alcohol, control over sexual desires, right use of speech, and control of anger. (More on this later in Chapter 16 on Christlike character.)

Acquiring self-mastery is an indispensable step along the path to using independence and freedom wisely. It will help our children make good choices about who their friends will be, how they spend their time, what music and books they will enjoy (when you're not looking over their shoulders), and what courses to study.

Self-mastery is especially important for teens in the area of chastity. Cultivating the virtue of chastity is not the same as the simplistic "Just say no!" formula. The *Catechism of the Catholic Church* illuminates the positive and essential place chastity has in human formation. "Chastity means the successful integration of sexuality within the person and thus the inner unity of man in his bodily and spiritual being."[5] The proper vision of chastity is a lot easier to communicate to teens if it has been built on a foundation that stresses sexuality as something good (not shameful), but something so special because of God's purpose for it.

Parents have the responsibility to give their children accurate and appropriate knowledge about their bodies and their sexual development, all in the context of God's beautiful plan for mar-

---

[5] *Catechism of the Catholic Church*, no. 2337.

riage and the family. Simply handing your child a book and telling him to come to you with questions is not adequate. True sex education should be an ongoing conversation—a continual process of giving the right information at the right time. For example, the specific description of sexual intercourse that you give your early adolescent should not be the last word on the subject. And while your teenage daughter needs to understand her body's fertility cycle, charting her cycle is premature and inadvisable. Give information when they need it, not before.

Describing the image of a fire in a fireplace helps teens recognize the incredible power and beauty of their sexuality. Fire that is properly contained—used for the right purpose and in the right place—gives us warmth and light, beauty and happiness, and suggests well-controlled power. Used wisely, it brings us nothing but good. In contrast, a fire that is ignited and burns without boundaries leaves destruction, pain, and ashes in its wake. It rages out of control, ultimately destroying everything it touches. Our sexuality, both within marriage and without, is most desirable and beautiful when we use it within God's boundaries. Teens need to sense our own joy and humility in our sexuality—that it's a delightful gift from God that surpasses all expectations when we use it as He wishes.

Many parents foster this understanding in their teens by taking them out for a special dinner and conversation in which they encourage their teen to make a commitment to God and their future spouse to remain sexually pure for their wedding day. Some parents present their teen with a specific piece of jewelry (such as a ring or a small gold key on a necklace) as a symbol of this commitment. Together they agree to pray not only for the teen's own chastity but also for the purity of the person God has chosen as his future wife (or her future husband). It helps teens to think of reserving expressions of their sexuality not just for "marriage" but for marriage to a particular person and to make a commitment to that special person even though they probably have not even met yet.

Some parents feel uncomfortable discussing delicate issues of sexuality with their children. They may prefer to rely on parish sex-education programs to handle the more sensitive material they feel awkward broaching with their teens. Unfortunately, this not only sends a message to your teens that *you* are *not* the person whom they should seek out with their questions but also leaves your preteen or teen at the mercy of a program and presenters over whom you have no control.

It is imperative that as parents we give our children appropriate sex education that focuses on their need to commit themselves to chastity. One father challenged his children to imitate him and his wife by being virgins until marriage; at the same time he shared how wonderful his physical relationship was with his wife—better than ever. Unlike the classroom situation, where a teacher can make sex seem fraught with difficulty, disease, and risk of pregnancy, the home is the natural environment to share the freedom, security, and life-giving power of love in the context of marriage.

In public schools, current classroom practices in sex education often involve the following: children are told numerous names for private, sexual parts of the body in mixed classes of boys and girls to help break down their modesty; they are trained in the use of contraception (even practicing with condoms in class); they are taught about abortion; they are told about various immoral sexual practices (e.g., masturbation and homosexuality) as if they were value-neutral practices. Many of these same classrooms are visited by representatives of Planned Parenthood but are off-limits to pro-life speakers who would speak about chastity.

Parish sex-education programs usually avoid the extremes of the public schools. However, some parish programs convey ambiguous information on abortion, homosexuality, birth control, and premarital sex—at best, leaving teens confused and, at worst, leading them in the wrong direction.

Encourage your parish instead to hold sessions for *parents* that will guide them on how and when to talk to their children about sexuality, and on what to say. In some cases, joint parent–child sessions sponsored by the parish can be helpful. Yet, these do not substitute for individual conversations with each one of your children. (Don't assume the younger ones will have picked up the proper information or perspective from their older siblings.) Having the chance to help our children understand their manhood or womanhood and God's plan for creating new life is a beautiful privilege, not something to be shied away from or shirked. Let's embrace this wonderful opportunity to add a new dimension to our children's understanding of God, humanity, and the moral laws of the Church.

While one effect of self-mastery is often denying ourselves something good, that is not its purpose. The purpose of self-mastery in all areas of our lives, as with sexuality, is to acquire mastery over our will and our passions in order to use our freedom as God designed—to serve Him and others, according to His plan. In this way we can put all our human talents, our personality, and our education at His service. The *Catechism* emphasizes the relationship between self-mastery and authentic human freedom.

> Chastity includes an *apprenticeship in self-mastery* which is a training in human freedom. The alternative is clear: either man governs his passions and finds peace, or he lets himself be dominated by them and becomes unhappy. "Man's dignity therefore requires him to act out of conscious and free choice, as moved and drawn in a personal way from within, and not by blind impulses in himself or by mere external constraint. . . ." Whoever wants to remain faithful to his baptismal promises and resist temptations will want to adopt the *means* for doing so: self-knowledge, practice of an ascesis adapted to the situations that confront him, obedience to God's commandments, exercise of the moral virtues, and fidelity to prayer.[6]

Thus the prescription is clear. We need to help our children know themselves—both the weaknesses built into every human being as well as their own particular vulnerabilities. Self-knowledge helps them see the reality of tempting situations. Our children need to practice small and large ways of sacrificing their own

---

[6] Ibid., nos. 2339, 2340, quoting from the *Pastoral Constitution on the Church in the Modern World*, no. 17.

wills—whether that comes in denying a desire for a particular food, possession, or simply their own stylistic preference. This builds their ability to control their desires, delay gratification, and put someone else's good before their own.

Yet it is important to realize that our teen's efforts to be virtuous and develop good character will, like our own efforts, be marked at times by failure. The Church demonstrates her wisdom in this regard, again using chastity as an example.

> Chastity has *laws of growth* which progress through stages marked by imperfection and too often by sin. "Man . . . day by day builds himself up through his many free decisions; and so he knows, loves, and accomplishes moral good by stages of growth."[7]

Although our teens' physical development will heighten their temptations against chastity, never lower the moral standards you expect your children to follow. (God doesn't, after all!) But, as God does with us, always use forgiveness, compassion, and love in guiding your teen toward a more complete fulfillment of the Christian life. Be patient with your teen, as God is with us. Our kids are only human and need time to change and grow in Christ, just as we do. Self-mastery is desirable, not as a measure of perfection for its own sake, or simply as a mark of adulthood, but in order to put all the human gifts that God has given us at His disposal.

One concrete way of growing in self-mastery is to focus on it within the context of developing one particular character trait at a time. For example, if your child is working on temperance, he can practice by moderating his consumption of soda or sweets. Or he might break up his recreational time with a small act of service to someone in his family—such as coming in from playing basketball and asking mom if there is anything he can do to help her. To help keep the focus positive, remind your teen that the emphasis is not so much on denial as on making choices and using his freedom to serve God better.

---

[7] Ibid., no. 2343, quoting from *The Christian Family in the Modern World*.

Human Formation:
Independence and Responsibility

Most teens complain that their parents fail to give them the independence they feel they deserve. Ideally, their growth in maturity would keep pace with their desire for independence. But whether it does or doesn't, home education gives you a better vantage point from which to judge their maturity and to give them new opportunities to show their responsibility.

Parents can cultivate independence and responsibility through an older child's relationships with his siblings. "They need to feel responsible and respected by their younger siblings. Parents can provide opportunities for this", observed one mother. Using your older children to help teach the younger ones is an easy way to do this. Sibling tutoring not only solidifies the material learned by the older one and helps him realize that it is useful, it also makes the older child feel he has accomplished something worthwhile when he helps the younger child succeed. In addition, it brings out another dimension in the sibling relationship.

One mother of six shared her efforts to give her two teenagers responsibility compatible with their desire for independence.

> I'm trying to find more things for them to do on their own and to let them do things I want them to do, but on their own. . . . I give them more responsibility [such as] letting them pick [their] choice of several books to read or subjects to write on or countries to study in geography. It makes them more self-directed.

Self-motivation, self-direction, and self-control are all valuable indicators of our teen's growing maturity.

Differentiate levels of responsibility, and the privileges that go with them, according to age and demonstrated good judgment. An older teen who works diligently on his own to complete his schoolwork quickly is ready for greater freedoms and privileges. In the words of one experienced mother who home schooled several children through the high-school years:

Teens need more scope. [This means] letting them try their wings in the world, so they'll feel that they can get along in the real world. They want to use their talents and realize they are of real use. Realizing they can make money, feeling that they can make friends and have something to give the world, and succeeding in a place other than the family, are all tremendously important for older teenagers.

Teaching teenagers to set up and live under the constraints of a budget is a necessary part of teaching independence and responsibility. One excellent resource in this area is *Money Matters for Parents and Their Kids* by Ron Blue.[8] Make it a goal for your teen gradually to assume an increasing proportion of his own costs, such as clothing, entertainment, and perhaps "room and board". Within the total budget, set aside 10 percent for tithing and 10 percent for long-term savings to give your teen the opportunity to make financial giving and regular savings a habitual part of his life.

When he is ready for college or to enter the full-time work force, he will truly understand the scope of financial responsibility required for adults. Further, he will have developed the restraint, self-control, and maturity to plan for the future and defer immediate gratification.

Choosing entertainment is one potentially "sticky" area where your teen may feel he is entitled to exercise increasing independence. According to the Teenage Research Institute, "teenagers watch 50 movies a year in theaters, and 80 percent are rated PG-13 or R! (Teens also view another 50 movies a year on video.)"[9]

It is imperative for parents to *know* what their children are seeing and listening to, not to assume it's "probably O.K." because the rating is only PG or PG-13. Realistically, however, most parents lack the time to screen every movie, show, or piece of music their teen wants to view or hear. Parents can exercise vigilance over the media to which their teen is exposed by subscribing to a monthly

---

[8] Ron and Judy Blue, *Money Matters for Parents and Their Kids* (Pomona, CA: Focus on the Family, 1988).

[9] *Focus on the Family* magazine, April 1995, p. 6.

publication such as *Parental Guidance*[10] that reviews the latest movies, TV shows, and music from a Christian perspective.

When they can, parents should watch movies or TV shows with their teen, as this allows the parent to initiate discussion of the moral choices portrayed in the program or video. This is especially important when the negative natural consequences of a character's actions are glossed over or ignored.

Occasionally, in spite of your best efforts, your teen will be exposed to immoral scenes or influences. Yet, don't fall into the deceptive trap of relaxing your oversight simply because "They've seen everything there is to see." Images stick. And repeated images can do irreparable damage by subtly shaping your teen's expectations of what is "normal" behavior.

For example, a show whose characters constantly engage in premarital or extramarital sex, even if nothing explicit is shown, wears down the viewer's initial repugnance at such behavior—especially when the characters are appealing and exhibit virtues in areas other than sexuality. Frequent exposure to anti-Christian values can erode a teen's convictions simply by making him accustomed to seriously sinful behavior. His tolerance for such behavior increases when he sees "good" people engaging in it. (This effect is not restricted to movies or music, as friendships with "nice" kids who live by different values can have the same effect.)

Through the teen years, parents must continue to supervise media choices. Yet, make your restrictions reasonable (don't decree that your teen can see only movies made before 1960), and continually discuss the reasons for your decisions. We want our teens to internalize our values in these areas, not simply abide by our rules until they are out on their own. A calm, reasonable approach accomplishes more toward that end than a fearful, automatic "No" to most requests.

---

[10] *Parental Guidance* magazine, Focus on the Family, Colorado Springs, CO 80995; telephone (800) 232–6459.

Human Formation: Discipline

In the midst of their many transitions, teens still need our discipline, but in a different way from before. Of course, every family—and every teen—is different. There are, however, some fundamental principles to keep in mind.

First, disagreements between parents and teens are inevitable. However, it is crucial for us to keep our own anger and emotions under control. If we do not act in a mature way, how can we possibly expect them to? Parents who lose their tempers and rant and rave, or parents who ridicule, soon lose their teen's respect. And that is not only counterproductive, it is potentially disastrous. Teens need heroes. If they don't respect their parents as men and women, they will inevitably go in search of alternative role models. In contrast, parents who present strong models of self-control reap the rewards of consistent behavior and genuine (if secret) admiration from their teens. Staying calm through teen crises has a practical benefit, too—it ensures that at least *one* person keeps the situation in perspective.

When your teen has "blown it", and his emotions are out of control, it may help to give him a "cooling off" period before you require him to express repentance and make amends. A teen who is required to leave the room and think through how he misbehaved usually reappears half an hour later chastened and repentant. Sometimes it's better to elicit an apology after the teen has had time to regain control and perspective. This ensures that his apology is heartfelt and reflective. In contrast, a surly "sorry" that is grumbled in anger teaches a child to mouth words of repentance without really changing his heart.

Second, don't argue. Our teens need to obey us because we are their parents, not because we are superior debaters. Some things shouldn't be argued over, because they are beyond question. Genuine moral standards and serious safety concerns simply cannot be relaxed.

Aside from morality and safety, we should be open to reasonable modifications of family rules, depending on the circumstances. Keep an open mind—arguments can be avoided when we initiate discussions. Also, consider negotiating with your teens on curfews for special events, in setting punishments ahead of time for specific infractions, and on the timing of chores or completing other responsibilities.

Third, be realistic. You cannot correct every trivial fault or guard against every far-fetched safety risk. St. Paul warns, "Fathers, do not provoke your sons, lest they become discouraged" (Col 3:21). The same thing goes for mothers and daughters. Besides, you need to "keep your powder dry" for the big battles. In the sixties, for example, too many good parents squandered their moral authority in unnecessary clashes over jeans and sandals and then had nothing left with which to fight the sexual revolution.

Fourth, punishments should be reasonable. They should "fit the crime" and should tend to be swift rather than prolonged. Punishments that are long and drawn out over a period of time (for example, being grounded for two weeks) are less likely to be followed through on by parents and more likely to engender bitterness in teens. *Never* give your teens (or your other kids) the "silent treatment". It only erodes your relationship.

Punishments that are naturally related to the transgression are more likely to be remembered. For example, a teen who stays out too late one night may lose his privilege of driving the family car the next night.

On the positive side, parents can obviate a lot of problems if they provide their teens with frequent opportunities to release pent-up physical and emotional energy. Introduce adventure into their lives, particularly for your sons. Campouts, rafting trips, sleep outs, and amusement-park trips keep your teens from being bored and restless. Giving them extra privileges to do things outside the home helps them to be more responsible and happier at home.

As a final thought, keep in mind that teens want to be seen as young adults rather than as children, even as they struggle with immature behavior. Make their entry into the teen years a positive initiation into the adult circle within the extended family. Allow them to stay up later and join adult family members on occasions when the younger children are not invited or are already in bed. One family honors each new thirteen-year-old in the extended family with a special dinner sharing memories of him and welcoming him into the ranks of the older family members. Creating positive expectations helps motivate your teen to live up to those expectations.

Human Formation: Social Development

Friendships are necessary and wonderful for your teenager. Help your teen build solid friendships that reinforce the values you stress. Peer relationships that are based on similar faith and values provide great reinforcement for all that we teach them at home. Good friends can challenge our teens and hold them accountable for their actions in ways that parents often can't. Friendships shouldn't be approached reluctantly by parents. As the Church reminds us in regard to chastity,

> The virtue of chastity blossoms in *friendship*. . . . Chastity is expressed notably in *friendship with one's neighbor*. Whether it develops between persons of the same or opposite sex, friendship represents a great good for all. It leads to spiritual communion.[11]

Parents can help their teens build healthy friendships by encouraging and planning supervised social activities. Kids need to find a peer group, whether through the home-school support group, the parish youth group, or clubs (either parish, school, or community based, such as 4–H, sports, dance, theater, music lessons, youth groups). Academic clubs are another good way of encouraging social development within the home-education environment. Teens form fast friendships with others in the group while they are stretched academically and personally by competition and the desire to perform well before others.

Home educator Mary Anne Greene observes that, through home schooling, children "are able to develop naturally without

---

[11] *Catechism of the Catholic Church*, no. 2347.

the artificial constraint of the modern peer group determining attitudes and activities. They are interested in a broader spectrum of activities, with people of all ages." Yet, parents need to help teens find the opportunities for group socializing—just plain having fun with others their own ages.

One group of dads in Steubenville, Ohio, established a regular time for "pick-up" basketball games for home-educated teenage boys. The games appealed to the teens' eagerness for good competition and physical activity and also provided an opportunity to develop close-knit friendships. With a little imagination and effort, parents can help create the circumstances that foster good friendships.

What about Dating?

During the teen years, parents must deal with the issues of dating and socializing with the opposite sex. Distinguish for your kids the difference between socializing (it's great, natural, healthy, and fun!) and dating to find a spouse (more appropriate to a particular age). Encourage (and provide lots of opportunities for) your teens to mingle with the opposite sex. Socializing in group activities, or on occasional dates, helps your teens feel comfortable socially with *all* their peers in different types of social situations.

Discourage steady dating before a reasonable age. What is a reasonable age? It depends. It may not be best to set a "magic" age, such as sixteen, when a teen can begin solo dates or "have" a boyfriend or girlfriend. What is appropriate will depend on each child's maturity, the circumstances, and their life plans. (For example, a teen who intends to join the work force full time after high school and a year of vocational school may be closer to marriageable age than a teen who plans on four years of college and several years of graduate school.)

When you do choose to allow your teen to date, set limits on the amount of time spent alone. Acknowledging that more time alone together will bring more temptations against purity is not the same as communicating that you don't trust your teen. It is simply a realistic view of how powerful our passions can be. Research has shown that dating one person steadily and spending long periods of time alone together are risk factors for teen sexual activity.[12]

Encourage teens to build their friendships with each other in group settings, talking over the phone, and in other appropriate settings. Emphasize enjoying the activity together and getting to know each other's personalities and interests.

As your children reach the upper teen years, help them focus on discerning their vocation. Some teens never stop to consider that God may be calling them to the priesthood or the consecrated life. Encourage them to pray specifically for openness to God's call and the wisdom and generosity to respond to His desire for their lives.

At the same time it may be appropriate to begin evaluating their relationships more in terms of finding a future spouse. As they mature, they will begin to narrow in on the type of person with whom they feel most comfortable. It is important that parents take advantage of this period to discuss the qualities they should look for in a future spouse. (One long-term impact of virginity worth pointing out to your teens is that the divorce rate for those who are not virgins when they marry is a staggering 71 percent higher than it is for couples who marry as virgins.)[13] Especially if your teen plans to attend college away from home, you need to help him realize the goal of serious dating: a chaste relationship that brings both people closer to God, as well as each other, as they discern whether to marry.

[12] Research sponsored by the U.S. Department of Health and Human Services Office of Adolescent Pregnancy Prevention, and conducted by Dr. Stan Weed, President of the Institute for Research and Evaluation in Salt Lake City, UT, identified four key factors in predicting whether a teen will become sexually active: (1) whether he believes in higher values, including a definable "right" and "wrong"; (2) peer influence (What are his friends like? What do *they* think about premarital sex? What are their dating patterns? What are their drinking patterns?); (3) drinking (Does he or doesn't he?); (4) dating patterns (Did he begin dating early? How often does he date? Does he have one person whom he dates regularly?). Research information is from *The Marriage Savers*, by Michael McManus (Grand Rapids, MI: Zondervan Publishing House, 1993).

[13] McManus, p. 92.

Finally, keep in mind that our own actions toward our children build the important psychological foundations that will help them resist sexual pressure and avoid destructive relationships. One Christian chastity-education program[14] identifies five ways parents can positively influence teens to be chaste and help them choose a future spouse wisely:

1. Set out clear *standards* of right and wrong behavior.
2. Show that you *accept* your teen, thus creating a sense of security.
3. Show *appreciation*, so that teens feel they are significant and can accomplish significant things.
4. Be *available* to them, so that they will know we consider them important.
5. Show *affection*, so our teens will know that they are loveable.

Parents who commit themselves to loving their teenager in these ways will have succeeded in providing their teens with a solid basis for a lifelong marriage relationship.

Intellectual Formation: Where to Begin

A home-educated high-school student can expect to spend more time studying than the typical two to three hours spent by younger children. Parents will also need to make a greater time commitment; the time required, however, shouldn't fill all your available hours or consume your life. Students this age are well suited to doing independent study and should have the self-discipline to stick to the task before them. However, they do need specific times set aside for discussion, analysis, and guided in-depth projects. Mary Anne Greene, the mother of two teens, cautions that teens are able to work alone but that "they want to be engaged in meaningful conversation and enjoy a challenge. It's hard for them to work alone for most of the day, without real exchange or feedback."

When parents spend time with their teens discussing weighty

---

[14] Josh McDowell's "Why Wait?" chastity education program.

topics, that serves as food for thought and as a catalyst for discussions. As Susan Waldstein shares,

> We've spent hours reading aloud to them. . . . It's a time for fruitful discussion. We read adult novels, such as *Pride and Prejudice* by Jane Austen and *The Count of Monte Cristo* by Alexandre Dumas, that gave us the opportunity to talk about virtue and vice. . . . We're reading to them not just for the literary value but to awaken them to what is really beautiful and noble.

She emphasizes that the literature you choose for your children during these years is as important to their intellectual formation as the written and analytical training they receive. "Teens have a great desire to fall in love with great things. They deserve to have you give them the best. Give them adult books about the saints, not saccharine stories about them. Let them see what really heroic people are like."

Home educating an older child can be a real opportunity for a parent to provide a more traditional, classical approach than what the area schools offer. Students can delve deeply into the great works in literature and philosophy as well as pursue advanced math and the sciences from a classical perspective.

Not only college-bound teens benefit from home education. The non-college-bound student, because of his home-education schedule, may have an opportunity to do a work-related internship, or apprenticeship, that will better prepare him for the working world or teach him the trade he intends to practice. Families can create internships by trading work opportunities with other home-educating families who own their own businesses. Another possible avenue is to contact businessmen listed in the local guide to Christian businesses that many communities now publish. Word of mouth may lead to more possibilities as well.

Parents should keep as many options open for their teens as possible—whether college, technical school, apprenticeship, or full-time work. While the Church certainly doesn't require us to provide a college education (indeed, not everyone may be suited to college), we want to maximize our child's choices. So don't foreclose his possibilities too early by electing, for example, not to teach any math beyond ninth grade.

Home education often creates additional options for our children in academic, cultural, or athletic pursuits. For example, a child with unusual talent on the violin may have the chance to pursue excellence in his music by practicing four hours a day—an opportunity that might have been foreclosed in a school setting because of time constraints or negative peer pressure. Or a child interested in nursing might take the opportunity to accompany family friends on a short-term medical mission.

Parents who lack training in advanced math either will find themselves learning along with their children or may consider finding a tutor in those subjects or trading with another home-educating parent. One Catholic home-study supplier has just begun offering college-level courses to parents who want to home educate their older children but are worried about their own educational deficiencies.[15] Franciscan University of Steubenville now makes available for home study (non-credit) some of its best courses in theology, history, and philosophy.[16] Courses include a written study guide. Other universities offer similar programs. It *is* possible to stay two jumps ahead of your children!

Intellectual Formation: What Skills Do Teens Need?

The three key intellectual skills your teens need to develop during these years are communication skills (written and oral), analysis skills, and independent study skills. All subjects require a certain level of proficiency in each of these three skills. For example, a student taking a chemistry lab course must be able to conduct his experiment and analyze his data independently. His results must be

---

[15] Seton Home Study Institute will be offering a college-level curriculum, tentatively beginning in the fall of 1995. For more information, call Seton at (540) 636–9990.

[16] For information about the Distance Education program, contact Franciscan University of Steubenville, Distance Education, 100 University Blvd., Steubenville, OH 43952; or call (800) 466–8336.

communicated descriptively, accurately, and effectively in a written lab report, and possibly an oral report as well. Not surprisingly, these skills are necessary not only for college success but also for career advancement.

While our children have gradually been acquiring the ability to explain, describe, analyze, and discuss facts and opinions all through the elementary years, they need to perfect these skills, both verbal and written, during the teen years. To help your child develop the appropriate oral skills, you must set aside enough time to talk over substantive issues. Discuss with him why he thinks what he does. Question his explanations to help him describe more precisely what they mean. Encourage his involvement in speech or debate contests to practice using his verbal skills in a more public forum.

Marion Smedberg of Sterling, Virginia, notes that the challenge in educating her high-school-age son at home is finding the time to discuss, one on one, the classical "great books" that form the cornerstone of his education. They solve this by reading the works aloud to each other in the afternoon (while the younger children nap) or in the evening. She rightly observes that teenagers have a real need for a serious intellectual relationship with an adult and for discussions about the larger questions raised by these classic works of philosophy and literature.

In addition to verbal skills, effective writing skills are crucial. One recent study by the U.S. Education Department found that "only 2 percent of eighth-graders and eleventh-graders were able to write effective responses to questions."[17] Another study, released in January 1995, revealed similar alarming results.

> Even among eighth-graders, only 12 percent of narrative papers tell a developed story and only 4 percent of informative papers present a developed discussion. . . . Among eighth-graders, only 4

---

[17] "Tide of Mediocrity Ebbs As U.S. Scores Math, Science Gains: Schools' Reading, Writing Levels Are Stagnant, 20 Year Study Says", *The Washington Post*, August 18, 1994, p. 3. Article reported findings from the National Assessment of Educational Progress, analyzing 1992 data.

percent of persuasive papers present a developed argument that is
something more than a thinly supported opinion.[18]

Writing well for older high-school students means more than
simply constructing grammatical sentences. It means organizing
thoughts not only logically but also in the most persuasive manner.
They must learn to support their ideas with concrete facts and
thorough analysis—not relying on mere assertions that their idea is
true. Effective writing requires finding words, beyond trite phrases,
that will express their thoughts and feelings so that others will
understand them.

Related to the ability to write and speak persuasively and clearly
is the ability to think critically—to analyze. Some curricula materials now include exercises in critical thinking. Another vehicle to
develop this skill is to compare two different stories on the same
topic and analyze why the stories are different. Help your teens
notice the difference the author's perspective, beliefs, and experience make. Susan Waldstein explained how their family encourages deeper analysis of what they read.

> We're reading together articles from magazines and newspapers and
> talking about them. It's important for helping them develop their
> own norms and to see what the current situation is like and to
> judge it . . . also to see what the media are like. For instance, we'll
> have them read two different presentations of an event such as a
> pro-life march. They will read the newspaper and a religious news-
> paper. This lets them see the difference perspective makes.

Analytical skills are especially important for the college-bound
student. Not only will he need to analyze in many of his subjects,
but you will want him habitually to analyze and to think critically
about what he hears or what others say to him. This is especially
important if he will be going to a nonreligious school or even a

---

[18] "Students' Writing Falls Short", *The Washington Times*, February 2, 1995, p. A5,
reporting results of the National Assessment of Educational Progress Writing Portfolio
Study, which sampled actual written work of approximately 1,800 eighth graders and
1,800 fourth graders. Fourth graders' percentages were even lower than the eighth-
grade results cited here.

religious university where his faith is likely to be challenged by erroneous ideas mislabeled as Catholicism. He needs the ability to see the underlying premises of an idea, follow them to their logical conclusions, and judge the truth or falsity of the idea on that basis. An introduction to formal logic can be helpful at this point.

One good way to perfect analytical skills is by analyzing poetry. Your teen may be surprised to discover that probing the ideas, assumptions, word choices, and meaning of a well-written twenty-line poem is no easy task. If he can write a two-page analysis of a twenty-line poem, he will have learned to look beyond the obvious for deeper, more subtle meanings. Other subjects, such as advanced math or science courses or an in-depth look at the U.S. Constitution, provide opportunities for in-depth analysis as well.

The high-school years are also the time to hone the study skills needed for college. A student must work independently (home-educated teens typically excel in this area), read quickly, and skim and sift through large amounts of material for the key points, take notes on them, and analyze them critically. He must compare, organize, and synthesize notes and materials pertaining to a course. In addition, college-bound students need to develop the ability to work on a long-range, comprehensive project in manageable increments.

Note-taking skills can be acquired from listening to and taking notes from audiotapes covering various topics. Also, many home-educated teens take lecture-style classes at the community-college level, both for the advanced credits they can earn toward a college degree and for the opportunity to practice those skills, such as note taking from lectures, that are essential to college success. (Occasionally, high schools will count college classes taken early toward the credits needed for high-school graduation.)

You can have your high-school student choose a semester-long project to plan, organize, and write. Assign reading and writing projects frequently. Reading and writing, like riding a bike, are perfected with practice. A home-taught student may wonder why he must write so much when he can simply explain it orally to you.

There simply is no substitute for writing. To write well you must write often.

Because of the flexibility home education offers, the parent is in a good position gradually to move to an academic approach similar to what colleges use. For example, you might move to an every-other-day schedule for some subjects, assigning larger amounts of independent reading to be completed prior to the next time for that subject. A home-school routine where you have to prepare for the next class on your own and review and summarize material on your own is not only easier for mom but definitely to your teen's benefit.

Intellectual Formation: What Colleges Are Looking For

Keeping options open means being aware of college requirements *before* the last year of secondary education. For example, if a college you are likely to consider requires two years of lab science prior to admittance, you need to be aware of that prerequisite far enough ahead of time in order to fulfill it (for example, through community college classes, cooperative effort, or cooperation with local school officials).

Start looking ahead to college at least by the end of the ninth-grade year. Contact several state schools and several private universities that are likely possibilities for your child's college applications. Request admissions materials, including admission requirements. These will spell out how many years of core courses (math, English, history, science) must be completed during high school in order to be eligible for admission. A good rule of thumb is as follows (but please be *sure* to check with the specific colleges you are considering):

English (including literature)	4 years
foreign language (same language both years)	2 years
history (including U.S. history)	3 years
math (including algebra and geometry)	3 years
science (including biology and one year of lab science)	2 years

Ask also how the admissions office treats multiple scores on the standardized tests. For example, if your child takes the SAT (a standard college admission test) three times, will the admissions office look at only the highest score, average the scores, or apply some other formula in evaluating the test results?

Set up your high-school curriculum plan with college course requirements in mind. If you are not already doing so, begin to keep a transcript (or record) of what courses your child is studying, what year each course was taken, and the grades earned each quarter. Most colleges and universities automatically require a transcript for admission, even though their evaluation of your child's application is more likely to rest on three other factors: standardized-test scores, the personal interview, and a writing sample.

One consistent word of advice comes from parents and admissions counselors alike: become familiar with the standardized tests required for college admission. In most cases, this means the PSAT, SAT, and ACT exams.[19] Students should be acquainted with the format of the tests, the types of questions asked, working within a time limit, what to do when they are unsure of the answer (guessing usually pays off better than leaving the question unanswered), and how to check their answers in the remaining time.

Some parents of home-educated students advocate letting your child begin taking these tests years before he actually has to worry about college admission, for example, in eighth or ninth grade. "Early and often" is the test formula that has worked well for many parents, as their children benefit from being familiar with and comfortable with the format and material on these crucial tests. (In some parts of the country, regular high schools have adopted this early testing practice as well.) Just remember that all test scores received and not only the best scores will be sent to the college to which your child applies.

[19] Information about testing dates and registration for the PSAT and SAT can be obtained from most high-school guidance offices or by contacting the College Board SAT Program at P.O. Box 6200, Princeton, NJ 08541–6200; telephone (609) 771–7600. Information about the ACT exams can be obtained also through local high schools or by contacting The American College Testing Program at the following address: ACT Registration, P.O. Box 414, Iowa City, IA 52243; telephone (319) 337–1270.

Other parents feel that repeated early test taking may lead a college or university to discount a high test score earned when it counts, in the spring of eleventh grade. In order to accomplish the same purpose of familiarizing their child with the standardized tests, they rely on practice tests or test-preparation booklets and courses.

Maximizing the possibility of high test scores is important, not just for admission to college, but also for enhancing your scholarship possibilities. The PSAT, given in the fall of the eleventh grade, is the qualifying test for National Merit Scholarships. These scholarships help economically; in addition, even if a scholarship is not awarded in this particular competition, the student's admission prospects are enhanced by his designation as a "Commended Student" or "National Merit Semi-Finalist" winner in this prestigious competition. Other scholarships as well are based on test scores. It is well worth the effort to prepare conscientiously for these tests.

Colleges and universities generally require home-educated students to fulfill standard college admissions test requirements. Franciscan University of Steubenville, for example, requires home-educated students to have taken either the ACT or the SAT. Margaret Weber, the Director of Admissions at Franciscan University, explained that these tests are the "only means we have of comparing them [home-taught students] with other students coming in."

Similarly, the University of Notre Dame requires applicants who are home-educated to take the ACT exams in all five subject areas, English, math, science, history, and a foreign language. In the words of Admissions Counselor John Imler, "We need some comparative and objective data."

Most colleges and universities require students to submit a writing sample or an essay on a particular topic as part of the admissions application. Pay attention to the limitations on length—more is *not* better. One admissions counselor listed three mistakes that are almost guaranteed to sink all but the most spectacular applicant: failure to *answer* the essay question (especially after writing pages on the topic!), grammar and syntactical errors, and typographical errors. Although it is generally considered "fair" to have a parent proofread a writing sample, it's not fair for anyone but the student to edit or revise it.

If the application offers a choice of questions from which a student may select his essay topic, some counselors advise choosing the most difficult option (assuming you think you can do a decent job answering it). As one admissions officer explains,

> Remember, it's a human being who is reading this essay. We do our best to be fair, but it's only human to get bored sometimes, especially when most applicants select the easiest question to answer. A credible attempt to answer the most difficult question will generally earn you more points than one more essay making the same obvious points about the easiest topic.

Finally, several counselors stress the need for sincerity in filling out the application. "We can tell when someone is trying to snow us", one counselor reports. (For example, one applicant described his personal hero as Pope Paul VI, yet his essay revealed a complete lack of familiarity with the Pope and his accomplishments.) Honesty, sincerity, and integrity will accomplish more than trying to engineer the "right" answer.

Across the board, college admissions counselors recommend campus visits and interviews for home-educated students, mostly for the student's benefit. Some universities state plainly that an admissions interview will have no bearing on the final decision whether to admit the student or not. For other schools, a good interview might enhance an otherwise tenuous application. Determine in advance what each particular school's policy is.

Campus visits and interviews can prevent your child from choosing the school that looks best "on paper" but that would be disastrous for him personally. Margaret Weber from Franciscan University urges parents and prospective students to come and visit: "The environment is why most students choose to come here, and there's no way to communicate that through brochures."

Finding the right atmosphere where your child can "feel at

home" will ease the transition to the college environment. A shy or quiet teen may feel lost on a large, seemingly anonymous state campus. The type of housing (coed dorms, single-sex dorms, no dorms) offered at each school may affect your decision as well. Sometimes just a walk through a campus dormitory tells you more about the moral climate of the school than all the printed material ever could.

"Parents also need to look for a match spiritually", before finalizing their choice, says Notre Dame's Imler. Not all Catholic universities or colleges offer the same degree of support for your child's faith, and some will undeniably be dangerous to it. On the other hand, a truly Catholic university or college (a few do exist) may meet all your requirements for orthodoxy yet not suit your child's temperament or intellectual strengths. Spending a few days soaking up the atmosphere and taking into account all the "intangibles" will help you and your child make a more informed decision.

Knowing the admissions requirements years in advance not only will help your curriculum planning but will also spur you to search for ways your child might earn college credits early. In some areas, your teen may be able to earn Advanced Placement credits either through satellite schools, local high schools, or through junior-college or community-college classes. Because these are college-level classes, your child may be able to receive college credits for courses taken during high school or to score high enough on university placement exams that certain core course requirements will be waived.

Parents inevitably worry that their home-schooled children will be at a disadvantage when they apply for college admission. Yet, assuming the children are well prepared academically, these fears seem baseless. In fact, in the words of one admissions counselor at a large university, a home-taught student with the same test scores as a traditionally educated high-school student may even be better off. "If I saw a home-schooled kid with the same test scores, I would be inclined to look *more favorably* at him because of all it took to achieve those scores" on his own.

Several counselors at other colleges echo the thought that each student is looked at individually, so in effect home-schooled teens are evaluated no differently from other applicants. Most universities and colleges stress that although they publish "average SAT scores" for their students, students are evaluated on a broader basis than scores alone. In an effort to find well-rounded students and to achieve a diverse student body, admissions counselors will take into account an applicant's extracurricular activities and accomplishments (such as music or sports awards), leadership positions, and unusual circumstances (living abroad, financial disadvantage, handicap or disability, family background, and—in some cases— home education).

Margaret Weber notes that generally the home-educated students admitted to the Franciscan University "bring a wealth of experience and a giving attitude. While they've been home schooled, most haven't been spending six or eight hours studying at home during the day. They're involved in church groups and youth groups. Most of them want to be involved and they are involved" in campus life.

Do home-educated students feel they are at a social disadvantage once they begin studying at a college or university? One college freshman who was home educated all through high school and then enrolled in a large university comments that, in college, "everyone starts over. There are kids from big schools, little schools. . . . You're all on the same plane."

While the number of applications that universities receive from home-educated students is still small, more and more schools are not just receptive to their admission, they actively recruit them. Home-schooled students have been admitted to most of the Ivy League schools, as well to many Catholic universities and colleges, including both large universities and small, tightly knit Catholic colleges. With the right preparation, no home-taught student should be at a disadvantage when it comes to college admissions.

Yes, It Is a Challenge

No matter how daunting it seems to home educate your teen, it is a choice that can work and has worked well for many families. It will not be easy, but neither should it be overwhelming. With diligent preparation and conscientious formation, our home-educated teens can excel. In addition, the Bratten family reminds us to keep our perspective and to remember our most powerful support—prayer.

> I suspect each parent–child relationship is strained in different ways during the teen years. Home schooling actually makes this period easier because you are more aware of the changes and struggles your teen is facing. You also have fewer occasions of conflict (that is, school dances, parties, peer-group pressures). Open communication, continual affirmation, commitment, and consistent standards help, but I think prayer is the most important resource we have as parents and teachers.

Perhaps the final word on what makes home educating a teenager possible was best expressed in an inspirational passage discovered by one teenage boy. Expressing admiration for his mother's sacrifices and the challenges she met in teaching him at home, he read the following: "With God's grace you have to tackle and carry out the impossible, because anybody can do what is possible."[20]

What Home Educating Teens Is All About

1. The teen years are naturally turbulent, as teens straddle the line between childhood and adulthood; yet, they still can be wonderful years resulting in deeper relationships with our teens, especially when we home school.

2. Home schooling allows the parent to focus on, or consciously deemphasize, a particular area of development, according to the teen's overall best interests.

---

[20] Josemaría Escrivá, *The Forge* (New York: Scepter Press, 1987), no. 216.

3. Set concrete goals for your teen's spiritual formation, human formation (including personal maturity and character development), and intellectual formation.

4. Spiritual development focuses on a deeper prayer life, greater familiarity with and love for Scripture, a stronger sacramental life, and instilling an attitude of service in our teens.

5. Human formation takes into account the physical changes our teens experience. It requires growth in self-mastery, independence, responsibility, and social development.

6. Intellectual formation includes acquiring communication skills (oral and written), analysis skills, and independent study skills. These skills should be applied in every substantive area of study.

7. Colleges admit home-schooled students on the basis of a written application (usually including an essay), standardized test results, and (occasionally) a personal interview. Colleges look favorably on home-taught children because of their initiative and ability to think and work independently.

8. While schooling teens at home can be a challenge because of the added time required, the more difficult material to be mastered, teens' emotional peaks and valleys, and the pressure of college admissions, it not only *is* possible but also bears great fruit for teens and parents alike.

13

Time Out for Assemblies

Support Groups

We've already recommended several times that you look for (or start) a support group near your home. Now it's time to discuss support groups more fully. Don't skip this! Even if you're the independent, self-sufficient type of person (as many of us tend to be), a support group can spell the difference between success or failure in home education.

Support groups are helpful to almost everyone who undertakes home schooling. Statistically, families who are involved in support-group activities enjoy their home-education adventure more and continue it longer. Families who are not involved are more likely to drop out of home schooling after a short time or suffer burnout after a few years. They will have joined the ranks of home educators who are needlessly frustrated and become too tired and disillusioned to continue.

If you are a newcomer to home education, a support group lends inestimable practical help and moral support. As a novice home educator, you can absorb the wisdom of moms who have juggled new babies, toddlers, and mounds of laundry and still managed to teach their children well. The "veterans" can offer hundreds of insights on teaching strategies as well as schedule possibilities and their favorite (or least favorite) books and resources. Most home-educating moms love to share what has worked for them—with tips on managing toddlers, finding a gymnastics class for home schoolers, or answering neighbors' questions.

Support groups often can provide you with the easiest and most efficient way to compare curriculum materials, especially when you are first starting out. Holding the "real thing" in your hands, rather than relying on a catalogue description, not only lessens the mistakes from trial and error but also is infinitely more inspiring. More important, you can talk directly with the mother who teaches from it, probing what she likes and dislikes about it, how she uses it, and whether it has any weak points that need supplementing.

On a very practical level, a support group may help you keep your teaching load manageable, especially when you have a large family. Field trips, academic clubs, and team-taught subjects all serve to give you, the teacher, a break—either for a day or on a regularly scheduled basis. Kari Harrington, veteran home educator from Richmond, Indiana, describes another advantage busy moms reap through support-group cooperation: "Through support groups, many home schoolers find families that want to share teaching times together. This can lighten a teaching load, as one mom may teach history, while another, science."

Within the support group, moms unofficially tend to "check" their pace and their child's progress against the pace other families keep—not as a way of gloating over the successes of their own child, but for reassurance. One of the most common worries expressed by first-time home educators is, in the words of one mother of two, "I have no idea whether we're doing too much or too little." Looking through the window of others' experience can give you a better perspective on your progress toward your own objectives. For example, if you are the only one in your support group spending six hours a day teaching a second grader, you will quickly realize that *something* is not right! Frank conversations with other moms will help you discern whether your difficulty stems from lack of organization or from expectations that are too high.

Remember, though, that bouncing your schedule and teaching process off someone else won't necessarily yield the perfect plan for you. Be careful not to let it backfire into a source of greater anxiety. ("Oh, no. Sarah only spent three weeks teaching Mark the times tables. We've already spent thirteen. I must be doing it all wrong!")

The questions, "Are we moving at a reasonable pace?" and "How can I improve our school day?" can only be answered with any finality by looking at your own circumstances. Find the pace that allows you to reach your goals in a way most suited to your own family. Home education flourishes when families find the unique combination of curriculum, schedule, and pace that suits their own family situation. No two families—indeed, no two days of teaching—are ever exactly alike.

In a good support group, you will find plenty of novices and veterans with whom to exchange ideas, but without the pressure to fit into a certain mold. Joan Stromberg from Pennsylvania found this openness crucial to her own willingness to try home schooling. "This is what I found universally about the moms I met through TORCH [a nationwide network of Catholic home-schooling support groups]—gently encouraging without being judgmental or dictatorial."[1]

Even the more experienced mom, already content in her curriculum choices and schedule, will continue to benefit from support-group involvement. No matter how long you have been home educating, a conversation with other moms almost guarantees that you will pick up new ideas that may work for you. Be ever on the lookout for new resources, approaches, and ideas for keeping the fun in your day. Besides, the energy and enthusiasm newcomers bring is contagious! Their delight and fresh motivation help us remember the reasons we chose to make this commitment to our children in the first place.

It is important, too, to realize that *our* experience is a valuable asset to the other moms in the group as well. Matthew 25:14 (the parable of the talents) reminds us that whatever we have been given, we must return with interest. Your experience and wisdom can be a great blessing to those who are just starting out. Our ability to home educate is itself a gift from God, and one that we must be generous in sharing.

---

[1] Joan Stromberg, *TORCH: A Lighthouse for the Faithful* (available from TORCH, P.O. Box 2, Danville, PA 17821), p. 5.

Being part of a support group helps us avoid the "lone ranger" syndrome. Some people fall into the trap of thinking that they are better off alone—that because they are the ones doing the teaching, they should find all the solutions to their problems on their own as well. Besides, they tell themselves, home education is so all-encompassing that there just isn't time left over for friends and spontaneity. This lone-ranger mentality opens the door wide for burnout in many families. Your children need the peer support a support group provides. You, in turn, will discover that your burdens are lighter when you find other moms who will listen to you, cry with you, laugh with you, and pray for you. Although you don't necessarily have to be "super-involved", *do* take advantage of support-group activities, both for your own family's sake as well as for the families who may need *your* support.

Besides practical advice, both first-time and veteran home schoolers will find encouragement and draw emotional support from other support-group families. They, unlike some of your family members, neighbors, and coworkers, will completely understand the challenge you have undertaken. They will allow you the freedom to feel discouraged or to have a bad day without telling you, "You must be making a mistake. Why don't you put the kids back in school and go a little easier on yourself?" Not surprisingly, for many home-schooling families a support group also provides a natural circle of friends with similar values. However different your backgrounds or interests, the values and priorities you share can forge many lasting friendships.

While a support group can greatly benefit parents and families as a whole, it may be even more crucial to your children's adjustment to home schooling. Your support group forms a natural peer group of children who are taught at home just as your children are. Without support-group contact, your child may feel he is the only one not going to "real" school. Kids get a huge boost when they attend occasional large gatherings of home schoolers in your area. When 150 home-educated children skate together at the ice rink, they *know* they are not alone!

In a similar way, a Catholic support group can strengthen your child's sense of being a part of the Catholic Church. Many Catholic support groups (most notably the TORCH network) desire to foster Catholic culture within families and as part of the Church as well as to provide more typical home education activities. Your child can experience the richness of his Catholic heritage as your group celebrates Catholic feast days together or when an activity highlights a particular saint's life and virtues.

Lisanne Bales, wife of a former Protestant minister, has watched her six children absorb the beauty of Catholic culture through contact with families in her Virginia support group. She appreciates the opportunities her children have to develop good relationships with priests who attend support-group activities.

> One of the substantial benefits of home schooling for our family has been the introduction to and relationship with a diverse number of priests through support-group activities and hospitality. A recent Chair of St. Peter Feast Day activity included an address by one priest on the subject of papal authority and another priest's impressive introduction to Salvadore Dali's "Last Supper of Christ" masterpiece, which the group was scheduled to see the following week at the National Art Gallery.

Draw in priests, sisters, and consecrated lay people to participate in your support-group activities. Marsha Jacobeen, mother of five boys, enjoys seeing her sons find good priestly role models through her support group.

> Through our home-schooling support-group activities, my children have come to know priests as "regular" people. They have discovered that priests enjoy some of the same activities that they enjoy. My boys shared fly-fishing stories with one priest. After watching another priest juggle everything from balls to fire torches, my oldest son decided he could learn to juggle, too (balls, that is!).

These opportunities allow priests or religious to share about their vocations and nurture our children's openness to serving the Church in whatever way God asks.

In your smaller circle, a support group offers your child a network of friends—friends of different backgrounds and ages as well as those who are similar in age and interests. Because of the diversity of ages in a typical support group, every child has the chance to be "bigger" than some children and to look up to others. In addition, deep and lasting friendships are usually built on the strength of shared values. Your child is more likely to find in his support group a good friend who believes the same things, lives by similar restrictions, and has similar goals than he would in the typical class of thirty students.

Support groups also provide an arena for healthy, positive competition for your child. The prospect of competing (whether for prizes or recognition) can become a powerful incentive for your child to work harder and to reap an additional reward for his efforts. Spelling and geography bees, sports activities, science and project fairs all become outlets for this competitive drive. Parents ought to encourage their children to take part in competitive activities offered by the support group. Some children are reticent about attempting something new or exhibiting their proficiency (or lack of it) in front of a crowd. However, when the group sets specific ground rules for an event (i.e., no criticism, laughing at another's mistakes, or rooting against one another), the chance to prepare and test their skills should be a positive one for *all* students involved, regardless of who ends up in "first place". After one group's spelling bee, the most enthusiastic advocates for repeating the event next year were those who *didn't* advance very far in the competition. As one girl explained, "We had so much fun!" Competition can be a real confidence booster for all involved.

Through support groups, parents often pool their talents and resources to give their children an incredible number of opportunities for learning and fun. For example, an artistic mother might tutor your child in sketching while you tutor hers in music or computers. Parents who enjoy unusual hobbies or sports (such as kayaking) can share their passion with others through the support group.

Finally, participating in a support group may offer you and your child academic and social opportunities that otherwise would not be available to you. For example, visiting a local planetarium that accommodates only group tours, not individual visits, becomes a possibility when you are part of a support group. Group discounts on recreational and cultural events are an added bonus, too. Another example is the placement of group orders in the God's World and Scholastic Book Clubs for great discounts on a variety of excellent literature for children at inexpensive prices.[2]

What Kinds of Support Groups Are Out There?

While most home education support groups tend to be secular or generically Christian (not explicitly associated with a particular denomination), more and more Catholic groups are forming across the country. It is better to become involved in or start a Catholic group than to become part of a non-Catholic or secular group.

If you are the only Catholic in the area who home schools, it is probably better to be part of *some* support group, rather than home schooling in isolation, but be aware of potential problems. Some Evangelical or generic Christian groups require members to sign a faith statement, listing the core beliefs to which members of the group adhere. Catholics need to read such statements carefully, as some are outright anti-Catholic, while others maintain the primacy of Scripture as the only authority for the truth. In addition, some groups are given to proselytizing and let Catholics in only for the purpose of trying to convert them.

Secular groups may present problems as well. Some of them are held together by strongly humanist philosophies. Other secular groups attract families that specifically shun religious values and discussions. These groups certainly would be less likely to offer genuine friendship and support for your undertaking. Further, they may, in subtle ways, denigrate or undermine your own faith or the more fragile faith of your children.

Catholic support groups, on the other hand, are far more com-

---

[2] God's World Book Club, P.O. Box 2330, Asheville, NC 28802; Scholastic Book Club, Scholastic, Inc., 2931 E. McCarty St., Jefferson City, MO 65101.

mon today than they were five years ago. New ones form every month across the country. As more and more Catholics discover home education, they are drawn together to start their own groups, rather than relying on the Christian or secular ones that exist already. (If you are interested in beginning a Catholic support group, it can be done! Read on!)

At its best, a Catholic support group strengthens the families involved, but not simply by passing on the practicalities of effective home schooling. More importantly, support-group members can help each other really live their Faith and know the beauty of the Church's teaching on marriage and family life, especially as it is lived out in the specific context of Catholic home education. As Catholics in a post-Christian society, we want to retain a distinctively Catholic identity, in lifestyle and teaching. At the same time, we want to avoid creating a fortress mentality that refuses to engage the "nasty, terrible world out there".

Support groups can play a key role in the "New Evangelization" that Pope John Paul II has stressed for the Church. It begins by families connecting and passing on parts of the Faith and the human wisdom needed to live the Faith fully. From that beginning, families continue to pass on Catholic Faith and culture in the broader context of local groups, the parish, and society in general. As the Pope stated in his 1994 "Letter to Families",

> It is important that families attempt to build bonds of solidarity among themselves. This allows them to assist each other in the educational enterprise: parents are educated by other parents, and children by other children. Thus a particular tradition of education is created, which draws strength from the character of the "domestic church" proper to the family.

Our efforts toward the New Evangelization must aim for an authentic, rich, and fully integrated Catholic culture.

Some people wonder whether creating a Catholic support group necessarily excludes non-Catholics or lapsed Catholics. Support groups can remain open to non-Catholics, or non-practicing Catholics, so long as they are never allowed to dilute the group's identity as one faithful to *all* the Church's teachings, including the documents of Vatican II and the postconciliar encyclicals. Group leaders, however, should not hesitate to exclude those who are vocally anti-Catholic or who are outspoken against some or all of the Church's clear teachings, as these might lead others astray.

Support groups come in a wide assortment of shapes and sizes. The big difference, besides that in the founding philosophy, is in structure.

How They Work

Ranging from the most casual get-togethers in the park to highly structured activities happening on a regular basis, support groups tend to assume the characteristics most desired by their members. Some mothers are looking merely for a regular, but informal, chance to chat about curriculum, schedule, or teaching difficulties. They might meet in a park and talk while the children play. Alternatively, they might meet for lunch once a month on a Saturday, leaving dads at home in charge of the kids. They simply enjoy being with each other and take advantage of the time together to compare notes, share their problems and difficulties in home education, and build friendships. Other groups, while still informal, meet on an occasional basis for the more focused purpose of combining an educational experience for their children with the opportunity for them to build friendships. This kind of group might schedule their get-togethers around a field trip, holiday party, or religious feast day.

Other groups are more structured, holding meetings or activities on a regular basis. A few groups or networks are incorporated and insured and put out monthly newsletters for all members. They organize children's activities around a specific purpose, whether to teach specific academic skills, enrich the families' sense of Catholic culture, or to broaden the children's understanding of a current event or particular liturgical feast. In addition, some groups may offer activities aimed at involving the whole family by holding family potluck dinners or field trips on a weekend so that dads can participate.

The kinds of activities support groups undertake are as varied as the members themselves. Once the group knows its goals (i.e., does it exist primarily for the mothers to share experiences, or for the children to participate in group activities, or some combination of both?), the events offered will be a natural offshoot of those goals.

The most common type of activities offered, or ones you might consider doing with your support group, are listed below with a description and specific ideas following each.

Mothers' Forum (or "Parents Only" Meetings)

Moms (and a few dads) get together to share problems, solutions, resources, and new ideas on a regular basis. Often the group will host an outside speaker on topics ranging from new curriculum offerings to time management.

Begin with an organizational meeting in August. It will help new people feel on top of things and start the new year with enthusiasm. You might distribute to each family a packet that would include the following: a list of members' addresses and telephone numbers, a calendar of the major events for the next six months, brief descriptions of upcoming events with the name and phone number of the organizer, a sheet outlining state law, a current listing by grade level of state standards, information on all available sports teams and music lesson opportunities, information on activities of interest at the local university, information on local museums (fees, times open, group discounts, programs) plus a map of those museums, deadlines for local competitions (geography bees and programs such as Book-It,[3] sponsored by Pizza Hut), fall Mass and Confession schedules at all local parishes, a phone tree for emergencies with clear instructions for use, and information on how to register with local authorities.

[3] Book-It is a reading-incentive program from October through February—each child earns a free pan pizza (small) if he reads an amount designated by the teacher (mom) each month. For more information, you can call 1–800–4BOOKIT.

Holding meetings in someone's home contributes to the warmth and openness of your gathering, again making newcomers feel part of the group. If the group is large, it might be better to meet in a parish hall or a business basement. A comfortable yet roomy locale helps to set a welcome atmosphere. You might want to designate one or two official greeters who would introduce new people and make sure everyone gets the agenda, a name tag, and any other important materials.

In addition, your leadership team might offer subsupport-group meetings for the half-hour before or after the main support-group meeting. These smaller groups could focus on a particular need— new home schoolers, teens, children with learning disabilities— without adding another evening out. Or perhaps you could offer new home-schooling moms an opportunity to pair up with a veteran willing to offer some one-on-one advice during that time slot.

Meetings often last approximately two hours, with the first half devoted to business and organizational concerns and the second half to a presentation or sharing on a particular topic. Follow a set agenda to keep meetings productive, printing as much information as possible to minimize note-taking and for the benefit of those not present, who can receive a copy of the agenda from a friend attending.

Specific discussion topics during the course of a year might include: one night each on curricula for math, science, history, English, foreign languages, logic, computers, and geography; coping with toddlers; challenging your teens; boredom busters for the winter; unit studies; household helps; time management for busy moms; preparing for Advent or Lent; deepening your prayer life amid diapers, dishes, home business, and math problems; and disciplining and building character.

Children's Activities

One of our guiding principles has been that we can provide any fun and worthwhile activity that an institutional school offers.

This does not mean that the institutional schools set the agenda for our activities, but rather that we can duplicate the best of their ideas.

For children's activities, families gather on an occasional or regular basis, either in someone's home, a parish hall, or at a park, for an organized activity on a particular theme. The theme might be academic in nature, spiritual, or celebratory. For example, the children (usually divided by age) might hear a presentation by a mom or outside speaker on Roman history, then make a map of Italy or do a craft related to the topic. If the topic is spiritual, a priest might come in and do a presentation to the children on Advent, followed by a craft, such as making an Advent calendar. The variety of topics your group can cover is limitless! The children benefit from being part of the group as well as from the change in routine from their usual studies.

In some locations, home-educated children take part in programs and events sponsored by local churches and community groups, such as team sports, geography and spelling bees, science fairs, and children's plays, choirs, and bands. When there are no community-based options, or when community or parish programs are undesirable, support groups often organize bands and choirs, debate teams, and sports teams.

Support-group activities offer a ready forum for displaying your child's work or rewarding his efforts. Many groups do their own science fairs, art exhibits, or project nights, where students display their work for the admiration of all the families involved. Some groups also hold spelling and geography bees for their students, often in combination with other local support groups.

Support groups can also offer your children classes in hobbies and skills such as sewing, quilting, crochet, clay sculpture, woodworking, car care, art, etc. Similarly, many groups increasingly sponsor a wide variety of academic clubs. These clubs, which can range from writing clubs to math or Latin clubs, gather students on a weekly or biweekly basis to study one subject or work on skills together in a particular area. A writing club, for example, gives the children a chance to share their writing with others and to hone their writing skills through a variety of exercises when the club meets.

Field Trips

Here, too, the possibilities are endless. Our groups have scheduled trips to orchards, museums, symphonies, newspaper offices, weather stations, banks, airports, police and fire stations, bakeries, hospitals and nursing homes, local businesses, historical sights, aquariums, zoos, the statehouse, monasteries—you name it!

As home-school groups acquire reputations for having orderly, well-mannered children, even more doors will open to us. (At the same time, many local school districts are cutting back their field trips because of liability concerns, discipline problems, and lack of chaperons.)

One important thing to keep in mind, however, is that children often benefit most from a field trip designed for their age level.

Many groups organize some field trips geared specifically to the preschool or kindergarten set and others appropriate only for junior-high and high-school students. You might want to designate specific people to arrange field trips for each age group as well as for the more general trips open to entire families. Teens need some time for age-appropriate activities, including trips, without younger siblings trailing along. (Cooperative baby-sitting by group members frees up some moms to accompany the older children.) Similarly, much younger children (preschool and kindergarten) benefit immensely from trips designed for their pace, interests, and shorter attention span.

Preteen and Teen Activities

Teens in support groups often meet for discussion or classes that focus on history, literature, politics, or apologetics. Your teen coordinator might organize special evenings for teens to go to the movies (or watch a film together in someone's home) or attend plays or concerts at a local university, thus meeting the needs for both intellectual stimulation and fun.

In order to strengthen the spiritual lives of children this age, some support groups organize youth groups or coordinate their children's involvement in specific spiritual and apostolic works. Resources in this area include the Junior Legion of Mary, youth groups organized by the Legionaries of Christ or Opus Dei, Catholic Young Life, Teen Life, and parish youth ministers. In addition, some parents encourage their teen's participation in a monthly pro-life event—attending a pro-life convention or rally, assisting at the local crisis pregnancy center, or praying outside an abortuary.

Select a host couple for each teen event, whether or not the activity occurs in their home. This couple coordinates the nitty-gritty of the activity (transportation, cost, refreshment details), supervises attitudes and actions of the peer group, and guides the activity until it is finished. We must remember that peer pressures are strongest in this age group. Unsupervised time together as a group can lead to difficulties; however, a well-organized event can be a blessing to everyone.

Support Groups for Special Interests

Some support groups encourage their members to meet as sub-groups to address various family needs. For example, parents of teens, children with disabilities, or children in that crucial transition year after being taken out of school and beginning home education benefit enormously from time spent exchanging ideas with other parents in similar situations.

Family Activities

In an effort to include dads more in the home-education experience, groups often plan weekend activities for the whole family. Ideas include family retreats, family potluck dinners, sports days (with dads doing the organizing, coaching, and refereeing), camp outs at a local state park, project nights, science and art fairs, pilgrimages to shrines, and group picnics.

Communications / Resources

Support groups often publish some sort of newsletter that includes more than just schedule information. Some newsletters contain columns or articles pertaining to Catholic culture, curriculum, dads, moms, or teens. Features may include a children's page, written and edited by home-schooled children from the support group, or a "question and answer" column edited by the veterans in your group. Newsletters can provide much-needed support and encouragement to support-group members who live a fair distance away from the other members and need to feel connected to the larger group.

In addition, many groups put together lists of the resources available to home-educating families in their local area. Lists may include all sorts of activities, not just technical academic resources. Sports-minded families find it heartening to learn that choosing home education does not rule out sports for their children. A list of local sports leagues, teams, or lessons available, including the details on age groups, the costs of joining, the names of coaches, the training given, and practice and game locations can be invaluable. Similarly, groups can list information on music and art lessons, such as teachers, opportunities for local bands or youth choirs, costs, and recital opportunities. Other "miscellaneous" activities, such as sewing lessons, woodworking, cooking, or craft lessons, can be included as well.

Certainly, the same information can be shared informally, by word of mouth. However, it is more valuable to newcomers if the information is written and immediately available (kind of a written "Welcome Wagon"). The same information can be given to those considering home education, who need concrete information on all the opportunities available to their children before they take the plunge.

Larger groups often catalogue the academic resources members use and are willing to lend to others. Handouts for members might list everything from Cuisinaire rods to spelling texts and children's dictionaries—or a group could choose to note only those hard-to-find items, such as microscopes or out-of-print books. Another way to accomplish the same result is to circulate a notebook at every group meeting that lists each family's curriculum recommendations or resources they are willing to share with others.

Where Can I Find a Support Group?

Begin Informally

Probably the most common way of finding out about a support group in your area is through informal contacts with other home schoolers. Whether you are first starting out or just considering home education, take advantage of every conversation with other home educators to ask whether they are involved with a support group. Those who are involved are usually very open about inviting newcomers to attend a support-group meeting or an upcoming activity.

One of the first questions someone who is considering home education often asks is, "What about socialization—how do you find friends for your children?" This question quite naturally elicits an enthusiastic response about the children's activities, including support-group events. Word of mouth also allows you to find out about home-schooling families or mothers who get together for the same purposes as a support group without ever calling themselves a formal group.

Another typical way of discovering a support group is through notices in the local home-schooling newsletters. Newsletters put out on a monthly or bimonthly basis by a support group in the area often include information pertaining to other events, including other support-group meetings. Sometimes a subgroup of home schoolers (such as those from a particular neighborhood or who share the same faith) will put a notice in the newsletter letting others know of their activities.

For Catholics, a time-honored way of finding support-group members is through bulletin announcements. Existing Catholic support groups frequently run announcements in the local parish bulletins, listing a contact person or describing their activities. Occasionally individuals will place an ad, asking other home-educating families to contact them.

Within some parishes, support-group leaders have introduced themselves to and cultivated relationships with both the parish priests and the parish school principal. Besides creating a positive impression of home education, these relationships can turn into an important referral network. Some principals have even referred families who are leaving their school in order to home educate to parish support-group leaders.

Tap into National Resources

On a larger scale, the National Association of Catholic Home Educators[4] maintains a regularly updated list of Catholic contacts in every state. These people stay in touch with Catholic home educators throughout their state. Either they, or someone they know, will probably be aware of Catholic support groups in your area. In addition, NACHE sponsors several Catholic home-education conventions in different parts of the country each year. Conventions are a good place to pick up information about the support groups in your area.

Similarly, the major Catholic curriculum suppliers often keep a list of contact people and fellow subscribers who are from your state. They may be willing to put you in touch with someone who uses the same curriculum, thus forming a nucleus for a support group. The major curriculum providers also host mini-conventions in sites around the country. This, again, provides a good opportunity to meet people.

The largest network of Catholic support groups is based in Baltimore, Maryland, and goes by the acronym TORCH—Tradi-

---

[4] National Association of Catholic Home Educators, 6102 Saints Hill Lane, Broad Run, VA 22014; telephone (540) 349–4314, fax (703) 264–5831.

tions of Roman Catholic Homes.[5] TORCH has its own network of contacts all over the country, including those places where local TORCH chapters exist. TORCH activities are designed, not just to support families in the nitty-gritty of home education but, more important, to help families grow in their Catholic faith and practice. Cultivating a rich and vibrant sense of Catholic culture and faith is central to TORCH's mission. Local groups who are not interested in becoming official TORCH chapters are welcome to get ideas from the mission statement of TORCH as a guide to establishing their own group. One of TORCH's hopes, according to founder Miki Hill, is eventually to have chapters in all major cities, much like Couple to Couple League or La Leche League. Anyone new to an area could seek out the TORCH chapter leaders for sound, practical help in their home schooling and in living their Faith.

Another official way of finding support groups is through the state home-education organizations. They usually have lists of contact persons in most towns and cities throughout the state. Although these contact people may not be part of a group you are interested in joining, they usually are "plugged in" to area leaders and can give you names of people to call. A state organization, however, probably will not distinguish among different faiths or philosophies. You may end up making quite a few phone calls in order to find a Catholic or Christian connection. At the very least, the state organization should be able to tell you about any home-education newsletters that serve your area.

Form Your Own Support Group

But now, how do you start a support group when none is available? First, find a few other families who are home-schooling and who are interested in getting together on a fairly regular basis. Depend-

[5] Miki Hill, TORCH Director, 1700 New Hampton Lane, Woodstock, MD 21163. Or Joan Stromberg, TORCH National Network Coordinator, P.O. Box 2, Danville, PA 17821; telephone (717) 271-0244.

ing on the number of people who will be involved initially, you may want to designate a leadership or planning team.

Next, agree on your goals—are you networking in order to provide friends and activities for your children, or for moral support and information for the parents, or a combination of the two? A mission statement is a helpful tool for defining the group's agreed-upon purposes and communicating your philosophy to prospective members. (However, don't spend months crafting the perfect mission statement before putting it into practice—the important thing is to begin!)

Third, don't "reinvent the wheel". Begin by finding out, through friends who home school in other cities, or through TORCH or NACHE, what kinds of activities other support groups offer and how they structure them. Discuss the types of events you might want to offer now or in the future. Decide what your immediate needs are and how frequently you want to meet. Discuss where to hold your meetings, whether in a home or a parish hall. (Keep in mind that some parishes or other facilities may require group members to sign a waiver of liability or to procure group liability insurance. TORCH or NACHE can give you more information on ways to meet these requirements.) Agree on a small membership fee to cover the costs of copying and mailing newsletters and to underwrite group activities. This eliminates the need for later fund-raising projects.

Finally, divide up the responsibilities. A simple model for your leadership team could include four positions: (1) an overall leader, who makes the agenda and runs the leadership and group meetings; (2) a newsletter or communications person; (3) a social-events organizer; and (4) a teen group leader (or preschool coordinator, depending on where the concentration of ages falls).

Another more comprehensive division of labor could look like this:

Field Trip Coordinator
> Schedules field trips chosen by the leadership team or age-group coordinators.

Religious Activity Coordinator

Finds priests, sisters, consecrated religious to speak to children about vocations, feast days, saints' days. Coordinates or connects with youth groups or different local groups offering spiritual formation. Plans ways for the members to deepen their understanding of different liturgical feasts and saints' days throughout the year.

Age-Group Coordinators (preschool coordinator, teen coordinator, early elementary coordinator for ages five to eight, elementary coordinator for ages eight to twelve).

Coordinators plan activities, projects, and games for appropriate age groups to accomplish objectives set by leaders (e.g., teach children about Rome).

Craft Coordinator

Finds volunteers to direct or plan craft activities in conjunction with age-group coordinators.

Snack Coordinator

Finds volunteers to bring snacks to group activities.

Newsletter

This person is the key! Types and circulates copies of the newsletter or schedule, usually once a month.

Membership / Phone Tree

Puts together a list of members, including names and ages of children as well as addresses and phone numbers—this helps in finding playmates and baby-sitters from among home-schooling families. Sets up a phone tree to keep members posted on the latest schedule changes or special events.

RSVP Contact

This person receives RSVPs from members for certain events.

Librarian

Keeps track of materials available and who has checked out what. Is responsible for bringing the library to the monthly meetings.

Depending on your size and the degree of organization you want, your group may need volunteers for some, all, or none of these responsibilities. It doesn't need to be complicated. Having a support group can be as simple as one family inviting two or three other home-schooling families to join them on an outing to the local museums (or asking each family to plan a special activity for the group one month out of the year).

Remember Your Purpose

Support groups are there to provide you with the practical know-how and the friendships and encouragement you need to home educate well. But most important, in the words of TORCH founder Miki Hill, "We're there ultimately to work within the heart of the Church to build the Church."

Support Groups—Too Good to Miss

1. Support groups provide newcomers with an unlimited source of curriculum ideas, organizational tips, and moral support.

2. Veteran home schoolers continue to benefit from others' ideas, resources, and enthusiasm through their support groups. In addition, they bring an invaluable wealth of knowledge and experience to share with others.

3. Children benefit from support-group involvement, as it provides them with a natural peer group and a ready source of friends, competition, academic activities, and socialization opportunities.

4. Families draw inestimable moral support from support-group families who share similar values and experiences and a common desire to live their Catholic Faith deeply.

5. Support groups range from highly informal gatherings of a few families who meet for occasional field trips to more organized groups that publish newsletters and meet on a regular basis for academic, social, and spiritual activities.

14

Test Questions

Short Essay Questions and Answers

The following questions and answers have been written in short-paragraph format for your convenience. If one question does not pertain to your situation, please skip ahead to one that does. We hope you find this section helpful.

I am a single parent. Can I home educate my children?

Yes, you can.

Home educating as a single parent has its own unique challenges, just as parenting alone does. Every single parent may not be able to home educate, but many can if that is their desire.

The emotional needs of a child are compounded when a parent is missing through either death or divorce. The greater the child's emotional needs, the more difficult it is for him to do schoolwork; he is adjusting to a major change in his life, so his energy is dissipated. Here's where home education could be a helpful tool.

You can combine meeting the emotional needs of your children with their academic training. As you home educate, you share more than information—you share yourself. This can be more than an opportunity for a better education—it can be time for personal attention, quality sharing, physical affection, and a deeper bond of love.

One single mom, Cathy, said, "It has been such a blessing to see my daughter's self-esteem grow as we spend time studying together and cooking together. I have been very, very pleased with this choice for her."

Home education always requires a certain amount of flexibility. The single parent needs even more adaptability. While most children attend school between the hours of 9 A.M. and 3 P.M., your child can follow a different schedule. You are not limited by the hours of a typical school day—teach when you are available.

Inevitably, there will be stress as you make changes. Do you think you can handle the added stress so that home education works for your family? The more flexible and tolerant you are as you work with changes in the schedule and format of education in your home, the more likely you will succeed. For more schedule ideas for single parents who work, see the next question.

Consider the option of home educating one child at first. Ask yourself if there is one child in particular who would benefit from home education. It's a real possibility to home educate one or two children without teaching all of them. There's no one "right" way to home educate.

Initially, family and friends might not support your decision to home educate. They may worry that the burdens you already carry are too heavy. Point out ways home education will strengthen and unify your family during this adjustment period, giving greater stability to each family member. If you feel confident that home education could be a good option for your family, let your support network know your need for their encouragement.

After the death of her spouse, Tani said, "We were handicapped as a family—it was hard to find peace within our family." Tani and her children appreciated the help other people offered, but they struggled to feel like a family in the midst of their grief. Drawing the children home from school helped. As they worked, studied, and had fun together, they grew in their mutual support of each other and rediscovered their sense of family. "Now", Tani says, "we feel like a family again. We still need the help of others for support, but not because we are not stable."

One of the challenges of a single parent is substituting other kinds of help that would normally be provided by a spouse. A close friend who home educates or a local support group can give you encouragement and creative solutions for various problems. Area clubs and tutorials can supply teachers who fill in the gaps in subjects that might have been taught by a spouse. "Above all," Tani says, "having the Faith is critical." If the Lord is the One opening this door for your family, then He will provide the necessary strength to do it.

I am a working parent. Can I home educate my children?

Yes, you can.

Flexibility is the name of the game. Often we think school can occur only during normal school hours, but that's not so. Adjust your "school hours" according to your work schedule. Your child can do independent work while under the care of a sitter or at the home of another home-educating family during your work hours. Teach the subjects not covered by independent work when you are available: early in the morning, in the evenings, or during the weekends.

If there are times your spouse is available when you are at work, perhaps you could divide your child's subjects between you. Or you could hire a tutor for certain subjects and then complete the school day at your convenience.

Some people have altered their work schedules to accommodate home education: they work four longer days and are free three; or they change shifts to have more hours free during the day; or they work weekends instead of weekdays; or they choose to work part time instead of full time. Whatever arrangement best suits your family, be sure you know your state's laws so that you can fully comply with their requirements for the percent of class time a parent must provide and the percent a tutor can provide.

Some people change their work place from outside the home to within the home. You might set up a desk for your child near you at home and go back and forth between giving him your full attention for tutor-intensive subjects and giving him independent studies while you complete your work. You would be available to answer questions and yet accomplish your job.

A few people have flexible situations at work where they can bring a home-educated child to work. A study station could be set up close to mom for the child. This is an unusual situation, but some employers provide this flexibility.

As you and your spouse think about the possibilities, pray that the Holy Spirit will help you think of creative solutions to your particular situation. Again, if God is the One directing you to home educate, He will provide what is needed for your success.

I am pregnant. Can I home educate my children?

Yes, you can.

What difficulties does pregnancy cause you? Tiredness, nausea, varicose veins, and being emotional may challenge you in addition to home educating your crew. How can it all work?

If you are tired, adjust your schedule in the morning or get help to allow for an afternoon nap. In the morning, your schedule for school can always start a little later than what you consider ideal— an extra hour of sleep might do all of you a lot of good. In the afternoon, hire a sitter or use an older child to free up time for a nap.

Your children will help you more because they are home than if they were gone all day at school and then needed your help later with homework. If you have children who do not need a rest time when you nap, plan some independent work for them during your rest. Some families have a quiet hour after lunch for everyone so that mom can rest. Older children can read or do quiet activities while younger children nap.

If you are very nauseous, plan the most demanding hours of your schedule for when you feel best. Part of your educational plan can include older children assisting the younger children while you oversee progress from the sofa. Incidentally, if you have a good lesson plan, you can easily direct traffic from the floor or a sofa while resting those varicose veins, as the doctor ordered.

Perhaps you need to adjust your overall goals. Feel free to revise the number of courses you wanted your children studying for a few months or even for that academic year. (You can always pick up

French or art class next semester.) Ask other families to include your children with them on field trips or cancel your family's involvement on field trips altogether until you feel better.

Utilize available assistance—planning is the key. Children can check off a list of course work accomplished if you provide the list. Your husband can oversee some of the children's work until you feel better. Perhaps tutors could fill in as substitute teachers temporarily.

Remember: nausea and tiredness will pass, but the opportunity to instruct your children this year, including them in a special way with this pregnancy, will only happen now. Share your needs; see how your husband and children rise to the occasion and help out so that your home-education endeavor succeeds.

I have (or will have) a newborn. Can I home educate my children?

Yes, you can.

Often people find that only a short break is needed before the school schedule is reestablished. Resuming routine often gets the family through the adjustments to the new child. Even a small amount of work done regularly helps the family feel back to normal.

Organize as much as you can before you have the baby. Encourage your children to work ahead, doing extra credit so that they can get a break when the baby is born. Design your post-baby schedule so that you need a minimum of time planning each day.

Since newborns typically just eat and sleep, you can accommodate their schedule to your schooling activities. You can feed your baby easily while continuing your lesson plans if you place a comfortable chair nearby. It might save you time and stairs if you set up a baby-changing station in your schoolroom. (Changing a baby in the schoolroom keeps to a minimum the chaos that can develop if you leave the room for a time.) It is not too difficult to juggle a young baby in your arms while explaining a math problem, for instance.

Besides your arms, there are other safe places for your baby while you tend to the needs of your other children. You can focus your attention elsewhere, knowing your young one is secure in an infant seat, swing, or playpen. If you invest in a baby monitor, you can be downstairs or even outside while the baby's napping. You will have peace of mind that the baby is all right while you use your baby-free time to focus on the other children.

Fussy times do happen, and it helps to have a strategy. If necessary, you could coordinate teaching certain tutor-intensive subjects with one child while your other children take turns caring for the baby in another room, thereby minimizing distractions.

As your baby begins crawling, think safety first. Clear off lower shelves in your schooling area for age-appropriate toys. Block off any areas that are not child-proofed with safety gates. As long as the environment is safe, the baby probably will play happily near you, even though your attention is focused on another child.

Some babies do not establish routines for a while. In that case you may need a flexible schedule that designates certain subjects for the least chaotic parts of the day, whenever they may occur. Plan your concentrated sessions of math or language arts to coincide with his nap time. This may work well in the morning; however, if you have to wait until afternoon for baby-free time to do certain subjects, you may be teaching a child when both of you have less energy and interest in studies. What works best for your family may change during the year as the baby's schedule changes.

Realize that having a baby is a positive learning experience for everyone in the family. Studying the newborn's development can be a great project for older children. And there will be more opportunities for everyone to serve the family, which is good for the character development of all involved. In fact, your children will have more opportunities to develop a relationship with this new little one because they will have more time together. You can make the whole experience of including a newborn as part of your home education work well with planning, prayer, and a positive attitude.

We have only one child. Can I home educate successfully with only one child?

Yes, you can.

You have the opportunity for individualized tutoring without the distractions or interruptions from other children. You have preparations for one grade level rather than juggling the curricula and schedules of several grade levels. What a blessing—you can focus your time and attention on your child and his needs in all the areas that encompass home education: spiritual, emotional, physical, and intellectual.

The social development of your child may be your greatest concern. Though your child may miss daily social contact with a classroom full of peers, that interaction is not necessary for true socialization and academic success. For more specific information on questions about socialization, see Chapter 5.

How can you provide for the real social needs of your child? Link up with your area home-education support group and participate in group activities. Look into clubs and sports activities through church and community groups. Team up with another family for one subject area for some planned social time with an academic goal. In addition, you can always invite children regularly to play and offer hospitality to families with children who can develop friendships with your child.

Some mothers find that an only child struggles with laziness—the lack of competition can discourage diligence. Offer extra-credit incentives or plan special field trips when your child has attained certain goals. Talk to other moms of only children—how do they motivate their children and provide them with good social experiences? There are creative solutions to the difficulties you face as you home educate your only child.

Can I home educate one of my children without teaching all of them?

Yes, you can.

First, there is no state law that prohibits teaching one child unless you teach them all.

Second, you know the needs of each of your children. One child may have a greater need to be home with you than the others. This is especially true when you are thrust into this decision midyear due to a crisis with one child. Besides, home schooling one child might give you a better idea about the feasibility of teaching all of the children the next year.

You may run into difficulties as you juggle the challenges of both home education and parenting children who attend school outside the home (e.g., teaching one child all day and helping the rest with homework at night; or having the home-schooling day interrupted by car-pooling the others to their schools). In other words, it could be the best of both worlds, the worst of both worlds, or somewhere in between. Many families who have tried to home educate and be involved in a school have eventually simplified their lives and made a decision one way or the other. Any arrangement is possible—just think through, with your spouse, what God wants you to do and how to do it.

We have a special-needs child. Can we still home educate?

Yes, you can.

Many people have had mixed experiences with "experts" in public schools. The professionals may have special training that could help your special-needs child; however, the negative social-ization that can occur in school and the lack of one-on-one care (even though the class may have a small teacher–student ratio) can limit your child's progress.

A study released August 30, 1994, by Steven F. Duvall, Ph.D., entitled *The Effects of Home Education on Children with Learning Disabilities* revealed a marked improvement for those children who were home taught.

> Results indicated that home school students were academically engaged about 1.5 times as often as public school students. Fur-thermore, home school students averaged six months gain in read-ing compared to one-half month by public school students, and eight months gain in written language compared to less than 2.5

months for public school students. Both home and public school students averaged 13 months gain in math.[1]

Your special-needs child could benefit greatly from the individualized tutoring you can provide through home education. You have the love for and commitment to your child that no one else has. You could provide the time and individual attention critically needed for your child's improvement. Talk about an individual education plan!

First, assess your child's ability in the areas of prereading, math, and speech skills. You can acquire a copy of the Revised Brigand Diagnostic Inventory of Early Development from the Home School Legal Defense Association.[2] It covers development from birth through second grade.

In addition, you may need the help of a professional. Your involvement with a professional may be limited to assessing your child's needs and making therapy recommendations you can provide in your home. Or you may need a qualified therapist to come to your home on a regular basis or see your child regularly for office visits. Whatever the help provided, a professional's assessment may guide you to the most beneficial curricula.

Second, look through the catalogues, magazines, and books recommended by NATHHAN (National Challenged Homeschoolers Associated Network) for specialized resource guides. *The NATHHAN Resource Guide*[3] lists resources according to specific learning disabilities and handicaps for home schoolers teaching special-needs children.

In addition, there may be very helpful materials from standard educational books and supplies. The more resources and support you find, the more secure you and your spouse will feel about your

[1] "Study Concludes That Home Education Benefits Learning Disabled Children", *Home School Court Report*, September/October 1994, p. 18. The article describes the results of a study done by Dr. Duvall comparing home-taught and public-school children with learning disabilities.

[2] Home School Legal Defense Association, Box 159, Paeonian Springs, VA 22129; telephone (540) 338–5600, fax (703) 264–5831.

[3] Kathy Salars, *The NATHHAN Resource Guide*, NC 31 51–N–91, Midland, TX 79707.

decision to home educate. One recommended guide, by Sharon Hensley, is entitled *Home Schooling Children with Special Needs*.[4] For more resources, write to *The Teaching Home* and request a copy of their July/August 1994 issue entitled "Teaching Children with Special Needs".

Third, connect with other home-educating families with special-needs children. NATHHAN has a matching service for families with similar situations. What an advantage for you to benefit from the research and experience of others who have gone before you. It could also be a blessing to them to share what they have learned.

> In addition, there is a growing network of professionals, many of whom also home school, who are willing and interested in assisting families in the areas of testing, educational counseling, and the various therapies.[5]

Since some friends or family members may not be supportive of your decision to home educate, look for support from other families in a situation similar to your own.

The nurturing environment of your home can be ideal for developing parent-directed occupational, speech, or physical therapy, which involves the whole family.

> Parent-directed, home-based therapy is a viable and positive alternative for homeschool families. Numerous studies have shown family involvement in a therapeutic program to be a key factor in the child's progress.[6]

Home-based therapy can free up time and money otherwise expended outside the home for therapy. In addition it can involve the

---

[4] Sharon Hensley tackles many issues related to teaching children with a variety of disabilities: curriculum, behavior problems, and discouragement. *Home Schooling Children with Special Needs* (Gresham, OR: Noble Publishing Associates, 1995).

[5] Janet Wayne, "How Home Schooling Helps Your Special-Needs Child", *The Teaching Home*, July/August 1994, p. 40. Janet Wayne is the Special Needs Coordinator, Home School Legal Defense Association.

[6] Marcia Lapish, "Parent-Directed Therapy at Home", *The Teaching Home*, July/August 1994, p. 42.

whole family in the growth and development of your special-needs child. At appropriate times, professional evaluation would be helpful.

Fourth, contact the Home School Legal Defense Association for the specific legal requirements in your state for instructing your special-needs child at home.[7] They will send, free of charge, a packet of information on home schooling a special-needs child.

Fifth, prepare your home for schooling so you minimize distractions.

> TV, radio, pets, and even pictures on walls or in books may hinder concentration. Earplugs or a shield around a desk may help, or have your child work facing a blank wall. Use cards to block out distractions on a page.[8]

An atmosphere of reduced noise and decreased visual stimulation can increase the effectiveness of your teaching.

As important as academics are, you may find a great deal of your time will initially be spent in attention training and basic discipline. On the one hand, structure your day to bring a sense of peace and order to your child. On the other hand, be flexible with your schedule when your child is having great difficulty settling down to work. You can still follow your plan, but you may have to adjust the time frame per task.

Remember: this special-needs child is a gift from God to you. Since He is the One who has given you this child, ask Him in prayer for the specific resources and support you and your spouse need to be faithful stewards of his soul and mind. First Peter 5:7 says, "Cast your anxieties on Him, for He cares for you."

---

[7] See Christopher Klicka, *The Right Choice—The Incredible Failure of Public Education and the Rising Hope of Home Schooling* (Gresham, OR: Noble Publishing Associates, 1992). It includes a full discussion of the legal issues involved in home educating special-needs children.

[8] "Tips for Teaching Your Special-Needs Child", by the staff, *The Teaching Home*, July/August 1994, p. 44.

We have a large family. Can we home educate successfully?

Yes, you can.

Organization is key to successfully home educating a large family. One family of eleven has established a schedule where the four oldest children each spend one weekday managing the household, making meals, and doing creative activities with the younger children while mom teaches the others two days' worth of course work. Friday is a day for group activities for everyone, and Saturday is a general cleaning and errand day. Everyone learns more than a regular five–day schedule would allow, they all contribute to an ordered household, and they gain life-skill experience while Mom focuses on educating the other children.

There are a number of possibilities for coordinating the studies of more than one child. Some families train older children to teach some lessons to younger children or assist in child care while mom teaches more tutor-intensive subjects. Some families provide computer programs or video programs as excellent extra "teachers". Other families pair or even group their own children according to ability for math or grammar studies. Unit studies can be a lot of fun with a wide variety of ages: each child reads materials on his own level and contributes to projects with the whole family in one particular subject, such as history. Mealtimes and snack times can be valuable moments for group discussion.

Some food for thought—maybe you could limit extracurricular sports to those the family can do together, such as tennis, golf, or volleyball. That way the remainder of the day following school-work does not become a frenzied car-pool whirlwind. However, some families have found sports such as basketball, baseball, or soccer to be a lot of fun for the family. And, since there is no homework and the family has spent time together during the day, there is less sense of being frantic than when these sports are added onto a regular school day.

My parents and close friends are not supportive. Can I home educate successfully without their encouragement?

Yes, you can.

If you suspect that family members or close friends will question your decision about home education, pray about and prepare for the time you will tell them. Wait until you know what you are doing before you share your decision with them. If they misread your cautious presentation of the idea as a hesitation or lack of confidence that this is the right decision, they may express their negativity more strongly. On the other hand, if you present the idea politely and firmly, you may be pleasantly surprised at their initial response.

Listen to their concerns. Perhaps they have been unduly influenced by something they saw on TV about home education or by a family who was a poor example of home education. If they are open to discussion, and you think it would be helpful, share material you have gleaned about the benefits of home education (perhaps lend them this book) so they can know this is a well-thought-out decision. Assure them that home education is legal.

Your detractors may not even be aware of the prejudices they have against home education, but information you have could dispel their fears or concerns. Point out that home schooling is getting favorable press whereas public schools are not. For instance, *Better Homes and Gardens* recently published an article entitled "When School Is at Home".[9] The research to which it refers as well as the quotes from home educators were very positive. Keep a folder of some of these articles from the secular press handy as backup for your assertion regarding the success of home education.

Point out to your critics that home education is a natural extension of all you have already taught your children. Include them in an open house where your children's work is on display. Or invite them to a Christmas program so they can see your children perform and interact with others, and you can introduce

[9] "When School Is at Home", *Better Homes and Gardens*, March 1995, pp. 40–44.

them to other home educators in your area. You may even think of something they could teach your children so they could be included in your home education. What a special opportunity it could be for grandparents in particular to get to know the grand-children well.

If family members or friends try to manipulate your emotions or, worse, cause dissension between you and your spouse over this decision, perhaps you should spend less time with them until you establish your program. If they strongly oppose you, let them know it is not a subject for discussion. Then gently remind them that the decision to home educate your children is between you and your spouse. Cathy Gualandri, home-educating mother of four, shares, "Just simply say that you feel called by God to do this since you as parents have the primary role in the education of your children. Then be silent to combat evil."

Sometimes people have actually lost friends over their decision about home education. On the one hand, we should not convey an attitude of superiority over our family members or friends, as if *we* are the ones who *really* care about Catholic education for our children and they do not. On the other hand, some people may be offended by our decision, in spite of our best efforts to be sensitive. It may be that God will provide new friends through the local home-education support group—people who have similar values and are in similar situations.

My pastor is not supportive. Can I still home educate
my children without the approval of the parish priest?

Yes, you can.

As much as you may desire your parish priest's support for home education, you are not required to get his approval. You can listen to his concerns, but ultimately God has called *you and your spouse* to be the primary educators of your own children. Share a copy of John Paul II's "Letter to Families", in which the Pope speaks about the principle of subsidiarity in the area of education, opening wide the door for Catholic home education.

Perhaps your husband could speak privately with your priest, man to man, so that Father can understand how much thought and prayer have gone into your decision. If Father is managing a Catholic school, he may feel betrayed by your decision. Show him that you are being faithful to the Church's teaching, and demonstrate your continuing support for Catholic education in general. Emphasize the positive reasons for your choice so he will not feel you are condemning his school.

Remember: Actions speak louder than words. Hopefully, your priest will see how well mannered your children are and how much they are learning about and living the Faith. That may change his opinion about home education, if he is negative. You may be surprised how supportive your priest can become when he understands the reasons behind your decision.

Realize that many priests *do* support Catholic home education. Teresa Cunningham, of Oakton, Virginia, tells how her family's

> morale and sense of purpose in home schooling was given a real boost when one of our children overheard two priests talking at a home-schooling function. One priest mentioned that he believed that the priests should be spending more time with home schoolers, as home schoolers were the hope for the future of the Church.

These words are encouraging. A few quotes from these priests can strengthen your resolve when the lack of your own pastor's support causes you to question your decision. (Our parish priest has become the spiritual advisor for our group. That enables him to keep the pulse of the group and helps us connect with our local parish.) In short, pray for peaceful solutions to conflicts, for the good of all, and see what doors the Lord opens.

*What can I tell my children when they are criticized
for having school at home?*

Model your instruction to your children: Do not be defensive. There are good reasons you home educate. Make sure your children understand them. Then they can share them with others. Though your children might be tempted to lash out at others who are making fun of them, they should respond in a Christlike manner. Let your children see you calm and confident—they will imitate you.

It could be that the neighbor children are being negative because they are actually jealous of your children. In fact, some may have asked or even begged their parents to home educate them only to be told negative things about home education that are not true. Talk with the neighbor children about their criticisms. It is not necessary to be negative about other schools in order to share positively about what is going on in your home.

You might diffuse a tense situation with neighbor children if you invite them in—show them your schoolroom and supplies so they can see it is a "real" school. Perhaps you can include them on a field trip on a day they are home from school and you are in session (such as a teacher in-service day). If you include them, they are less likely to turn on your children with unkind comments.

In reality, despite your best efforts, criticisms may continue. Reaffirm with your children that you made the best choice for them and shield them from ongoing and hurtful criticisms as best you can.

I don't know anyone else in my area who home schools.
Can I home educate my children without a support group?

Yes, you can.

First, decide whether or not home education is the best educational option for your family. If it is, God will give you the strength to do it, even if it means standing alone in your community. You could feel isolated at first. Rather than thinking of yourselves as the *only* home educators in town, think of yourselves as the *first* home educators around. Who knows how many people you may encourage in the same direction, once they know of your decision.

Second, share your ideas with friends and check out their response. Perhaps one or more of them has been toying with the idea but has not pursued it for the same reasons you have waited. It only takes two families to form a support group.

Third, contact national home-education networks, such as NACHE, TORCH, and state home-education networks to see if they know of other home educators living in close proximity to you. Even if a family lives an hour away, you could plan a field trip halfway between you just for the fun and support of being together.

Fourth, let the local library know you are home educating your children. Often home educators moving to a new community will check with the public library for a contact of a local support group. Also, check with the local paper—perhaps articles have been done on area home-education support groups. That might give you a lead on other families in the area you can meet.

Fifth, two sources of long-distance support are magazines and phone calls. There are a growing number of home-education magazines filled with great articles that provide creative solutions to various situations you may be facing. Pen-pal sections offer direct contact with women for a more personal response to a concern. And don't forget that sometimes calling a dear friend long distance for support, suggestions, and prayer may be money well spent, even if you are on a limited budget.

Finally, remember that home education does *not* mean you should give up your friends, nor should your children give up theirs. You may have to make a special effort to get together because of the change in your schedule, but maintaining friendships is worth it. Often friends who do not home educate their children will still give you the support you need to pursue your goals.

I have almost no money for home-education materials. Can I home educate my children?

Yes, you can.

Home education is excellent private Catholic education at a fraction of the cost of other private schools. And the expenses can be cut further, if you cannot purchase curricula right now. Here are a few suggestions how.

World Book Encyclopedia has a listing by grade level of what is ordinarily covered in each subject. State education departments usually will send you for free the standards of learning for each grade. Some families use these as guides for checking out books from the library for most subjects except math. Collections of household objects, such as buttons, keys, rocks, or shells, can be used for math along with placing problems on the blackboard or a piece of paper—a textbook is not required.

You might want to invest in the appropriate grade level from the series by E. D. Hirsch, Jr., entitled *The Core Knowledge Series.*[10] Each volume contains a comprehensive explanation for what a child in that grade should know in each subject area, including math. Additionally, you would need to check out the library books that Hirsch recommends and make up your own math worksheets for your child's practice. Besides the initial expense of the book, there are no additional costs. Since it is nonconsumable, you can reuse it with each child.

Some local public schools allow home educators to borrow books. Your taxes paid for them, after all. In addition, teachers may accommodate home-educating families with the extra materials available. Access to these materials may be a phone call away.

Home-educating families in your area may provide other workable solutions for you. Perhaps they may lend you curricula they are not using currently. Or they might include you and your children in the subject area you need, such as science or history.

Check out used-book shops or book fairs at home-education conventions for bargains that will stretch your dollars. Ask relatives for specific curricula as gifts that may be a combination toy and educational tool, such as books, maps, and educational games.

If this is a new venture, gradually work educational materials into your budget. Perhaps money previously spent on school

[10] For example, E. D. Hirsch, Jr., *The Core Knowledge Series—What Your Second Grader Needs to Know* (New York: Doubleday, 1991). "The Core Knowledge Series" covers kindergarten through sixth grade.

lunches, bus fare, extracurricular activities, and school supplies could be transferred to your new school budget. Make this a matter of prayer—the Lord has the creative solution your family needs if home education is His plan for your children.

I do not have a separate room for a classroom. Can I home educate my children?

Yes, you can.

Though a separate room might be nice to have, it is not a necessity. The key is not whether you have a "classroom", but whether you have a place for children to use that is well lit, safe, comfortable, and convenient.

Some people put desks in the children's bedrooms. This works particularly well with children who are independent learners and can be trusted to complete their tasks without mom standing over them. It also helps those children who might otherwise be distracted easily by siblings. Often children already have desks in their bedrooms and may not have used them often. Now they can be put to good use.

Some people teach in their kitchen, using the kitchen counter or table for a work place and making room in the corner for a bookshelf for books and materials. Others similarly use the dining room or family room. There may be a few more distractions for you (housework needing to be done) and for your children (toys, TV, food) in these rooms than if you had a designated school room; however, routine use of these rooms for school—and not permitting the distractions to get the best of you—will help you all focus on the task at hand.

Do I have what it takes emotionally to home educate my children?

In your own strength? Probably not.

One mother expressed her fear this way, "Every character flaw in my personality, and every defect, would become apparent under the constant strain." Possibly. If, however, God is the One calling your family to home educate, He will supply what you are lacking spiritually and emotionally. Philippians 4:13 says, "I can do all things through Christ who strengthens me."

Some moms don't feel patient enough to pull it off. Mary Anne Greene, who home teaches four children, testifies to the ongoing challenge.

> Home schooling, at least for this mother, requires heroic perseverance in the practice of deliberately good thoughts and actions, habitually, while keeping the long-term goal of eventually developing permanent virtues fixed firmly in my mind, eagerly awaiting the attendant fruits of those virtues to show their pretty little faces! It's been a struggle, but I have learned my strengths and weaknesses, and how to work all things for a purpose. In some ways I could say I have grown beyond my old self, and sometimes experience the joy that comes with serving and sacrificing.

Remember: patience is something that grows.

Perhaps the very child you gratefully send off to school because of the personality conflict you have with him is the very child who needs you the most. Home education can intensify the conflict; yet, as you rub on each other—which you will do—you will both grow as a result. Perhaps what bothers you about that child is something that bothers you about yourself.

Your relationship will not improve by not being together. Whether the conflict between you and a child is a personality clash or just plain ol' rebellion, dealing with it, rather than running away from it, is the better solution. Remember: God holds you, not a teacher in a school, accountable for your child's training in discipline. Again, the key is doing it in *God's* strength, not your own.

Some moms are concerned they will become lazy and do permanent damage to the education of their children. Though that is possible, it is unlikely. Lazy people typically are not drawn to the formidable task of teaching their children at home. Even if an entire year was, in a sense, wasted, your children would get back on track in no time the next school year. Families who have gone through major crises that greatly impaired their ability to home educate properly for a year have found that their children still tested well at the end of the year. In our school district, a passing grade is anything above 24 percent—you can certainly do better than that!

You love your children and want the best for them—you are highly motivated to teach them well. Remember: you have been teaching them since they were born—keep up the good work and refine it, by the grace of God.

I tried home schooling once and quit. Can I try it again?

Yes, you can.

First, why did you stop? Many reasons parents take a break from home education—the birth of twins, a health crisis for a parent or child, financial difficulty, feeling burned out—may no longer exist. Perhaps you've had a change in life circumstances—it's never too late to resume home education.

Second, if you stopped home educating due to burnout from a particular method, curriculum, or schedule, there's good news— you have *lots* of options. (See Chapters 8 and 10.)

Third, placing your children into institutional schools temporarily may have given you a needed break to regroup. Hindsight may reveal more success academically than you thought at first. Perhaps your goals had not been realistic, but now you are ready to adjust your expectations for a smoother year.

Fourth, you may see now some of the benefits of home education that you did not see before. Lori Bortz, home-educating mother of five, brought her children back to home education after a year-long break.

> Even though school was sufficient, I lost all control of what they were learning, how fast they were learning, and whether or not they were learning something applicable to life. Each child was getting pieces of the puzzle of knowledge, but no one was putting it together for them. I, on the other hand, can keep the big picture in mind and not only teach them the pieces but also explain where they fit.

After a year off, the Bortz family reports an excellent year of home education. They recommend that families who stopped home educating for a time feel free to reevaluate their decision and reconsider the advantages and disadvantages. It might give you a fresh perspective on the best option for the new year. Remember: sometimes it may take more than one year to see the benefits accrue.

How do I avoid burnout?

Make a plan—be flexible—alter the plan—be flexible—make another plan—be flexible. . . . You get the picture.

Burnout occurs when mom and/or the children struggle with feeling stress over school at home. Since our goal is not reproducing school at home but rather home education, let's avoid avoidable stress.

On the one hand, without a schedule, you might feel swamped by all that is not getting done. The more you feel out of control, the more discouraged you become, and your attitude influences the children's attitudes. On the other hand, you may be feeling the kind of stress that precedes burnout due to a rigorous schedule. According to home-education experts Dr. Raymond and Dorothy Moore, authors of numerous books on home education, including *Home School Burnout*, burnout occurs when we lose sight of the goal of home education.

> True home schooling is tutorial, hand made, customized to each child. Such parents respond to their children in a loving, informal way, a balance between systematic structure where needed and a great deal of freedom for youngsters to explore.[11]

The Moores point out the natural tendency for us to educate our children at home the same way we ourselves were educated. However, we need to think through our experience—what worked and what didn't—before importing that into our home education.

> Since most of us were taught in conventional schools, we have a strong tendency to teach the way we were taught. This method is

[11] Raymond S. and Dorothy N. Moore, *Home School Burnout* (Brentwood, TN: Wolgemuth & Hyatt Publishers, 1988), p. 15.

generally rigid, detailed, and includes many textbooks, work-books, tests, and long hours. But if parents are sensitive to the developmental needs of their children and note their response to heavy structure and pressure, they will move toward a more flexible approach. Books will be used as resources more than texts, skills will be used largely in connection with projects or units of study, and meaningful dialogue will abound.[12]

Sometimes curricula written specifically for home educators repeat failed classroom techniques and transport that experience into our homes. The Moores warn, "Parents and children quickly burn out from several hours of dull routine a day with little opportunity for exploration and working out their own creative ideas."[13]

Let's capitalize on the delight our children naturally have toward learning—don't let drudgery dull their enthusiasm. Sometimes moms pack their schedule with so many hours of seat work that they think they cannot afford the time for a field trip! If you find yourself in that place, it's time to reevaluate your program. Number one, you are not a slave to your curriculum—it is there to serve you. Number two, you need a schedule that is flexible enough to alter for a field trip without feeling guilty about time not spent at desks.

Sometimes mental or intellectual exhaustion is preceded by physical neglect. Keep an eye on your family's nutrition and the amount of fresh air, sunshine, and exercise you get. This is true for mom as well as the children.

Evaluate how you are doing with basic discipline and training. Perhaps you feel overwhelmed by discipline struggles you have with one or more of your children. "Open your heart to your children and demonstrate the constructive discipline and selfless, unconditional love that is so essential for your child's development."[14] Remember: character building is an important aspect of the education you are providing your children.

[12] Ibid., p. 107.
[13] Ibid., p. 17.
[14] Ibid., p. 100.

For those of us who have perfectionist temperaments, we must be careful. Moderation in all things should become our motto. We must accept our limitations, under the circumstances, because no plan will go exactly according to our expectations—there are too many human factors at work. We can lessen how stressed we feel if we remember this: even when things are not going according to our plan, they are still going according to God's plan. It helps to set goals, but let's remember to commit those plans into God's hands and trust Him with the outcome.

If you feel as if you are on the edge of burnout, take some time for prayer and reflection. Hire a sitter, if need be, for the kind of time that will help you regain perspective as to why it is you began this venture in the first place.

Jot down ideas from this book and try them. Compare notes with other home-schooling moms and see what works for them. Mix fun with your work—if you are not bored, most likely your children won't be either. If you must change curricula, even in the middle of the year, do so. It could be that you have too many subject areas and should cut back on the hours seat work is taking. Perhaps you are overconcentrating on one area—academics—to the neglect of other areas of home education.

One of the most important ways you can avoid burnout is talking things over with your spouse. Keep him abreast of what is difficult for you or your children. Ask his advice. He may have the necessary detachment to see solutions that are right under your nose. If he is the one suggesting a simpler schedule or more free time for you, take advantage of it.

If you already feel burned out, we highly recommend you get a copy of the Moores' book *Home School Burnout* for lots of practical advice and numerous personal examples of those who have come back from burnout. It's not too late to enjoy home education!

My teen is having difficulty adjusting to home education. He
was very popular at school and does not like being with
siblings all day. What can I do?

Get a sitter, and, with your spouse, take your teen out to his favorite eatery. Have a specific agenda in mind (with the ground rule of respectful conversation at all times): share reasons you believe home education is so important to this young person, and listen to his concerns, fears, and frustrations. The point of the discussion is not for him to dissuade you from your decision for home education but to improve your communication, making home education benefit from both sides giving a better effort.

Tell your teen the specific benefits you see in this new direction for him. Stress the flexibility he will have in his studies—mixing necessary academics with subjects he's always wanted to study but was unable to get in school. He will have more time free for learning an instrument, working part-time, being with friends (without homework hanging over his head), or pursuing hobbies.

Listen carefully to his perceived needs. Pray for creative solutions to the problems he mentions. Perhaps he needs some time alone with you or your spouse or some private time away from siblings during the day.

Take seriously his desire to be with friends. Express your willingness to drive him to their homes so they can have time together, since they will not be seeing each other in class. Tell him you will work with him on special field trips with other teens who are being home educated. Perhaps he can accompany your spouse on some business trips. Communicate how endless the possibilities are.

Finally, work with him on incentives that will motivate him to accomplish assigned schoolwork quickly and neatly. This will lessen the pressure you feel and help him assume more of the burden of achieving his own goals. His growth in self-motivation will bless the entire family's home-education endeavor.

What to Say When People Say . . .

"Why not give your children's education to a competent teacher?"

"I can, but I would rather become a competent teacher for my children. I can show you some statistics about how well home-educated children have done academically, if you are interested in the facts."

Remember: nothing succeeds like success, and time helps demonstrate your success.

"Maybe you're interested in home educating your children because your friends are doing it—because of peer pressure."

"It's actually helpful that you've raised this concern. Part of the reason we are making this choice is that we do not want our children unduly influenced by their peers. In making our decision to home educate, we don't want to do the same thing.

"Our friends who home educate have not only set a good example for us, but they have given us literature to read so that we are basing our decision on well-thought-out reasons. Peer support should not be misinterpreted as peer pressure, especially when peers are influencing good choices.

"Though home education is gaining in popularity, especially among Catholics, it's not a fad; rather it's a return to the way education has occurred throughout the centuries for millions of people, many of whom had far less money and a weaker educational background than we do. We offer academics as part of a broader education in life, rather than the narrower offering from an institutional school."

Remember: criticisms often help us be more thoughtful in our reflection on the reasons for our decisions. A decision to home educate our children cannot be based on what our peers are doing but rather on what is best for our family.

"Your child will miss out on so much. I'm just concerned for his well-rounded education."

"True—our children will miss out on a number of things: exposure to drugs; sex education taught as if it were value-free; peer pressure regarding clothes, music, and possessions; exposure to students' disrespect toward authority; and foul language from students and sometimes adults.

"Seriously, if you are referring to music, sports, field trips, or other extracurricular activities, let me share something. There are many opportunities for private lessons for various instruments in our area, and the local parish includes home schoolers in the children's choir. Sports teams are available through the community in general, including some public schools that opened their teams to home schoolers this year. We had more field trips this year than our school district for several reasons: we chaperon, provide transportation, and take the insurance risk for accidents.

"Local science fairs, the National Geography Bee, the National Spelling Bee, and many other competitions are now open to home-educating families. The possibilities in home education are limited only by our lack of creativity.

"Tell me again, what will our children be missing?"

"What are you going to do if your child wants to return to a conventional school?"

"Our child must take seriously our decision for home education, and we must take his concerns seriously as well.

"First, we must help our child understand that this decision is primarily our responsibility to make, but we cannot make it work without his support. It is important that our child yield his will to ours as a matter of obedience, though he may need time and space to reconcile himself to our decision.

"Second, we should ask our child what he thinks would be missing were we to home school him. Most likely it would be the social, rather than the academic, climate he would miss. We then need to think creatively with him about possible solutions—activities with his friends during off-school hours, field trips with other older students in our home-school support group, and possibly youth-group activities."

*"All you need is an excellent Catholic school. Why can't you
help our parish school be excellent?"*

"I may have some concerns about our parish school, but those are not the primary reasons we are choosing home education. When we assess the environment in which we want our children instructed, the materials we prefer to use, and the benefits of tutoring, we see home education as a positive choice.

"We will support the local school, but we do not think this is the time for our children to attend. We are interested in the school's success and will continue to support it financially through the parish."

Remember: our primary obligation is the solid instruction our children receive whether at school or at home, not how we should support the parish school.

*"If you delay school (or do not send your child to preschool),
your child will be behind."*

"There is no indication that is true. Have you ever heard of Dr. David Elkind? He argues effectively against much of what is touted as 'early education' in terms of psychological and developmental readiness. In fact, he demonstrates in his book, *Miseducation—Preschoolers at Risk*,[15] that 'early education' can be 'miseducation', even to the point of permanently damaging a child's sense of self-worth.

"The goals of preschool education are best accomplished at home with the child having special time with mom. A local school in our area charges $750.00 for preschool, and their supposedly

[15] Dr. David Elkind, *Miseducation: Preschoolers at Risk* (New York: Alfred A. Knopf, 1987).

innovative approach includes group time with three-, four-, and five-year-olds. That's the environment I already have in our home! If I spend a fraction of that amount, I can have lots of fun with the creative curricula I can use with my own children."

"Are you going to home educate all the way through high school? How can you do that? Won't your child miss out on a lot?"

"We are making our decision to home educate this year, and we'll make that choice one year at a time. Our children are not in high school—we'll face that decision when we come to it. If we home school one year, we will not have failed. The goal isn't high school —the goal is having a successful home-school year this year."

Remember: only God knows the future. There's no reason to get into an argument about the future when you don't know what the future holds.

Summary

Each one of us has particular concerns and questions regarding the feasibility of home education for our family. Hopefully this chapter has given you some handles on solutions. If your questions have not been addressed yet, keep reading. God bless you as you search for answers.

PART FOUR

CATHOLIC EDUCATION —
HOMEWARD BOUND

A Vision for Catholic Family Life

Catholic parents today face real challenges in understanding and living faithful Catholic family life. Some of us were raised in close-knit, orthodox Catholic families who prayed together, studied the Faith so they could live it better, and appreciated the sacramental life together. The rest of us were raised with a different religious upbringing, be it nominal Catholic, nominal or faithful Protestant, Orthodox, agnostic, or even atheistic.

All of us can learn more about being a strong Catholic family. And unless we set goals for our families, we may simply repeat our own experience of family life, good or bad. However, if we develop a vision for Catholic family life, anything is possible. Through Catholic home education, we can implement this vision for family life—a vision that is much broader than, but certainly includes, academic excellence. We can all gain a better understanding of God's design for our families, regardless of our backgrounds in religious training.

First, we look to Jesus to set the agenda for our families. When He was asked what commandment was the most important in the entire Scripture, He responded, "You shall love the Lord your God with all of your heart, and with all of your soul, and with all of your mind." How can we, as individuals and as parents, lead our families to love God with our heart, soul, mind, and strength (Dt 6:5)?

15

A Mother's Guide to the Sacraments

And I am sure that He who began a good work in you will bring it to completion at the day of Jesus Christ (Phil 1:6).

The sacraments are the primary channels of God's grace to begin the good work of salvation in us through Baptism and to bring it to completion in a holy death. The sacraments are not mere symbols of grace. They are the means God uses to impart grace—His own life—within us. Let's look briefly at how the seven sacraments provide grace for us and for our children so that we can faithfully love God with all of our heart.

Baptism

When we hold our newborn babes, it's hard to imagine that already there is distance between our child and God because of the sin of his or her great-great . . . grandparents, Adam and Eve. How thankful we are that God initiated the restoration of His relationship to our child through Baptism.

God calls us to bring Him our little one in the sacrament of Baptism so that, by water and the Spirit (Jn 3:5), he will be reborn to eternal life. Baptism washes away the stain of original sin (Titus 3:5) and restores our children as God's children with the gifts of faith, hope, and love.

This is just the beginning; it is a foretaste—but not a guarantee—of heaven. Just as our children anticipate inheriting from us, so baptized children of God anticipate inheriting eternal life from their heavenly Father. However, in both cases, they must mature as faithful and obedient children in order to inherit. On the one hand, inheritance is not the same as wage earnings; on the other hand, it can be lost due to faithlessness and disobedience.

St. Peter compares Baptism to Noah's ark (1 Pet 3:20–22). All of the people on board were saved at the time of the flood, but at least one of them—Ham, Noah's son—abandoned the faith later on. Likewise, St. Peter refers to the people of Israel who were "baptized into Moses", but due to their unfaithfulness to God, they were "overthrown in the wilderness" (1 Cor 10:1–5). We must not presume upon the grace of Baptism but rather build on it with maturing faith.

Baptizing our helpless infants is a wonderful picture for us—and for our older children—that God is the One who transforms us. After all, we did not initiate our rebirth by Baptism any more than we initiated our natural birth. "We love because He first loved us" (1 Jn 4:19).

Confession

No matter how wonderful you and your spouse are, at times selfishness or a lack of charity disrupts the peace and joy of the home. And no matter how adorable children are, at times they push, shove, call each other names, and defiantly disobey. All of us demonstrate the effects of original sin, even though we have been baptized to remove original sin from our souls. When disharmony occurs in our home, we ask for forgiveness of each other and make amends. When disharmony results between God and us, we gratefully go to Confession for reconciliation.

First, we approach God, truly sorry for our sin. This is not the same as remorse for the consequences of our sin or regret that we got caught doing wrong. True contrition means that we have sincere sorrow for rejecting God's love and goodness, and we have a firm intention to change.

Next, we confess our particular sins—no vague apology accepted—to the priest who stands in the place of Christ, the One to whom we confess our sins and who prays for us. Then, we hear the wonderful words of absolution. Later, if we are tempted to wonder whether or not God has forgiven us, we can recall the objective event of this sacrament—"I know that I am forgiven because Christ has absolved me from my sins."

Finally, we are given a penance to help repair the damage our sin has caused. The penance is not proportionate to our crimes. For example, for the sin of lust, the penance might be five Hail Marys! But we are given the opportunity to demonstrate our ongoing sorrow and to participate in healing the breach caused by our sin. Sometimes, as Americans, we are so individualistic that we do not see how our failures affect others. Similarly, we often miss how much our sins have wounded the Body of Christ.

This is an example of how God our heavenly Father parents us with great love. For we know that good discipline of our children means more than their saying the words "I'm sorry." They need to mean they are really sorry when they say it, and they need to prove they are sorry by making amends.

For example, a young boy spray-painted terrible things about his father around town. When he repented, he did more than ask for forgiveness—he painted over those mean words, and he told people good things about his dad. He repaired the damage he had caused and thereby strengthened his relationship to his father.

Some people ask, Is it necessary to go to a priest? Can't I just tell God I am sorry for my sins and trust He will forgive me? First, we go to Confession because we are commanded to go. "Therefore confess your sins to one another, and pray for one another, that you may be healed. The prayer of a righteous man has great power in its effects" (James 5:16).

Second, we can always tell God we're sorry for our sins—the sooner the better—but one of the effects of sin is our difficulty in being totally sorry or in fully intending never to sin again. The sacrament perfects our intentions so that we can be forgiven completely. We must remember that we are very young children in relationship to God. Like a toddler who cannot totally clean his own dirty diaper, our efforts to confess sins privately are inadequate. We should examine our conscience and confess our sins daily and lead our children to do so as well. In addition, we need the transforming forgiveness that flows from the sacrament of Reconciliation. What a deal! We bring our sin, and we leave with sanctifying grace that empowers us to live in a way that pleases our Lord. Rather than Confession being the time God exacts His pound of flesh for the ways we have sinned against Him, it is His gift of love to us.

But is Confession necessary when we haven't committed any serious sins, like infidelity or murder? Confession is God's provision to restore our relationship to Him. Whether or not they are serious sins, our breaches of charity wound our souls and weaken our relationship to God. We need God to remedy the situation.

How strong would our relationship to our spouse be if we apologized only for major offenses and ignored the countless small ways we fail in our love? Daily we commit sins and we omit acts of charity we ought to do. These unconfessed sins against God and others can make our spiritual vision cloudy; Confession helps us see God and ourselves clearly. We want and need that clarity of spiritual vision so that we can grow in grace.

A few years ago, Catholic schools provided a regular time for Confession for schoolchildren, but today many schools do not. We are the ones responsible for taking our children for regular Confession so they can receive the grace they need (and we need them to have) to live their lives in a way pleasing to God. Regular Confession takes planning—home education makes planning for Confession easier.

Like us, they only *have* to go once a year, according to canon law. But if Confession is like a spiritual bath, just think how much we could stink in a year's time! (That goes for our children, too.) Let's not go for the minimum but, rather, for the maximum, since our goal is holiness. Many spiritual directors encourage Confession once a month, or more often, both for us and for our children.

Frequent Confession strengthens our resolve and makes our conscience more sensitive to those areas of sin in our lives on which we need focused prayer and attention. It is especially helpful to have a regular confessor. He can discern patterns of sin and reveal them to us. He can identify specific points of wisdom for spiritual growth in our lives and hold us accountable regularly for our response to his spiritual direction.

We all know how important accountability can be when we are on a diet—trying not to eat some foods and trying to do certain things. It makes a difference when we know we will be weighed weekly; it makes it easier to see progress or deal with the lack of progress in keeping the weight problem in check. Likewise, there is accountability with a confessor who knows our struggles, prays for us, and monitors our progress spiritually on a frequent basis.

It's also important to encourage our children to have a regular confessor who can give them suggestions for countering a pattern of temptations. When our children are old enough, a spiritual director can help them mount a planned attack against the vices in their lives and the obstacles in their relationships with God and counsel them in growing in virtue. We should remind our children how crucial full repentance and true forgiveness are.

We must not get discouraged with slow progress. One man said, "I don't know why I bother writing a list of sins every time. I ought to just photocopy it." We can feel this way sometimes, too. However, it's important to realize that even if we are struggling with the same sins regularly, the fact that we are going to Confession with the intention of not committing those sins again, doing penances, and acquiring more grace to strengthen us *is* progress.

It is crucial for our children to see our positive response to the opportunity for Confession. It is not an awful thing that Catholics have to do; it is a privilege to know we are loved and forgiven so completely by our Lord.

We model forgiveness and repentance in our own lives through frequent Confession, spiritual direction, seeking forgiveness from others when we offend them, and by forgiving our children and spouse the way God forgives us. Complete forgiveness is not optional; it is a commandment of Jesus Himself. Our children will become more eager for Confession when they see us go with a thankful heart and return humble and penitent.

Eucharist

First and foremost, the Eucharist is the gift of Christ Himself to us. Jesus became man so he could be the perfect sacrifice for our sins through His life, death, and Resurrection. Then He took that gift of Himself into the Holy of Holies of heaven as the perpetual, once-for-all sacrifice on our behalf. During the Mass, God transforms the bread and wine on the altar, through the ministry of the priest, into that very same Body and Blood of our crucified and risen Lord Jesus Christ that is in heaven.

We then receive Christ into our bodies, making us living tabernacles. Through the Eucharist He empowers us to go out into the world and live the sacrificial life to which He has called us. (What a precious gift it is to receive the Lord when we are expecting a baby; our child is so close to Him!)

We help our children love God by taking them with us to meet Him in the Eucharist. It may challenge our sanctity at times, but it is so important that we bring our little ones to Jesus for a blessing (like the mothers did as recorded in the Gospels). They are in His presence, and their hearts are touched by the Sacrifice of the Mass in ways we do not perceive. Sometimes when people stare at us (or even glare) because the sounds of our young ones disturb their meditation, we feel bad for having brought them. But Jesus told His disciples to let the little ones come to Him, telling them that their littleness was a reminder of how childlike all disciples are to be.

Sometimes people dilute the Church's teaching on the sacrificial nature of the Mass because they do not believe children can understand it. Children may not understand the unbloody sacrifice on the altar, but they can appreciate the mystery of Jesus' sacrifice, and they can learn to offer their worship through the Eucharist as reparation for sin. By virtue of their baptism they are part of the priesthood of all believers. Thus their participation in the Mass—assisting in the Offering of the Sacrifice—is an act of their priesthood.

There is so much about life children do not comprehend; consequently they struggle less with mystery than adults often do. For their sake, don't downplay Jesus' sacrifice of perfect obedience, even to death on the Cross. Share the truth—live the truth—of this mystery, and eventually your children will grasp the significance of God's work for them and in them.

Pope John Paul II has stated in his "Letter to Families",

> There is no other power and no other wisdom by which you, parents, can educate both your children and yourselves. The educational power of the Eucharist has been proved down the generations and centuries.[1]

Not only can we receive Jesus in the Eucharist, but we can also come before the tabernacle and adore our crucified, risen, and ascended Lord in the Blessed Sacrament.

We should teach these things to our children, especially as we prepare them for First Communion. Will the emphasis be the celebration of the Mass or the celebration afterward? Will the focus be the presence of Christ in the Eucharist or the presents received later?

Recently, a young boy preparing for First Communion was diagnosed with cancer. One session of treatments ended the day before the special Mass. Though he was weak, he did not want to miss Mass. After receiving the Host, he returned to his family. But his mouth was so dry from treatments, he did not have the saliva to swallow. So his father had him take the Host out of his mouth and place the Host in his hand. Then the father kissed it and consumed it. This was a father who had helped prepare his son and who demonstrated that he believed what he had taught. This was a young boy who knew what First Communion meant.

Just as our family is strengthened when we take time to eat meals together, so the larger Family of God is strengthened when we meet at the table of the Lord to eat the heavenly food He has provided—His very own Body and Blood (Jn 6:53–63).

Around the dinner table our sense of community is strengthened when we appreciate the food that has been provided and enjoy

---

[1] John Paul II, "Letter to Families", no. 18.

conversation. Likewise, our sense of community within the Church grows when we appreciate the sacrificial meal provided for us by Jesus through the priest. We appreciate the unity we have in Christ since we have received the Bread of Life together.

When we take time to give thanks, rather than bolting from the table at home, we honor the one who has so generously provided for our hunger. So also, when we take time to thank our Lord for His gracious gift to us, rather than trying to beat everyone out to the parking lot, we honor the One who has so generously provided for all of our needs, most importantly our spiritual food.

If Jesus is the food of our souls, some people are on a starvation diet! In contrast, when we make attendance at Mass a priority, our children experience the reality and the vitality of our faith. Sometimes children question the need to attend Mass more often than just on Sundays. Our response: "We don't *have* to go more often; we *get* to."

Sometimes there are difficulties in getting to daily Mass, but if we can add one more daily Mass than we are currently attending, that would make a difference. It is possible to fit daily Mass into our schedules in the midst of a typical school day, but it is much easier to plan academics around Mass and Confession schedules when we home school. Let's not miss the opportunity we have to bring our little ones to the Lord at Mass—there are so few years we can schedule this with them, and those years are passing quickly.

Confirmation

Through the sacrament of Confirmation we are called into a deeper commitment to Christ as Lord of our lives. We receive new spiritual strength at a time that new physical abilities are developing. The power of God is released in a deeper way than ever before when we are sealed by the Holy Spirit. St. Paul says,

> In him you also, who have heard the word of truth, the gospel of your salvation, and have believed in him, were sealed with the

promised Holy Spirit, which is the guarantee of our inheritance until we acquire possession of it, to the praise of his glory (Eph 1:13–14).

Through Confirmation, we become soldiers for Christ, commissioned to bring the good news of the Gospel to others, no matter what the cost.

We do not see home schooling as building a bunker where we can huddle down, hoping the enemy won't come over. Instead, home is the place where we prepare for spiritual warfare so that through us the Church will overcome the world. We do not foster a fortress mentality, building the walls high enough so that the world cannot scale them. Rather, we are gathering the necessary strength, through virtue and knowledge, to conquer the world for Christ by the power of the Holy Spirit.

A remnant mentality does not express faith, hope, or love. Jesus said to Peter, "And I tell you, you are Peter, and on this rock I will build my Church, and the gates of Hades shall not prevail against it" (Mt 16:18). The picture is not one of the Church standing strong against the attack of hell's gates. To the contrary, He gave us our marching orders; we know the outcome before the battle begins—we are more than conquerors through Christ, and hell's gates won't be able to stand in our way!

Earlier this century when a bishop confirmed children, he gave them a slap on their cheeks. Why? He reminded them to yield to the Lordship of Christ, no matter what suffering that might entail—humiliation, difficulties, and even death. And he anointed them for empowerment by the Holy Spirit so that they would be faithful. What a total contrast to peer-dominated situations where children feel pressured to conform!

Parents must resist the temptation to misuse this sacrament by delaying it until late in high-school years, just to keep children attending CCD and Mass. Children need the grace of this sacrament to meet the challenges of adolescence, to channel their argumentativeness into apologetics, and to remain pure. So many teens today wonder about the worth of their existence, their reason for living. We must challenge them: Commit your lives to Jesus Christ—*He* is Someone worth living (and even dying) for.

The essence of the Christian moral life, writes John Paul II in his 1993 encyclical *The Splendor of Truth*, "is not a matter only of disposing oneself to hear a teaching and obediently accepting a commandment. More radically, it involves *holding fast to the very person of Jesus. . . .*"[2] The crucial element in helping our children embrace the morality taught by Christ and His Church is leading them to a personal relationship with our Lord Jesus Christ.

Christian moral principles that are not embedded in a deep relationship with Jesus—knowing Him intimately, loving Him deeply, and serving Him personally—are doomed to crumble under the bulldozer driven by popular culture. Morality becomes a list of unconvincing "dos and don'ts" that are eventually tossed aside if they are ultimately unconnected to the reason—Jesus Himself.

A dorm director for a large Catholic university encountered many students whose sense of morality was based largely on a spiritual "to do" list and an intellectual acceptance of what was right and wrong, rather than a heartfelt relationship with the Lord. Most of these students eventually compromised, to a greater or lesser extent, the moral code that their good Catholic parents had raised them to believe. Their good intentions were not rooted deeply enough to withstand the stress of new temptations, intellectual challenges, and growing independence. Parents, bewildered and anguished at their children's immorality, sadly failed to grasp that true morality requires more than simply knowing or understanding something intellectually—it requires continuing conversion of the heart. The sacrament of Confirmation should be a public testimony of that kind of conversion.

---

[2] *The Splendor of Truth* (*Veritatis Splendor*), no. 19.

The Two Sacraments of Vocation:
Holy Orders and Holy Matrimony

When college students are asked whether or not they have a vocation, the answer is often, "No, I want to get married."

Something is missing in their understanding of vocation.

The choice is not, Do I want to be holy, or do I want to get married? Rather, the question is, Is God calling me to be holy as a celibate person or as a married person? By virtue of our Baptism, we are all called to holiness, whether our vocation is consecrated celibacy (possibly culminating in Holy Orders) or whether it is Holy Matrimony.

Before the "sexual revolution", Catholic writers referred to the development of the power to create new life as the paternal or the maternal drive (instead of the sex drive). When we see mature womanhood as motherhood and mature manhood as fatherhood, we see God's gift of our sexuality in a new light. Rather than asking ourselves if we want to enjoy our sexuality or throw it away, we ask the Lord how He desires us to express our sexuality in the most fruitful and sacrificial way to strengthen the Church.

The same qualities that make a faithful spouse and a good mother or father apply to whatever vocation God has for each one of us. When we teach our daughters to be faithful, hospitable, nurturing, gracious, tender, loving, and helpful, we are training them to be great wives and mothers. When we teach our sons to be good providers, faithful and self-disciplined men, encouragers, and servant leaders who balance power and loving sacrifice, we are training them to be great husbands and fathers. This focus should help us prepare our children for whatever is God's will for their lives as they yield the power of their sexuality to Him.

For those who choose consecrated celibacy, they channel their energy into spiritual parenting. St. Paul speaks of the benefits of consecrated celibacy in 1 Corinthians 7:32–35. The unmarried person is free from many worldly concerns and, therefore, can give the Lord undivided devotion and service. Consecrated celibates relinquish their right to earthly goods for the sake of the Kingdom of God. They are a sign for all of us, pointing us to the next life, where people will not marry.

In particular, the vocation of the priesthood is a call to spiritual fatherhood. Jesus refers to priests as "eunuchs for the sake of the Kingdom of God" (Mt 19:12). Eunuchs guarded the king's bride; so Jesus calls priests to protect, cleanse, and care for the Bride of Christ, the Church.

We must pray for our brothers and sisters who have chosen consecrated celibacy and in particular for those men who father us as priests and bishops. Their decision is a great sacrifice—something the world mocks and some in the Church trivialize because they do not understand. Let's acknowledge that sacrifice.

In addition, let's not criticize those God has set in authority over us in the Church, so that we guard our children's hearts (and our own) from cynicism. Instead, in a spirit of humility, let's pray for the priests and bishops to be united with our Holy Father, encourage them by our love and hospitality, and follow them as they lead the Family of God.

For those of us with the vocation of marriage, we become holy through faithfulness to our spouse. Faithfulness means so much more than not cheating on our spouse. It means growing in faith together, sharing in our spiritual life as well as our material goods.

> "For this reason a man shall leave his father and mother and be joined to his wife, and the two shall become one." This is a great mystery, and I take it to mean Christ and the Church (Eph 5:31–32).

St. Paul says marriage is a *musterion* (Greek for mystery), which is translated *sacramentum* in Latin (meaning sacrament). In Christ, marriage is elevated to the status of a sacrament. By virtue of our Baptism, we are the ministers of this sacrament. We reflect the mystery of the unity of Christ and His Bride, the Church, in each of our marriages.

We demonstrate our oneness when we renew the covenant through the marital act. This is especially true when the two become one so that the one is so real, nine months later we have to give it a name. We, too, take the powerful gift of our sexuality and give it to the Lord so that we honor Him. As we cooperate with His grace, He blesses our union with godly offspring (Mal 2:15). In total self-donation to each other and to the Lord, we demonstrate the life-giving power of love by divine design.

We must yield ourselves—time, talents, money, and, yes, our bodies—to the Lord as living sacrifices for our spouse and our children. This goal gives us many opportunities to grow in sanctity. Daily we submit our wills to the Lord in service to others, sacrificing our own desires: the father who plays catch with an eager three-year-old rather than resting after a busy day at work; the mother who spends afternoon hours car-pooling children to practices and events; the son who spends time explaining to a sister how to play baseball when he would rather play; and the daughter who makes a dessert for the family before calling a friend.

The meaning of married life is to form an interpersonal communion of life and love out of which flows the gift of life. We honor our spouse by living in harmony with the teachings of the Church regarding contraception. To renew the marital covenant *and* to contracept is tantamount to lying to each other with our bodies: I give myself totally to you and you to me, but I intend to destroy, if possible, that part of you that creates new life (i.e., the sperm and/or the egg). Instead, the Church calls us to keep every act of marriage open to new life and to cherish the children He graciously gives us.

As stated earlier, in the sermon by St. John Chrysostom, parents are the primary educators of their children in spiritual matters, especially character formation, as well as in academics. We teach our little ones by word and deed as we live the sacramental life and share our faith in our families. In imitation of the Holy Family, we consider everything we do as a family, no matter how mundane or routine, to be valuable.

God has given us spouses as primary channels of grace to us and us to them. At times, we are overwhelmed by the magnitude of our commitment to faithfulness, "in joy and in sorrow, in sickness and in health, for richer or poorer 'til death do us part". When we fail, as we will, the sacraments of Confession and the Eucharist fortify us, unclogging that channel so that grace flows to the family members through us again. This is the path of growth in holiness that we walk in Holy Matrimony.

Anointing of the Sick

For serious illness, God has provided the sacrament of the Anointing of the Sick. "This grace is a gift of the Holy Spirit, who renews trust and faith in God and strengthens against the temptations of the evil one, the temptation to discouragement and anguish in the face of death."[3] According to James 5:14–16, the combination of the priest's praying for and hearing the Confession of a person brings healing—spiritually and sometimes physically.

The difficulties we will face in the midst of suffering and dying give us special opportunities either to respond to grace and suffer for Christ, uniting ourselves to this saving work, or to reject grace and begin the downward spiral of doubt, anguish, and despair. The sacrament of Anointing of the Sick will strengthen us to endure suffering, granting us peace and courage to be faithful to the end. What a contrast between the Church's teaching of the value of uniting our sufferings with Christ's work versus the relativists' teaching in many schools that suffering is meaningless and suicide or euthanasia is merciful!

When we face death, we prepare for our homecoming.

> [The Anointing of the Sick] completes the holy anointings that mark the whole Christian life: that of Baptism which sealed the new life in us, and that of Confirmation which strengthened us for the combat of this life. This last anointing fortifies the end of our earthly life like a solid rampart for the final struggles before entering the Father's house.[4]

As we receive the Eucharist during this final sacrament, we echo the words of the Mass, "And may the Body of Christ bring us to

[3] *Catechism of the Catholic Church*, no. 1520.
[4] Ibid., no. 1523.

everlasting life. Amen." Both meanings apply—both the Body of Christ in the Eucharist and the Church as the Body of Christ, represented in the priest, bring us to everlasting life.

From new birth in Baptism to a holy death through the Anointing of the Sick, the Lord has given us His grace in the sacraments. He imparts His life to us so that we can grow as His sons and daughters. When we live the sacramental life and lead our children to understand and embrace that life, we know and love God as a family.

Sacraments—Channels of Grace

1. Baptism washes away the stain of original sin (Titus 3:5) and restores us as God's children with the gifts of faith, hope, and love.

2. The sacrament of Reconciliation restores our relationship to God through repentance, absolution, and penance. Frequent Confession strengthens our resolve and makes our conscience more sensitive to those areas of sin in our lives on which we need focused prayer and attention.

3. The Sacrifice of the Mass is the transformation of the bread and wine on the altar, through the ministry of the priest, into that very same Body and Blood of our crucified and risen Lord Jesus Christ. Through the Eucharist He empowers us to go out into the world and live the sacrificial life to which He has called us.

4. Through the sacrament of Confirmation we are sealed by the Holy Spirit and are called to a deeper commitment to Christ as Lord of our lives.

5. The two sacraments of vocation, Holy Matrimony and Holy Orders, call us to make a mature gift of ourselves in service to the Lord and His Church. Both require covenantal faithfulness and fruitfulness, spiritually for both and physically for most married couples.

6. The Anointing of the Sick provides a special grace that "unites the sick person to the Passion of Christ, for his own good and that of the whole Church".[5] In combination with the sacraments of Confession and the Eucharist for spiritual and physical healing, it prepares us to suffer for Christ and to be with Him in eternity.

7. The sacraments are God's gracious provision for us to mature as His sons and daughters so that we can enjoy Him now and prepare to be with Him forever.

---

[5] *Catechism of the Catholic Church*, no. 1532.

16

A Mother's Guide
to Character Formation

Do you sometimes feel overworked and underprayed? The demands of being a wife and mom or a husband and dad can be overwhelming. It is not enough to receive the grace of the sacraments—we must respond to that grace. As we respond, our desire grows to be with God and to become like Him in the character of our souls. This cannot happen apart from individual prayer time.

The Importance of Prayer

If our own spiritual reservoir runs dry of His wisdom, His guidance, and His love, we will have nothing within ourselves for our children. "Following Christ is not an outward imitation . . . , it touches man at the very depths of his being",[1] and it is possible only through the power of the Holy Spirit.[2] If we do not spend time alone in conversation with God (not just rote or scripted prayers), how can we develop our relationship with Him?

We know that in our relationship with our spouse, we want intimacy, speaking heart to heart about what matters most. If we simply exchange schedules or go over "to do" lists, we reduce our relationship significantly. If we want deeper love, we must spend some uninterrupted time together. Likewise, if our intimacy with God is to deepen, we need to spend at least ten to fifteen minutes each day in conversational prayer.

---

[1] *The Splendor of Truth* (*Veritatis Splendor*), no. 21.
[2] Ibid., no. 22.

If we do not make time with God a priority, how can we exhort our children to do so? Consciously or unconsciously, they will suspect that faith and the spiritual life amount to the pious things we *do* rather than a relationship we have with Jesus that calls us to do His will out of an intimate and simple love for Him.

Since we want our children to have an interior prayer life, we must set the example for them, and we must teach them how to pray, not just how to "say prayers". We guide our children as they share with their Creator in their own words what is important to them. We encourage them, even at a young age, to listen as God speaks to their hearts and minds. We know that the devil can tempt children; yet sometimes we find it hard to believe that the Holy Spirit can inspire our children. We must remember that a child's relationship with God, although "kid-sized", can be deep and loving.

As children move into the teen years, it is even more important that they know how to dialogue with God. A teen who has never spoken to the Lord more intimately than by reciting rote prayers or tossing a "please help me succeed" heavenward every once in a while will not likely turn to the Lord with his deepest problems for guidance, no matter how much doctrine he knows. It would be as difficult as having a heart-to-heart talk with an earthly father whose only communication with you was an occasional "Good game!" or a regular exchange of greeting cards.

A date with our spouse will happen if we designate a time and a place. Likewise, prayer time is more likely to occur if we designate a particular place in our homes where we typically meet for prayer. One thing some families do is make a family altar with pictures of Jesus, candles, a crucifix, and other religious articles. This family altar reminds the family of the importance of prayer.

Some examples of prayer that we have found helpful are the following: a morning act of consecration; prayer for Christians and, in particular, priests and bishops of a different country every day (Youth with a Mission has an excellent book that helps us called *Operation: World*; see Appendix C); spontaneous prayers through-out the day as the need arises (a siren always signals us that someone is in need of prayer); the Stations of the Cross; the Divine Mercy

Chaplet at 3:00 P.M.; a spiritual communion some time each day; an after-dinner decade of the rosary or a complete rosary as a family; special novenas for particular concerns; and an evening examination of conscience.[3]

We all need time with our Lord so we can become more like Him. Our children should have regular times for prayer so that their souls can become more Christlike. Then we follow up that time they have spent with God to form their character in godliness.

We might hope a classroom instructor would, with the same love and authority we have, guide our children in their character development. This is not realistic. A typical teacher has many other goals for class time. He can intervene when there is a problem, but the teacher cannot guide the development of virtue specifically needed for each child.

So, how do *we* go about doing this? We draw on the wisdom of the Church to know what virtues we should have and how to cultivate them in our young ones. We take great care (in terms of food, clothing, shelter, and sleep) for our children's physical bodies, which will die. How much more concern should we take for the care of their souls, which will live for eternity!

How Bad Habits Are Identified and Changed

When we mention bad habits, most people think of biting nails, sucking a thumb, or interrupting conversations. What we are discussing here, though, are the sinful habits that develop into vices, as well as the virtues that can replace those vices.

Throughout this journey of faith, we struggle in developing virtues and resisting vices. St. John identifies the sources of those struggles.

> For all that is in the world, the lust of the flesh and the lust of the eyes and the pride of life, is not of the Father but is of the world.

[3] Leaflet Missal Company sells a packet of sixty-five 5" x 8" cards with a variety of prayers and theological teachings, one per card. The print is large—very suitable for posting for family members to memorize. Leaflet Missal Company, telephone (800) 328-9582.

And the world passes away, and the lust of it; but he who does the will of God abides for ever (1 Jn 2:16–17).

The "Lust of the Flesh"

The "lust of the flesh" is our tendency to satisfy the desires of our flesh at the expense of our souls. As St. Paul says, "we all once lived in the passions of our flesh, following the desires of body and mind" (Eph 2:3). These desires include not only disordered sensuality but also the kind of laxity we have when we choose the most pleasurable way to do something, without regard for being faithful to God.

We must heed St. Peter's warning, "Beloved, I beseech you as aliens and exiles to abstain from the passions of the flesh that *wage war* against your soul" (1 Pet 2:11). For our children, the passions they may need to wrestle with include anger, no matter what the age, and sexual temptations, beginning with early adolescence. It is essential that we help our children control flirtation and develop modesty.

We weaken the tendency toward the "lust of the flesh" by resisting the temptation toward loss of self-control and, when we fail, repenting of our sin. We can arm our children to identify and to resist temptation, especially when they are adolescents and teens, by instructing them about what it means to be tempted, how to handle temptations, and why God allows temptations.

St. Paul's description expresses for our children what they undoubtedly have already experienced: "I do not understand my own actions. For I do not do what I want, but I do the very thing I hate. . . . For I do not do the good I want, but the evil I do not want is what I do" (Rom 7:15, 19). We must offer hope: "God is faithful, and he will not let you be tempted beyond your strength, but with the temptation will also provide the way of escape, that you may be able to endure it" (1 Cor 10:13).

Our own example is most important: when we sin, we humble ourselves to ask God and others for forgiveness. When our children fail, they must see that they have not only displeased us but have offended God by their sin. And if they repent, God will forgive them completely and give them the grace they need to do those things that please Him.

The "Lust of the Eyes"

The "lust of the eyes" is our misuse of and desire for material things for our own use instead of for the glory of God. We desire earthly things rather than spiritual things. The "eyes" see value only in material possessions (leading us to treat even people as objects) and are blind to supernatural realities. In reality, material possessions have limited value in themselves; if used for the glory of God, they can have eternal value.

We weaken the tendency toward the lust of the eyes when we see ourselves as stewards, for the Lord, of all that we have. In reality, we spend His money, we live in His house, we drive His car, and we care for His spouse and children.

We resist a longing to acquire by asking ourselves, How can we better serve our Lord? The answer still might mean buying a bigger home or a new car, but for the right reasons. In addition, practicing tithing and almsgiving helps us keep our perspective on money. Our goal is this: less attachment to our possessions and more of an eternal perspective on temporal things.

Sometimes we fail to see the gravity of materialism when the things we desire are inexpensive. Children are especially prone to this failing, but it is a temptation for all of us. For example, we can acquire an enormous amount of "things" cheaply through yard sales. To guard our hearts from greed and to keep "great deals" in perspective, we always pray for God's protection from temptation as we head out to the first sale.

Even children can "keep a loose grip" on their possessions when they share. We always say, "Jesus gives you this toy so that you can share with others." We teach our children about the needs of others and help them meet those needs through gifts of their toys (St. Nicholas Funds), clothes (the Rescue Mission), and money (giving as an act of worship at Mass).

The "Pride of Life"

The "pride of life" is the same independent self-love and pride that were the downfall of Satan. It is a haughty attitude. Rather than serving others as Christ did, someone can be led by the "pride of life" to look down on others, despising and mistreating them. It is the kind of boastful arrogance that is contrary to love, for "Love is patient and kind; love is not jealous or boastful; it is not arrogant or rude. Love does not insist on its own way; it is not irritable or resentful" (1 Cor 13:4–5).

When we acknowledge our total dependence on God, we are filled with thankfulness for the mercy of God. "Clothe yourselves, all of you, with humility toward one another, for 'God opposes the proud, but gives grace to the humble'" (1 Pet 5:5). Our desire increasingly becomes, "Therefore, whether you eat or drink, or whatsoever else you do, do all to the glory of God" (1 Cor 10:31).

We weaken the tendency toward the pride of life by choosing to serve. Children, too, can give glory to God by their little acts of obedient service: sharing toys and clothes, working with a good attitude, not insisting on their own way when playing with friends, etc. And those little acts form good habits, which, in turn, establish virtue.

Spiritual Warfare

We are in spiritual warfare daily (as are our children), wrestling back and forth between the new creation we are in Christ and our tendency to sin. We also struggle with the devil and his forces, who desire to thwart our spiritual growth by enticing us with temptations.

> For we are not contending against flesh and blood but against the principalities, against the powers, against the world rulers of this present darkness, and against the spiritual hosts of wickedness in the heavenly places (Eph 6:12).

For we know that "Your adversary, the devil, is a roaring lion, who goes about seeking whom he may devour" (1 Pet 5:8–9).

This should not fill us with fear but should be a reminder that our spiritual growth displeases the devil and his forces. In and of ourselves we are not stronger than Satan, but we are to

> Submit yourselves therefore to God. Resist the devil and he will flee from you. Draw near to God and he will draw near to you. Cleanse your hands, you sinners, and purify your hearts, you men of double mind (James 4:7–8).

Through the sacraments, sacramentals, thoughtful prayer, and spiritual direction, we can resist these supernatural forces and change sinful habits. It is not a matter of sheer will power, though we must all exercise our will in resisting sin. Rather, it is a matter of humility before God, acknowledging our weakness and His strength.

Pope John Paul II urges families to ask St. Michael for protection on a daily basis.

> St. Michael, the Archangel, defend us in battle. Be our protection against the wickedness and snares of the devil. May God rebuke him, we humbly pray. And do thou, O prince of the heavenly hosts, by the power of God, cast into hell Satan and all the evil spirits who prowl about the world seeking the ruin of souls.

We need the help of St. Michael to put our struggle back into the hands of our heavenly Father. We must acknowledge our dependence on God, for the battle is the Lord's.

How to Reject Temptations

In addition to prayer, we must tell our children *how* to reject temptations. It might help teens to treat a temptation like an obscene phone call: don't stand there horrified that you've gotten one (or wonder what it's all about). Hang up on it; then take the phone off the hook so repeat calls can't get past the busy signal. In other words, don't analyze or negotiate with it—reject it, put it out of your mind.

Our nature is such that if we tell ourselves not to think about something—like large orange basketballs—that's what we will think about. (You did, didn't you?) Instead we must fill our minds with truth.

> Finally, brethren, whatever is true, whatever is honorable, whatever is just, whatever is pure, whatever is lovely, whatever is gracious, if there is any excellence, if there is anything worthy of praise, think about these things (Phil 4:8).

When we keep our focus on the Lord, He strengthens our resolve to resist temptation.

We also want to assure our children that having a temptation does not mean they have sinned already. Everyone, including Jesus, has been tempted. Rather we need to follow Jesus' example in knowing Scripture well enough that we can recognize temptations for what they are. For example, in the midst of a heated argument, we remember St. James' words in James 1:19–20: "Let every man be quick to hear, slow to speak, and slow to anger, for the anger of man does not work the righteousness of God." Since our anger won't produce the results we really want in this situation, we can change strategies: listen more carefully, say less, and slow down our angry responses.

For another example, whenever we are faced with the temptations of fornication, we are reminded to

> Shun immorality. Every other sin which a man commits is outside the body; but the immoral man sins against his own body. Do you not know that your body is a temple of the Holy Spirit within you, which you have from God? You are not your own; you were bought with a price. So glorify God in your body (1 Cor 6:18–20).

What a critical passage for our children to learn so that they can know what to do with sexual temptations: Flee! And this passage gives the reasons—our bodies belong to the Lord, who paid a dear price for our salvation. These bodies are now dwelling places for the Holy Spirit and should not be defiled by sexual immorality.

How Good Habits Are Formed

Each family member has developed virtues into good habits, such as a generous spirit, a servant heart, an ability as a peacemaker, and a strong sense of justice. And each one of us has some habits that show our ongoing struggle with sin, such as a quick temper, impatience, unkindness, a boasting spirit, and selfishness expressed in a variety of ways. When we begin the process of replacing vice with virtue—in our own lives as parents as well as through our discipline of our children—we realize that quite a bit of training may be involved.

Sometimes new habits are like new shoes that need wearing a while before they feel comfortable as our own—our souls have to grow into these habits. Some days we become discouraged—how many times must we teach the same thing? How many squabbles must we endure before we see the love between siblings grow beyond tattling and nit-picking? We must persist in teaching them wisdom, fortifying that teaching with our earnest prayer and their regular visits to the confessional. We must have the same patience with our young ones as God shows us; after all, God is not finished working on us, either.

Theological Virtues

God places within our souls the theological virtues of faith, hope, and love at Baptism. *Faith* is the response of our reason to the truths of why God has created and redeemed us. We look at creation and know Someone far greater than we is its creator. *Hope* is the response of our will to put our trust in God. We believe that the One who created everything cares for us and wants to redeem us from our sin. *Love* is the response of our soul whereby we are transformed by the love of God so that we become partakers of the divine nature (2 Pet 1:4). "We love because He first loved us" (1 Jn 4:19).

We cannot give these theological virtues to our children, because they are supernatural gifts from God. Nor, for the same reason, can we restore them to our children once they have lost them through their sins. But we can provide the environment in which their use becomes habitual, and we can pray for an increase for both our children and for us.

For just as we cannot give our children more muscles than they have at birth, but we can provide ways to strengthen the muscles they have, so we cannot give our children more of the theological virtues than they received through Baptism, but we can give them opportunities to exercise those virtues so they become stronger. Faith, hope, and love are strengthened in us through the sacraments, doing good works, and prayer.

Our *faith* is strengthened by understanding the reasons we believe what we believe. Catechetics and apologetics are the key. And our faith matures as we deepen our understanding of the Faith and then apply it in good works empowered by grace through the sacraments.

Our *hope* is strengthened by choosing to live a life of ongoing conversion. When we answer the question of whether or not we *know* we are going to heaven, our answer is, "That is my hope." Sometimes that is misinterpreted to mean "That is my wish." What we mean by hope is that God has given us proximate assurance that we are His children and that He will complete in us what He has begun, provided we are faithful children.

Our *charity* is strengthened by imitating God's example of total self-giving love. We see attitudes necessary for true Christian charity by examining 1 Corinthians 13. "So faith, hope, love abide, these three; but the greatest of these is love" (13:13). Charity never ends—it only deepens after our death, when we see face to face the One who has loved us from all eternity.

These supernatural virtues are "foundations of the spiritual life without which salvation is impossible".[4] However, these virtues can be weakened through venial sins and can be lost through mortal sins, just as the misuse of muscles can result in damage or even serious injury requiring a physician's care. When there are

---

[4] K. V. Truhlar, "Virtue", *New Catholic Encyclopedia*, vol. 14 (New York: McGraw-Hill Book Co., 1967): 705–9.

mortal wounds to our soul, we need the healing power of the Great Physician, our Lord Jesus Christ, through Confession. We must remind ourselves and our children of our need to respond to God's grace, especially through the sacrament of Reconciliation.

Cardinal Virtues

Unlike the theological virtues, which are infused supernaturally, the cardinal virtues are acquired. Good habits are the trellises on which the flower of virtues can flourish. Since these virtues can be cultivated, we can set goals for ourselves and our children in each of the four cardinal virtues: prudence, justice, fortitude, and temperance.

The development of the cardinal virtues is somewhat analogous to providing food for our bodies. As food is to the body, so virtue is to the soul. A few comparisons might help us better remember the importance of cultivating them in our children so we can harvest the rich fruit of righteousness.

First, some people have an abundant food supply, while others must work very hard to gather what is needed for survival. Likewise everyone needs to acquire virtue, but the amount of effort each one of us needs to make may vary. In both cases—with food and with virtue—the kind of soil used for planting will make the difference in the abundance of the harvest.

Second, the better the diet, the stronger the person; so the better the training in virtue, the spiritually stronger the person.

Third, food prepared carelessly will not produce the desired effect, in much the same way that hit-or-miss training in virtue will not produce the desired results.

Fourth, too much emphasis on one food to the neglect of others produces an imbalance. Likewise too much emphasis on one virtue while neglecting the others can thwart balanced growth.

Fifth, food can strengthen muscles; so acquired virtues can strengthen the theological virtues.

And sixth, just as food eaten together can strengthen the family so that they can work together, so virtue worked on collectively as a family can strengthen the whole family toward our goal of holiness. (For instance, everyone can look for ways throughout the day to demonstrate prudence and then share at the supper table the results of being more prudent.)

We need the guidance of the Church and the wisdom of Sacred Scripture for developing virtue and constraining vice in our lives and the lives of our children.[5]

Prudence—"Look carefully then how you walk, not as unwise men but as wise, making the most of the time, because the days are evil" (Eph 5:15–16).

Prudence is the virtue that equips us to make good decisions. Prudence assists us in weighing the thoughts, feelings, and motives of ourselves and others against our standard of right and wrong. Then prudence leads us to make a decision based on good judgment. It is the virtue that holds the other virtues in balance, so that we respond rather than merely react to varying circumstances.

We demonstrate prudence when we think through options with deliberation, gather wise advice, and follow through on our plans decisively and without delay. To do this carefully, we must reflect on the past, look at the present, and consider the future. We are helped by wise and mature counselors. And by example we teach our children to value guidance from others they respect, to use discretion, and to make prudent decisions.

Prudence restrains us from jumping to conclusions, thereby helping us to avoid prejudices. When we think in terms of standards of right and wrong, we control our passions rather than let them rule us. Prudence assists us in following through on our decisions rather than wavering. With prudence we use our common sense in conjunction with the other virtues to avoid sin.

[5] There are many more applications of the virtues than can be discussed here. For a more technical explanation, see Adolphe Tanquery's *The Spiritual Life* (Westminster, MD: The Newman Press, 1930). For an in-depth presentation on guiding our children in these virtues at age-appropriate levels, see David Isaac's *Character Building—A Guide for Parents and Teachers* (Kill Lane, Blackrock, County Dublin: Four Courts Press Limited, 1976).

When we explain why we believe what we believe to our children, we establish a firm foundation on which they can base their standard of right and wrong. We want them to apply that standard as they think through decisions with the goal of pleasing the Lord and following His way.

Justice—"Seek ye first the Kingdom of God and His righteousness" (Mt 6:33).

The virtue of justice is rendering to others what they are due. Justice toward God is giving Him the worship and obedience He is due, which includes following the laws of the Church, such as going to Confession at least once a year and attending Mass every Sunday. This obedience to God applies to all lawful authorities God has established: parents, the Holy Father and the bishops united with him, and civil authorities.

We must set the example of prompt and cheerful obedience to these authorities. If we procrastinate or grumble, we will teach our children by example to do the same. But if we respond eagerly and joyfully in obedience to our Lord and those He has established over us, our children will in turn obey us promptly and cheerfully. No matter how small, any task can be an act of love for God. Let's remember how Jesus, though He was the Lord of Lords, submitted himself to his parents, Mary and Joseph (Lk 2:51).

Justice toward others means we respect "all rights to bodily or spiritual goods, to life, liberty, honor and reputation".[6] We treat borrowed things with great care, repairing or replacing damaged articles. We avoid all debts unless we are sure of the means to repay them, and we repay them responsibly.

Not only do we respect others' property, but we protect their reputation as well. Therefore, we avoid, at all costs, gossip, slander, and calumny. (We must resist the temptation to gossip or slander under the guise of sharing prayer concerns.) In addition, sometimes we damage someone's reputation simply by jumping to quick judgments about another person on the basis of gossip. For instance, we

[6] Tanquery, p. 490.

should guide how our children regard new playmates, in case they misjudge them on the basis of what others have said about them.

Sometimes children demonstrate a lack of justice in our homes, causing dissension and difficulty. Tattling about minor offenses that could be dealt with by the children themselves can be a breach of justice. If our children taunt their siblings about offenses already forgiven, we should intervene; what has been forgiven should be forgotten. If the children play one parent off the other, causing strife, that should be identified and dealt with as an offense against the virtue of justice.

When we are with close friends or family members, we should avoid the temptation to catch one another up on the "news", if such sharing is really gossip. This is especially true if we share negative things about our spouse with our older children; that is divisive to our marriage. Note the seriousness with which St. Paul handles gossips when he lists them among those who will not inherit eternal life (2 Cor 12:20). And when we (or our children) have committed these sins, we should restore the reputation that has been besmirched by our actions. Reparation is needed.

Fortitude—"I will all the more gladly boast of my weaknesses, that the power of Christ may rest upon me" (2 Cor 12:9).

Fortitude is the virtue that gives us spiritual strength to withstand trial and, in the face of all kinds of fears, even the fear of death, to remain steadfast to the Lord and our convictions. We are strengthened in fortitude when we understand why we believe what we believe and take a stand for what we believe even though there is a cost.

Fortitude enables us to answer this challenge, "If you had no fear of failure, what would you attempt for God?" This may require generosity of money and possessions, which in turn helps lessen the grip that wealth can have on us. Though it may involve ridicule, a loss of friends, or financial cost, we want to follow Christ's faithful example and do what is right. So do our children. For example, they may share about God with their neighborhood friends, some of whom do not attend church. They go ahead and share, knowing they may be ridiculed. They exemplify the virtue of fortitude.

Fortitude is far more than enduring suffering for Christ. When we unite our sufferings (no matter how small) to Christ's, we participate in redemption. Jesus is our example of heroic patience, calmly resigned to the will of God for the glory of God. We can foster this in our children by gently reminding them of the value of offering up their sufferings in union with Christ. St. Paul said, "I complete what is lacking in the suffering of Christ for the sake of His Body, that is, the Church" (Col 1:28).

Fortitude is strengthened when we resist temptations. Instead of being controlled by the appetites of our flesh, we rely on the strength of the Lord for our growth in self-control. When we face difficulties, we do not complain or grow bitter. We count the trials as friends (James 1:2). Remaining constant in our convictions yields the rich fruit of perseverance.

Temperance—"For if you live according to the flesh you
will die, but if by the Spirit you put to death the deeds
of the body you will live" (Rom 8:13).

Temperance is the virtue whereby we enjoy the pleasures of this world in moderation, as gifts from God, using them for God-given purposes. In particular, temperance regulates self-control in the areas of food and sex. In the ongoing struggle to bring our bodies into submission to our Lord, it is temperance that helps us focus on honoring God with our bodies.

Faithfulness is the key in building our relationship to our spouse, growing in true devotion to one another. Daily there are opportunities to demonstrate trustworthiness. We must be on our guard— others are not as concerned with our marriages growing in fidelity as we are.

Temptations come. Often for women it is more of an emotional temptation, where another man listens considerately and "compassionately" in ways the husband does not. Often for men it is more of a physical attraction, where another woman responds to his advances and meets his "needs" sexually in ways the wife does not. It may begin innocently enough as a good friendship that develops into being spiritual soul mates with an inappropriate intimacy. No one commits treason overnight, and no one quickly plunges into the frothy, turbulent waters of adultery. We must guard our hearts in little and large ways so that we quench the fire of temptations to infidelity with the living water of fidelity.

Temperance helps us disagree agreeably, ever respectful of one another's thoughts and feelings. Temperance keeps a check on how we express our love physically, never misusing each other, but rather cherishing each other as Christ cherishes the Church (Eph 5:29). We must have pure intentions in our celebration of the act of marriage, rather than defiling it with the practice of contraception or using each other simply for pleasure. This virtuous attitude was expressed by Tobias, "And now, Lord, thou knowest that not for fleshly lust do I take my sister to wife, but only for the love of posterity in which thy name may be blessed for ever and ever" (Tobias 9:8).

Temperance leads to chastity. Temperance cautions us to guard our eyes from sexual impurity (avoiding pornography, for instance). It warns us to refrain from evil thoughts (impurity in imagination and daydreaming). And it calls us to good use of time, avoiding idleness, "For idleness hath taught much evil" (Wis 33:29).

In humility we want our children to distrust themselves and their own ability to put out the fire of passion once lit. Instead, by placing their trust in the Lord, they should honor their potential mates, in purity of desire and modest dress and behavior. Temperance leads them to flee fornication (in thoughts and words as well as deeds)—to flee it, rather than seeing how close they can get to the edge without falling.

Temperance is the virtue that leads all of us to acknowledge in humility that we could fail in purity because of our weak nature. Though we distrust ourselves, we place our confidence in God to preserve us from sin, for He will not tempt us beyond what we can endure (1 Cor 10:13).

Temperance should assist all family members in understanding the failings of others, which will in turn foster a forgiving spirit. This brings real peace in our homes and will enable true peace in our society.

Character Formation Reinforced by the Lives of the Saints

Character formation in the virtues not only strengthens each one of us individually, but it builds up the entire family: good examples encourage perseverance. This is frequently illustrated in the lives of the saints whose feast days we celebrate throughout the year. What a variety of people have been canonized! Some were paupers, and some were princes; some offered their sufferings as victim souls, and some lived healthy, long lives of service to God; some were celibate, and some were married.

Saints are examples of holiness attained in this life. They are real people who struggled with sin just as we do, worked on developing virtues just as we do, and pursued a life of faithfulness to God in whatever vocation God called them to just as we do. The variety of saints, in terms of their personalities, strengths, weaknesses, and calling, helps us realize there is no one particular mold for a saint. What they have in common is faithful love for God, which sanctified them—a goal that all of us can attain.

We lead our families into a richer understanding of the life of the Church by entering into the liturgical calendar at home. Our participation in the cycle of ordinary days, fasting (Advent and Lent), and feasting (holy days, Baptism anniversaries, saints' days, and the Lord's Day) connects us with the "Story of stories"—the life and work of our Lord.

> Stories not told are soon forgotten, and the truth they kept alive is eventually lost. The practice and celebration of religious traditions tell stories. They tell of faith. Another generation hears the religious story by continuing the traditions.[7]

[7] Greg Dues, *Catholic Customs and Traditions* (Mystic, CT: Twenty-Third Publications, 1989), p. 1.

We do not perpetuate traditions for their own sake. Rather we utilize religious traditions as aids in explaining the faith to our children.

Observances of the liturgical calendar in our homes remind us of God's great work in others and encourage us to believe that He can work in and through us too. We walk through the life of Christ with the Church worldwide each year. We see ever more clearly God's great love for us in providing salvation as well as the individual part we each play in the unfolding drama.

Since many of us have not been raised in homes where there was a traditional celebration of the liturgical calendar, we need resources to assist us. Please see the Bibliography—Family Life for a number of books that might be helpful for your family.[8]

In addition, the Church commends to us a number of devotional practices, including the following: making visits to the Blessed Sacrament, attending eucharistic hours including Exposition of the Blessed Sacrament and Benediction, celebrating the Enthronement of the Sacred Heart in our homes, honoring the Sacred Heart of Jesus through attendance at Mass on nine consecutive first Fridays, honoring the Immaculate Heart of Mary by attending Mass on five consecutive first Saturdays, praying the rosary, praying the Stations of the Cross, praying the Divine Mercy Chaplet at 3:00 P.M., going on pilgrimages to various designated shrines, and blessing our children, our homes, and our possessions.[9]

Keys to Christlike Character

1. To develop Christlike character, we need to spend time with Christ in prayer. If we want our children to have an interior prayer life, we must model it for them, and we must teach them how to pray.

---

[8] Some of the material is used specifically in conjunction with the pre-Vatican II calendar. It may have to be modified.

[9] See *Catholic Household Blessings and Prayers*. This was prepared by the Bishops' Committee on the Liturgy for the National Council of Catholic Bishops (Washington, DC: United States Catholic Conference, 1988).

2. We need to identify the particular ways in which we, and our children, struggle with the three categories of vice: the "lust of the flesh", "lust of the eyes", and the "pride of life". By the power of God, we then act to weaken our tendencies to sin in these areas, and we lead our children to do so.

3. The "lust of the flesh" is our tendency to satisfy the desires of our flesh at the expense of our souls. We weaken this tendency by resisting temptation and, when we fail, by repenting of our sin.

4. The "lust of the eyes" refers to our misuse of and desire for material things for our own use instead of for the glory of God. We weaken this tendency by understanding that we are stewards, for the Lord, of all that we have. Our goal is less attachment to our possessions and more of an eternal perspective on temporal things.

5. The "pride of life" is a haughty self-love that refuses to serve others as Christ did. We weaken the tendency toward the pride of life by choosing to serve God and others.

6. This process of weakening vices and strengthening virtues must be done by the power of the Holy Spirit; we don't have the inner strength to do this kind of spiritual warfare on our own.

7. The theological virtues—faith, hope, and love—are infused, supernatural gifts from God. They develop through the sacraments, prayer, and loving obedience toward God.

8. The cardinal virtues—prudence, justice, fortitude, and temperance—are acquired through diligent training.

9. Prudence equips us to make a decision based on godly judgment. It is the virtue that holds the other virtues in balance, so that we respond rather than merely react to varying circumstances.

10. Justice involves the rendering of proper respect due another person. Justice toward God means worshipping and obeying Him; justice toward others includes obeying authorities, respecting life at every stage, and honoring the freedom and property of others.

11. Fortitude gives us spiritual strength to withstand trial and, in the face of all kinds of fears, even death, to remain steadfast to the Lord and our convictions.

12. Temperance enables us to enjoy the pleasures of this world in moderation, as gifts from God, using them for God-given purposes.

13. As we study the lives of the saints with our children, we reflect on the development of Christlike character in their lives, and we can imitate them as they imitate our Lord.

14. Our family's observance of the liturgical calendar connects us with the "Story of stories"—the life and work of our Lord.

15. We strengthen our relationship to Jesus Christ and our resolve for His character to be formed in us and in our children through a variety of devotional practices.

17

A Mother's Guide to
the Faith of Our Fathers
through Scripture and Tradition

Our love for God is much more than feelings. It is an act of the whole person—mind, heart, and will—to submit ourselves completely to the One who made and redeemed us. "Jesus said, 'If you love me, you will keep my commandments'" (Jn 14:15). Yet how can we know His commandments if we do not study them? It is not enough for us to be Catholics simply because our family line has always been Catholic. We also must *choose* to be Catholics—to grow in our knowledge of the Faith through Scripture and Tradition and to submit ourselves without reservation to the Church.

It seems that many Catholics today are satisfied with a very limited understanding of the Faith. Catechetical instruction often ends after children receive First Communion or Confirmation until they are ready for marriage or they must meet with a priest for their child's Baptism. For example, many Catholics still use the examination of conscience they were taught in preparation for their first Confession, rather than deepening their understanding of making a good Confession as an adult.[1] How can this be?

The Bible Is a Catholic Book

There is a myth that, while Protestants emphasize the Bible—reading and studying it—Catholics can get by without it. This is

[1] See Fr. Richard Rego's *A Contemporary Guide to Conscience for the Sacrament of Confession* (St. Paul, MN: Leaflet Missal Company, 1990).

a popular belief, but it is not based on Catholic teaching. Remember: Catholics wrote the New Testament, Catholics compiled the canon of the New Testament, and Catholics, through the Magisterium, help us interpret the whole Bible. *We* are Bible Christians.

Listen carefully to Psalm 1:1–4:

> Blessed is the man who walks not in the counsel of the wicked, nor stands in the way of sinners, nor sits in the seat of scoffers. But his *delight* is in the law of the Lord and on His law he meditates day and night. He is like a tree planted by streams of water that yields its fruit in its season and its leaf does not wither. In all that he does, he prospers.

This is the kind of person each one of us desires to be—firmly rooted in the truth and yielding rich fruit for God. The key is delighting in and meditating on the Word of God.

The Church urges Catholics to read the Bible both privately and along with the Church, especially following the lectionary, which has the readings for Mass. (A lectionary can be purchased from Catholic bookstores everywhere.) We read the daily readings in the morning with our children before going to Mass. That way, they hear the same passages twice and can think about it before they hear a homily. Later in the day (or even on the way home from Mass), we can discuss the passage again, so that the Word of God becomes deeply planted in our souls.

An age-appropriate Bible (with pictures for little ones) captures the attention of our children and acquaints them with the basics of the Old Testament history of God's interaction with His people and with Jesus' life and teachings. But we want to do more than just jog our memories from childhood by reading simple Bible stories—we want to understand and apply God's living Word to our life *now*.

As we explore Sacred Scripture with our children, we unearth with them the treasured messages of faith, hope, and love that the Holy Spirit has inspired. Poring over the Gospels is the best way to know Jesus—an essential step toward imitating Him and becoming united with Him. One outstanding resource for teaching children Scripture is the Little Rock Scripture Study for Children.[2]

Since the Word of God is the sword of the Spirit (Eph 6:17), it is a vital tool of the Spirit for heart surgery on all of us. Reading the Word is not enough—we must study the Word of God. One very helpful tool has been the Navarre Bible Commentary series. Another helpful tool for many families is the series of Bible studies by Scott and Kimberly Hahn, available on audiotapes and videotapes.[3]

St. Paul admonishes us to "Let the Word of Christ dwell in you richly" (Col 3:16). For Christ's Word to *dwell* in us, we must do more than read and study Sacred Scripture—we should memorize it. Here again many Catholics think memorizing Scripture is a Protestant thing to do. But all Christians need to have the Word of God in their hearts for meditation and guidance. (Contrary to popular belief, Protestants do not have a special gene that makes memorization easier for them!)

Sacred Scripture is an important tool for the discipline of our children. We want our children to be pure, and yet we often overlook one essential way we can assist them: memorizing Scripture. Psalm 119:9, 11 says, "How can a young man keep his way pure? By guarding it according to Thy Word. . . . I have laid up Thy Word in my heart that I might not sin against Thee." By memorizing Scripture and meditating on it, we guard our hearts and our children's hearts from sin.

The same Church that gave us Sacred Scripture has preserved, by the power of the Holy Spirit, an infallible interpretation of it through Sacred Tradition, the teachings of the Popes, and the Magisterium. Again, how will we know what these vital interpretations are unless we study them?

[2] The "Little Rock Scripture Study for Children" series (Collegeville, MN: Liturgical Press, 1993) is a very good series. Colorful, with lots of kid appeal, it blends a serious look at the Faith as it is presented in one book of Scripture with the fun of age-appropriate games and puzzles. The studies for children correspond to the material for adults, so your family could study the same book together.

[3] More than two hundred tapes on Sacred Scripture and Roman Catholic theology by Scott and Kimberly Hahn are available from St. Joseph Communications, P.O. Box 720, West Covina, CA 91793; telephone (800) 526-2151.

We have ready access to the documents that represent Sacred Tradition. The Daughters of St. Paul reprint papal encyclicals very inexpensively so that lay people can read these important documents. In addition, paperback editions of the Vatican II and post-Vatican II documents can be acquired easily.

The *Catechism of the Catholic Church* is a gift to every Christian—the first catechism for the entire Church since the Council of Trent. If you do not already own a copy, we urge you to get one and begin reading it. (It's available in any bookstore.) Then you can look for opportunities to share it with your children, according to what they can understand. We should read these teachings of the Church so that our lives reflect the fullness of God's truth.

Know Truth to Know God

When we teach doctrine, Church history, or catechism, we should relate it to our children's personal relationship with God. The "what" without the "why" will not lead them into a more intimate relationship with our Lord or enable them to live holy lives.

Learning about God and the truth He gives us through the doctrines of the Church is much more than an intellectual exercise. When our minds are transformed by truth, we learn what God desires and how to live the life He wants for us. Then we can accomplish the particular work He has planned for each of us.

Through the prayerful reading and study of Sacred Scripture and Sacred Tradition, we are able to follow the teaching of St. Paul, "Do not be conformed to this world, but be transformed by the renewal of your mind that you may prove what is the will of God, what is good and acceptable and perfect" (Rom 12:2). If we desire our children to develop their catechetical understanding of the Faith, we need to set the example ourselves. The more fully our intellect is informed in the Faith, the more our will can truly submit to the Lord, all of which is an expression of our genuine love for God.

Applying Our Faith in Service

Each day we have opportunities to love our Lord by serving others, individually and as a family. Our desire to imitate Christ in ministry flows out of our developing interior life. God has so abundantly blessed us. In return we want to be a blessing to others through good stewardship of the money, time, talents, and bodies God has given us.

"The love of money is the root of all evils", according to 1 Timothy 6:10. One of the ways we break the power money can have over us is to give generously to the Lord. St. Paul provides us with some important guidelines for offerings that please the Lord: give generously, cheerfully, and freely (2 Cor 12:6–12). The starting place of Christian giving is the tithe spoken of in the Old Testament (one tenth of earnings); generosity beyond the tithe in almsgiving is urged by New Testament teaching. The psalmist speaks of our gifts for God as "lending to the Lord" (Prov 19:17). No matter how little money we have, we have the privilege of honoring our Lord through our donations. Remember—we cannot outgive the Lord. God always blesses us more abundantly than we give, especially when we give sacrificially. The wealth at our disposal has the potential for harm or for great good, depending on our attitude toward it and our stewardship over it.

Many of us may not have great financial resources at our disposal, but we do have time we can make available to the Lord by serving others. Setting aside time in our schedules for hospitality can be a great blessing to everyone. Perhaps there are college students who would enjoy sitting around a dining-room table, enjoying a home-cooked meal. Perhaps there are elderly people who rarely cook nice meals for themselves because they live alone, and who would appreciate the good food and even the hubbub of a family meal for a change. Maybe there are young married couples who cannot afford a meal out, or large families who, because of their size, never get asked over for a meal. The fellowship around a family meal might also be just the kind of encouragement that priests, nuns, or brothers need.

We show our children how their skills and abilities can be a ministry in a variety of ways. When families are having a new baby, we take them meals, offer child care for their other children so dad can go to the hospital or mom can rest, or do some errands for them. Some of the skills we have taught our children in yard work or housework can help these families or can assist elderly people who have no family close by.

In addition, we can use the pain, difficulties, and suffering of our bodies to love God in our weakness. For when we offer up our sufferings in union with the sacrifice of the Cross, we actively participate in Christ's work of salvation. No matter how small our children's sufferings may seem to us, they can be offered to God in sacrificial love as well. When one of our children had the flu, he asked God in prayer to use his suffering to keep some young mother from having an abortion. He still felt sick, but he knew his suffering was having a powerful effect since he had given it back to God through prayer.

Everything we have belongs to God—our money, time, talents, and bodies. Daily He gives us opportunities to demonstrate good stewardship over these gifts. Through good stewardship, we strengthen the domestic church, build up the Church, and witness to the world our love for Him.

We desire spiritual growth in our own lives and in the lives of our children. We want our children to know, love, and serve the Lord in this life so that they will join us in enjoying life forever with the Lord. That's why the Lord declares His desire for faithfulness to the marriage covenant to result in "godly offspring" (Malachi 2:15).

For our children to be "godly offspring", they must orient their lives more and more around Jesus as their King instead of around themselves. The holiness for which we (and they) strive is not a measure of ourselves—not something *we* achieve. Sometimes our pride whispers "congratulations" as we mentally check off each penance we undertake or as our self-righteousness smugly notes our faithfulness to Mass and prayer, which others fail to have. We can easily focus on *our* ability to get things done on our spiritual "to do" lists rather than on the Person for whom we do all these things—*Christ*.

Holiness for its own sake is not the goal. Rather, holiness is the mark of our love for our Lord—we want to become like the One we worship. The possibility for holiness grows in proportion to our desire to imitate Him and our willingness to let Him rule our lives. As we grow in holiness and lead our children to do likewise, we reflect more and more of the life of the Trinity in our homes.

Pope John Paul II has declared his hope that Christian families would

> become ever more authentic "domestic churches", in which the word of God is received with joy, bears fruit in lives of holiness and love, and shines forth with new brilliance as a beacon of hope for all to see. The faith-filled witness of Christian families is an essential element in the new evangelization to which the Holy Spirit is calling the Church in our time.[4]

How can we live this kind of a vision for Catholic family life without being overwhelmed by all that we can't do and don't know (yet)? First, the Lord is the One who establishes our marriages and blesses us with children. Then He reminds us of our vows to educate those children responsibly so that they know and serve the Lord they love. Finally, the Lord empowers us by His Holy Spirit so that we can obey this call.

A Solid Foundation for the Next Generation

1. It's not enough for us to be raised Catholic—we must *choose* to be Catholics—to grow in our knowledge of the Faith through Scripture and Tradition.

2. St. Paul admonishes us to "Let the Word of Christ dwell in you richly" (Col 3:16). For His Word to *dwell* in us, we must do more than read it—we must study, meditate on, and memorize it.

---

[4] John Paul II, personal correspondence for the *Totus Tuus* Conference in Pittsburgh, PA, October 10, 1993.

3. God not only gave us His Word through the Church, but He also provided an infallible interpretation of it through the Church. The new *Catechism of the Catholic Church* is an important tool for us to use and to share with our children.

4. The goal in knowing about God—through Sacred Scripture and Sacred Tradition—is to know Him personally.

5. Our desire to imitate Christ in service flows out of our deepening relationship to our Lord.

6. Through good stewardship of our money, time, talents, and even our bodies, we strengthen the domestic church (our family), build up the Church, and witness to the world our love for Him.

7. As we grow in holiness as a family, we reflect more and more of the life of the Trinity in our homes.

8. For a wide variety of reasons, there is a movement among Catholic parents toward taking primary responsibility for the complete home education of their children. This home-education movement is not in reaction to all that is not well with the world; rather it is in response to God's call fully to educate our children for a life of fruitful service to Him. Catholic education *is* homeward bound.

Now That You Have the Facts

Would home education enable you and your spouse to live more fully God's desire for your family life?

We have found, in our experience, that the challenge has been more than worth the effort. Day by day, our commitment to the education of the whole person is bearing good fruit. We see our children growing in the knowledge and grace of our Lord, individually and as part of our families. In addition, their academic achievements have been outstanding—they are getting the intellectual formation needed to pursue service for God for the rest of their lives.

Catholic home education has given us a great opportunity to practice stewardship over the money, time, talents, and physical strength God has given us. We pray that our diligence in response to His faithfulness will result in each one of us growing in sanctity,

> until we all attain to the unity of the faith and of the knowledge of the Son of God, to mature manhood [or womanhood], to the measure of the stature of the fullness of Christ; so that we may no longer be children, tossed to and fro and carried about with every wind of doctrine, by the cunning of men, by their craftiness in deceitful wiles. Rather, speaking the truth in love, we are to grow up in every way into him who is the head, into Christ, from whom the whole body, joined and knit together by every joint with which it is supplied, when each part is working properly, makes bodily growth and upbuilds itself in love (Eph 4:13–16).

Appendix A

OUTCOME-BASED EDUCATION

The following paragraphs are quoted from *The Phyllis Schlafly Report*, "What's Wrong with Outcome-Based Education?", published in May 1993. Each paragraph addresses a different concern. For more current information on specific states where OBE is now being integrated into the educational system, contact *The Phyllis Schlafly Report*, Box 618, Alton, IL 62002.

1. "OBE advocates continually use double-entendre expressions that parents assume mean one thing but really mean something different in the OBE context. When they talk about 'new basics', for example, they are not talking about academics such as reading, writing, and arithmetic, but OBE attitudes and outcomes. When they talk about 'higher order thinking skills' or 'critical thinking', they mean a relativistic process of questioning traditional moral values."

2. "OBE advocates are not able to produce any replicable research or pilot studies to show that it works. . . . The best test of an OBE-type system was Chicago's experiment in the 1970s with Professor Benjamin Bloom's Mastery Learning (ML), which is essentially the same as OBE. ML was a colossal failure and was abandoned in disgrace in 1982. The test scores proved to be appallingly low, and the illiteracy rate became a national scandal."

3. For years, secondary schools have established their criteria for graduation on the "Carnegie units". "Outcome-Based Education tosses these traditional units out the window and replaces them with vague and subjective 'learning outcomes' that cannot be measured objectively by standardized tests and for which there

341

is no accountability to parents and taxpayers. OBE will make it virtually impossible to conduct any kind of tests that allow comparisons with students in other schools, other states, or prior years. Under OBE, grades have no relation to academic achievement and knowledge. Colleges will have no criteria by which to judge whether students are ready for admission."

4. "OBE is a dumbed-down egalitarian scheme that stifles individual potential for excellence and achievement by holding the entire class to the level of learning attainable by *every* child. To accomplish this, children are placed in Politically Correct groups (race, ethnicity, gender, class) for 'cooperative learning' and may be given a group grade instead of individual grades. Cooperative learning researchers admit that the purpose of this strategy is to eliminate grading and competition in the classroom. This is the essence of OBE and explains why all measurable criteria—standardized tests, the Carnegie units, traditional subject matter, and report cards—must be eliminated. . . . The result is that all students demonstrate 'mastery' of mediocrity, and none can aspire to excellence."

5. "In an OBE system, academic and factual subject matter is replaced by vague and subjective learning outcomes. . . . A look at the outcomes that have so far been made public shows that they are heavily layered with such 'Politically Correct' notions as training for world citizenship and government (instead of patriotism), population control, radical environmentalism, and government 'solutions' for every problem."

6. "A high percentage of OBE 'outcomes' concern values, attitudes, opinions, and relationships rather than objective information. . . . OBE requires students to meet vague psychological objectives relating to self-esteem, ethical judgment, and adaptability to change. Moving from one level to the next, and even graduation, is dependent on meeting behavior-change requirements and government-mandated attitudes."

7. "OBE sets up a computer file on each child to track the

child's efforts to master the learning outcomes. These 'electronic portfolios' will take the place of traditional assessments and test results and will become the basis for the school's efforts to re-mediate whatever attitudes and behaviors the school deems unac-ceptable. The portfolios will include all school, psychological, and medical records and are to be available to prospective employers after graduation."

8. "OBE is a method for concealing and perpetuating the num-ber-one crime of the public school system—the failure to teach first graders how to read. OBE is wholly committed to the 'whole language', word–guessing method rather than the phonics method. This ensures that children will learn only to memorize a few words that are massively repeated. Teachers are cautioned not to correct spelling and syntax errors because that could be damaging to the student's self-esteem and creativity."

9. "OBE, of course, involves high costs for administration and the retraining of teachers in an entirely new system, which will be reflected in high [increased] school taxes. The computer portfolio system is reported to be five times as expensive as traditional assessment tests."

10. "OBE involves tightened state control at the expense of local control. Although OBE salespersons claim otherwise, the new system tightens the grip of state education officials and federal education laboratories because they write the required outcomes, develop the curriculum, train the teachers, and judge the perfor-mance of the students (all of whom must conform to National Goals). . . . Teachers will not be able to get around the OBE system, and teach the basics anyway, because the teachers are graded on how their class meets the outcomes."

"Alexander Solzhenitsyn, the famous Russian author and former political prisoner in Soviet Gulags, said in a speech in the mid-1970s: 'Coexistence on this tightly knit earth should be viewed as an existence not only without wars . . . but also without [government] telling us how to live, what to say, what to think, what to know, and what not to know.'

"Unfortunately, that's what Outcome-Based Education is—a process for government telling our children how to live, what to say, what to think, what to know, and what not to know. What the children say, think, and know must conform to the liberal Politically Correct ideology, attitudes, and behavior. What they do not know will be everything else. And because they won't know the basics of reading, writing, and arithmetic, they won't be able to find out. OBE is converting the three R's to the three D's: Deliberately Dumbed Down."

Appendix B

SUGGESTED RESOURCES—
KIMBERLY'S CHOICES

ART

Drawing Textbook, by Bruce McIntyre (grade 2 and up). Audio-Visual Drawing Program.

McIntyre believes all children should learn the basics of drawing so they will be literate in that medium, just as everyone should learn to read. He builds slowly and solidly from simple shapes to complex cities. It's a good bargain—thorough *and* inexpensive.

Drawing with Children, by Mona Brookes (grade 2 and up). Jeremy Tarcher, Inc.

Many children have learned how to use several art mediums because of Brookes' method. An older student could read the book by himself and experiment, or a parent could use it to instruct a child.

ART APPRECIATION

"Mommy, It's a Renoir!" (age 3 and up). Parent-Child Press.

This actually happened to us—my six-year-old saw a copy of a Renoir painting in the doctor's office and identified it for me!

Parents utilize beautiful reproduction art postcards to challenge the child from one level (matching identical paintings) to increasingly more difficult groupings (identify the artist, the painting, and the period when that school of artists painted). There are eight levels, each with varying difficulty.

BIBLE HISTORY

Bible History—Containing the Most Remarkable Events of the Old and the New Testament, with a Compendium of Church History, by Right Rev. Richard Gilmour (then Bishop of Cleveland). New York: Benziger Brothers, Inc., 1881.

Yes, 1881. Is it outdated? Since the Bible was completed before 1881, I don't think so. Seriously, this little volume presents a helpful overview of Bible history for children in grades 4 to 8.

CHURCH HISTORY

An Illustrated History of the Church, 12 vols. Winston Press, 430 Oak Grove, MN 55403. Out of print.

This series covers Church history from the time of Christ to the late 1960s. Each page is written at two levels—large print and simpler explanations at the top of the page; smaller print with more details at the bottom of the page. Very readable style with lots of illustrations. It's worth the search, if you can find it.

COMPUTERS

Pride's Guide to Educational Software, by Bill and Mary Pride. Wheaton, IL: Crossway Books, 1992. Available from Great Christian Books.

Whether or not you are a computer whiz, you will enjoy the helpful critiques for the gamut of educational software out there. It's a one-of-a-kind resource. For very helpful material on the various on-line services, see the magazine *Practical Homeschooling*.

20th Century Typewriting (grade 4 and up). Any good typewriting book will do. I use the one published by South-Western Publishing.

I prefer to teach my children how to type correctly rather than let them use the hunt-and-peck method. It's an important skill for life. Why not take the time to learn it the right way the first time?

CRAFTS

Learn to Sew with Dorcas, by Ellen Lyman. Vol. 1. Right at Home Productions.

This is a delightful resource chock-full of creative yet simple sewing designs. It includes patterns and instructions for sixty projects (other than clothes) with two levels of difficulty, depending on the child's abilities. Each project discusses some aspect of Christian character as well.

GEOGRAPHY

Daily Geography (grades 2–11). Evanston, IL: McDougal, Littell & Co.

Each day you ask two geography questions. Your child can (and should) use the geographical resources you have on hand to answer them. It's a lot of fun and doesn't take a lot of time.

Since this is a systematic program, you might want to order all of the books and ask more questions of your older children to bring them up to speed.

GeoSafari (preschool through high school). Available through Great Christian Books, Inc.

GeoSafari is one of the finest tools we have purchased for home education. It's great for independent work while you tutor someone else. We have all of the packets available—each one is excellent. Tell grandparents about it as a gift suggestion. By the way, it's worth the extra $10.00 for the AC adapter. Highly recommended.

Operation: World, by Patrick Johnstone. Youth with a Mission.

We have used this unique resource for five years. Every country is described in terms of recent political history and current political structure, religious make-up, population (current and projected), and specific prayer requests for that nation. We scan the page for a few important bits of information about one country each day and then pray for its people.

It is written and published by non-Catholics, so sometimes there is an anti-Catholic bias (less so with each edition), but it's a one-of-a-kind resource that is invaluable for encouraging mission-mindedness in our children. We began using this guide a few months before the Iron Curtain fell. Talk about the power of prayer! Our children believed—and rightly so—that their prayers made a difference.

Success with Maps series, A–F (68 pp. each for grades 1–6). Scholastic, Inc.

This series systematically teaches the principles of map reading. Each level is challenging for a given grade, so you will not go quickly through the series. If you are jumping into the series with children in the later elementary grades, however, I'd recommend beginning with book A and let them work until they reach their grade level. The principles build on one another. It's fun, colorful, and interesting.

Take-Off (age 8 and up). Resource Games, Inc. Available from Timberdoodle.

This is an outstanding geography game. You play on a 56" x 24" map, jumping from country to country, identified by the capital cities and the flags of each country. The goal is to move one's jet around the world first. A variety of levels of difficulty make play challenging for any age group, including adults.

GOVERNMENT

Our Nation's Government Series (grades 5–8). Scholastic Inc.

These twenty-four–page booklets on the judicial, legislative, and executive branches of our government provide a brief yet comprehensive overview of the historical development of the powers of each branch and the responsibilities each has in the balance of power.

HEALTH, SAFETY, AND MANNERS

The Family Book of Manners, by Hermine Hartley. Published by Barbour and Co.

This book provides a delightful overview of all kinds of manners we should develop and teach our children. Children can read this on their own (grade 3 and up).

Health, Safety and Manners (grades 1, 2, and 3). A Beka Book Publications.

This excellent series has brief explanations, attractive illustrations, and helpful comprehension questions.

HISTORY

A Child's World History, by Thomas Hilyers (grades 1–4). Out of print.

Check used-book shops—an excellent resource.

Greenleaf Guide to Ancient Egypt, by Cynthia A. Shearer. Greenleaf Press. First in a series.

Shearer guides students through a unit study that accommodates children at varying levels of reading and writing ability. The discussion questions lead either to conversation about the material (from age-appropriate books recommended) or to essays. This is a wonderful resource for a multilevel unit study with everyone contributing to projects according to ability and knowledge. Highly recommended.

The Old World and America, by Rev. Philip J. Furlong (grades 5–7). 1937. Reprint. TAN Books and Publishers, Inc.

This is a very helpful history text from a Catholic perspective beginning with the earliest civilizations up to the founding of the United States. The review questions at the end of each chapter provide a check on comprehension. Though the print is small and the illustrations are black and white, it is a text worth using.

Western Civilization, by Linville, Perry, Chase, Jacob, Jacob, and Von Laue. Vol. 1: to 1789. Houghton Mifflin Co. It also comes with a study guide.

This text was recommended to us by Dr. Dominic Aquila, Professor of History at Franciscan University. He uses this book in the history club we have for older children in our support group.

LANGUAGE ARTS

Alphabetter, by Dr. Edwin C. Myers (grade 2 and up). This comes in MasterPak I, by Providence Project (described under Mathematics—CalcuLadder, below).

This is a speed drill for alphabetizing. Very helpful.

English from the Roots Up, by Joegil Lundquist (grade 3 and up). 2 vols. Literacy Unlimited Publications.

This book identifies English words that have either Greek or Latin roots. You don't need a background in either language—I'm learning right along with my children. Children with an understanding of the roots of our language grow in their ability to speak and write in an articulate manner. Down the road this will translate into much higher scores on the SAT, not to mention a better facility with our own language.

Faith and Freedom Readers (grades K–8). Out of print. Ginn and Co. Check used book stores.

The younger grades are sweet stories that seem a little like a Catholic Dick and Jane series. It's more like cheap children's poetry than excellent literature; however, children enjoy it, and a small dose is not going to ruin their taste for better literature later. The books for older children are higher-quality material. I supplement with these books rather than base my program on them.

Handwriting—Basic Skills and Application, Books 1–6. Zaner-Bloser, Inc.

Each book is a colorful and creative workbook for improving basic handwriting skills. This simple yet effective practice yields good results in other writing projects.

Open Court Reading and Writing Program (grades K–6). Open Court Publishing Co.

Each reader provides students with a variety of excellent literature—fables, folk tales, an autobiography, a Bible story, poems, fairy tales, a scientific article . . . and includes a rich variety of illustrators. Two workbooks accompany each reader: one checks comprehension skills; one hones writing skills. The teacher guides are indispensable for instructing the teacher (you) how to read and write critically. The only negative is their phonics program, which I do not use.

The Sentence, by Martha Zook (grade 7 and up). Rod and Staff Publishers, Inc.

This 110–page booklet is the best resource I have found yet for teaching sentence diagramming systematically and thoroughly. What, you may ask, is the value of diagramming sentences? It illustrates the structure of sentences so that errors in writing can be remedied more easily. That, in turn, makes the structure of foreign-language sentences much more readily understandable, particularly a language such as Latin or Greek, each of which has a structure very different from that of our own language.

Short Vowel Readers and *Long Vowel Readers*, by Dolly Thoburn (K). Great Christian Books.

Each series has ten short stories with a moral. Each reader's vocabulary provides practice for a particular short or long vowel. These books are very nice for beginning readers. Children can color the black–and–white sketches.

Winston-Grammar, by Paul R. Erwin (grade 2 and up). 2 vols. Hewitt Educational Resources. Available from Great Christian Books.

This outstanding program teaches grammar in understandable increments, using cue cards and worksheets. You can begin as young as second grade if you go slowly enough and add sentences to drill one skill until mastery is attained. This program is excellent preparation for sentence diagramming. Highly recommended.

Writing Strands, by The National Writing Institute. There are several levels.

We have enjoyed this series for building writing abilities and encouraging imagination through story starters. Young children can listen and then share a story-ending with Mom; older children record their responses. When we share the stories, we demonstrate our appreciation for the imagination of one another.

LATIN

Artes Latinae, by Waldo E. Sweet (grade 3 and up). Bolchazy-Carducci Publishers.

I have never studied Latin before, but I'm learning alongside my children. Sweet uses the program method of instruction—you learn one bit of information at a time. He sprinkles the text with humorous illustrations and comments that help memory work. The tapes are invaluable if you are unfamiliar with Latin. It's been a great learning experience for us all.

LOGIC

Building Thinking Skills Series, by Critical Thinking Press & Software (K–Adult). Available from Great Christian Books. Levels include: Primary, Book I, Book II, Book III Verbal, and Book III Figural.

This company has produced a number of outstanding materials in logic. The original *Building Thinking Skills Series* covers a variety of figural and verbal analogies. We've found CTP's *Organizing Thinking Graphic Organizers* very helpful for training in organizing thoughts before writing or speaking in a group. We've had more fun during snack time with copies of *A Case of Red Herrings— Solving Mysteries through Critical Questioning* and the series *Do We Have an Understanding?—Analyzing Agreements.* We look forward to sampling more of their challenging and enjoyable materials. Highly recommended.

MATHEMATICS

Addison-Wesley Mathematics (grades K-12). Addison-Wesley Publishing Co.

This is an excellent series for several reasons: each concept is introduced thoroughly with a number of examples; manipulatives are included in books K-2; concepts from other chapters are reviewed regularly in "Skill Keeper" blocks; logic is introduced in "Thinking Skills" blocks; and each chapter ends with both a chapter test and a cumulative test. The teacher guides are excellent—more than just answer sheets. Our children have gone directly from *Addison-Wesley Mathematics 6* to *Saxon 87*. Highly recommended.

CalcuLadder, by Dr. Edwin C. Myers (six levels available—grade 2 and up). The Providence Project.

"CalcuLadders" are daily timed drills on math facts. A child does one drill a day (or more, if he accomplishes the task in the time allotted without errors). The goal is increased speed and accuracy on math facts. You can purchase twelve copies of every drill per level in a book, or you can purchase two MasterPaks. I recommend getting the MasterPaks—#1 gives you CalcuLadders Levels 1–3 plus ReadyWriter (a fun prewriting drill), and #2 gives you CalcuLadders Levels 4–6 plus AlphaBetter (an excellent drill for mastery of the alphabet). You can either photocopy the number of copies you'll need or put the originals in inexpensive plastic page-protectors and have the children use fineline erasable markers (my choice). Highly recommended.

Creating Line Designs, by Randy L. Womack. Golden Educational Center Publications.

Womack has created a series of four booklets, twenty lessons each, which combines math-facts drills with the skill of making line designs—solve the problems and connect the dots. This has been a helpful resource for improving accuracy.

Mathematical Reasoning through Verbal Analysis, by Warren Hill and Ronald Edwards (grades 2–4, 4–8). Critical Thinking Press & Software.

These two books lay the foundation for the kind of mathematical reasoning a child needs to do in order to comprehend higher math. Children work independently while you tutor someone else. You might want the teacher guide for the second volume.

Mathematics Their Way (grades K–2). Addison-Wesley Publishing Co.

This book introduces many basic mathematical principles through the use of a number of manipulatives—some you make and some you purchase. (We recommend highly Unifix Cubes; order from Didax, One Centennial Dr., Peabody, MA 10960.) It lays an excellent foundation for abstract math. I've limited its use to kindergarten.

Saxon Math—87, Algebra 1/2, Algebra I, Algebra II, and *Advanced Mathematics*, by John Saxon. Available from Great Christian Books, with the Answer Keys.

The principle behind this outstanding method of learning mathematics is simple—teach one skill and then practice that skill almost daily. You build in small increments—slowly and solidly. The Saxon series keeps all skills fresh—great preparation for end-of-the-year standardized tests, not to mention the SAT! Saxon textbooks are now available for K-12, but I prefer the *Addison-Wesley Mathematics* at the beginning levels.

MUSIC APPRECIATION

The Gift of Music, by Jane Stuart Smith and Betty Carlson. Westchester, IL: Crossway Books. Available through Great Christian Books.

This volume contains the biographies of forty composers. It's an excellent resource for background material to accompany any series of recordings of classical music.

The Music Masters Series, written by Marianne Kuranda and directed by Ward Botsford. The Moss Music Group, Inc.

Three sets of six tapes, each set presenting twenty different composers, include biographical information as well as snippets of major compositions. Have a tape handy to pique your children's interest during car travel, and then locate more of the composer's music for playing at home during afternoon hours.

PHONICS

Discover Intensive Phonics for Yourself, by Charlotte Lockhart (grades K–2). Available from HEC Reading Horizons.

Hands down, this is the phonics program I recommend. It is user-friendly, telling you what to say when and why. It's nonconsumable, so you can use it with all of your children, lend it to friends the years you don't need it, and still have it for grandchildren!

Charlotte's theory is this: if a child works at a blackboard, he uses more of his body in active learning. Phonics taught thoroughly does not need added games, songs, or prizes—learning to read is the reward. I especially like her application of principles to syllabication. Many friends have borrowed my book to teach this to their children. I highly recommend this resource.

Modern Curriculum Press Phonics A, B & C (grades K-2). Modern Curriculum Press.

These workbooks provide reinforcement to the phonics lesson a child has completed at the blackboard. The latest editions are in color. They are inexpensive and comprehensive.

PIANO STUDIES

Alfred's Basic Piano Library, by Willard A. Palmer, Morton Manus, and Amanda Vick Lethco. Alfred Pub. Co., Inc. (Also available through most music stores.)

Whether you are learning piano yourself or teaching your children, this is an excellent series of piano books. Six levels of difficulty coordinate Technic, Theory, Lessons, Recital, Hymn, Merry Christmas, and Fun Books. I have taught piano before—this series is the best I have seen for young children. Highly recommended.

By the way, when you teach piano through home education, I think you teach it more thoroughly. We do piano lessons right after devotions. Morning practice ensures its place in our day. Rather than building up to a weekly lesson, the children make progress with me daily. When they master a piece, we go on. There's less pressure for them, and they don't waste time repeating pieces all week before a lesson—they go on when they are ready.

RELIGION STUDIES

Catechism of the Catholic Church, published in 1994 by Libreria Editrice Vaticana. Available from Ignatius Press.

This is helpful with older children. We read a brief section and look up the footnoted Scriptures and Church documents.

Faith and Life Series (grades 1–8). Available from Ignatius Press.

This series of books for training in the Faith is excellent. Each book clearly teaches our children the Faith in a well-written and beautifully illustrated style. The workbooks help the child focus on applying the reading material. Teacher guides for home educators are in the works.

Family Devotional Time

Each morning our family gathers in the living room to do the following: make an Act of Consecration; read the readings for Mass that day from the *Vatican II Weekday Missal* (available in Catholic bookstores) and discuss them briefly; review and memorize Scripture; read about the saint for the day, using *The One Year Book of Saints*, by Rev. Clifford Stevens (Our Sunday Visitor); read about a country to pray for that day from *Operation: World* (by Youth with a Mission); and close with extemporaneous prayers from each family member, followed by an Our Father, Hail Mary, and the Prayer to St. Michael.

SCIENCE

Blood and Guts—A Working Guide to Your Own Insides, by Linda Allison. Little, Brown and Co.

This is a fun text that explains all about the human body and includes small experiments to demonstrate what is being taught. Children fourth grade and up could read it to themselves; you could make it understandable to children in first grade.

Good Science—Process Skills of Science, by Dr. Richard Bliss (grades K–3 and 4–6). Creation Life Publishers.

This science program takes you step-by-step through the skills needed to do physical and life science at each grade level. You learn technical terms, make predictions, conduct a variety of experiments, record data, and draw conclusions. You can take each chapter as a theme and integrate other science materials you have accumulated along the way. We enjoy doing this program with other families, taking turns teaching.

SOCIAL STUDIES

Konos Character Curriculum, by Carole Thaxton and Jessica Hulcy. Available through Great Christian Books.

Konos comes in three volumes, focusing on nineteen character traits through unit studies that cover all subject areas except math and grammar for grades 1–6. Use of a time line helps children see where significant figures in history fit in. We enjoy *Konos* as an opportunity to work together on projects, with each child contributing on his ability level.

When we do *Konos*, our children say, "Is this school? It's too much fun!" Some home educators build their program around *Konos*, but we use it as a supplement. We're eager to find out more about their new volume for high school.

SPELLING

Building on Ruth Beechick's idea that the best spelling list is made up of words each child has actually misspelled, I have developed a simple method for working on spelling.

Whenever a child misspells a word—in his daily journals, on papers or other homework, or even orally—it goes on his spelling list. I place the word on a sheet with three half-inch columns labeled Daily, Weekly, and Monthly. The day after he misses the word, he writes the word three times on the blackboard. The next day I test him on the word. If he spells it correctly, I check the daily column; if he misspells it, he writes it three times on the board.

The child must write it correctly three days in a row for the word to be on weekly review. Every Monday I ask him to spell the words on weekly review. After three weeks in a row with the correct spelling, I put the word on monthly review. After three months in a row with the correct spelling (done the first Monday of the new month), the word is retired. If at any time he misspells it, or misspells it again in his work, he goes back to daily review. This efficient method has been *very* effective in helping my children become very good spellers. Highly recommended.

SUGGESTED RESOURCES—
MARY'S CHOICES

In addition to the resources suggested by Kimberly (some of which I already use and some of which I can't wait to try!), I have used the following:

GEOGRAPHY

Rand McNally Discovery Atlas of the World (grades 1–4). Published by Rand McNally & Company, 1993, and available at most bookstores and Rand McNally stores.

This slim atlas covers the continents, giving separate maps and explanations of the terrain, animals found in that region, life on that continent, and the major cities and countries of each continent. The illustrations and photos used are appealing to young children.

IQ Games (*World Geography* and *U.S. Geography* game cards). Available through Educational Insights.

This easy game uses game cards with questions of varying levels of difficulty to drill children on basic geography facts. We use it to take a break from more traditional geography programs and map reading. My kids don't consider it "real" schoolwork because it's a game!

Maps, Charts and Graphs (levels A-H, appropriate for grades K–7). Available through Modern Curriculum Press.

These little books offer occasional practice in mapping and graphing skills, similar to the format on standardized tests. For this reason they are valuable, especially if this is a year when you are choosing to concentrate on other subjects but want your kids to stay proficient in geography skills.

Mapping the World by Heart (grades 5–12). Tom Snyder Productions.

Recommended by a friend, this one-volume, reusable text, though pricey, really teaches children to know the world and to be at ease with reading and drawing maps. If you are using it to teach more than one child, you can make copies from the available maps or order extra from the company.

HISTORY

My approach to history is to cover the key time periods through numerous works of historical fiction about each era. I usually introduce and follow up the novels with more general background reading from the textbooks suggested below.

For those who want to use the historical-novel approach to history, I recommend getting the God's World Books and The Elijah Company catalogues. Both catalogues divide works of historical fiction according to time period, making it easy to choose good books for your children. Elijah's listing tends to be more comprehensive, while God's World Books is more eye-catching and selective. Even if you end up getting the books out of the library, these catalogues will speed up your search for good materials.

A History of US, by Joy Hakim (ten slender volumes covering different periods of U.S. history, for grades 3–7). Available by the volume at most bookstores, including Crown Books. Published by Oxford University Press, NY, 1993.

These books are a wonderful choice for background reading. Unlike history textbooks that simply contain chapter after chapter of summaries of events, these books interweave stories about real people from the time period, explanations of events, and original sources, including letters, diaries, and documents. The author has an entertaining style and weaves in humor and and historical anecdotes in an interesting way. The volumes we have covered so far are relatively free from bias and political correctness, especially for secular texts.

Christ and the Americas, by Anne Carroll (junior high to high school). Available from Seton Home Study Institute.

Although this is a high-school text, with page after page of dauntingly small print, it can be a valuable resource, even for younger students. I highlight the paragraphs I want my children to read and spend a lot of time in discussion. The strength of this book (and its companion, *Christ the King, Lord of History*) is its interweaving of Catholic history and perspective with the standard historical material.

Childhood of Famous Americans biography series (grades 3–6). Available through God's World Books (see Appendix C for address) or at many regular bookstores.

These children's biographies are an easy way to acquaint your children with major historical figures. My kids devour them without my having to "assign" them as history readings.

The Usborne Book of the Ancient World (grades 4–8). Available through EDC Publishing.

Anyone familiar with Usborne Books knows that their layouts appeal to children. This particular book provides a good overview of different aspects of ancient cultures—Greeks, Romans, Egyptians, etc. Interesting reading to provide context for more in-depth study of the period.

LANGUAGE ARTS

The Christian Child Reading Series (readers for grades K–5). Out of print. These are the original Catholic readers that were written to accompany the Modern Curriculum Press phonics series. (Originally Reardon Baer published both the readers and the phonics workbooks.)

These readers interweave saints' stories and typical children's fare, all at the appropriate phonics level. I wish someone would update and reprint them—they dovetail so well with the Modern Curriculum Press phonics program!

Standard Test Lessons in Reading, Books A–C (reading comprehension tests appropriate for grades 4–8). Available through the Spalding Education Foundation.

These single-page tests mirror the form found on standardized tests. They offer an excellent way of keeping tabs on your child's reading speed and comprehension and make standardized reading tests a breeze.

A Beka Cursive Writing Skillbook (grade 3). Available from A Beka Books.

I use this book to introduce cursive writing. The text also integrates phonics review and reference skills. A Beka also offers handwriting books for levels above and below this, but this is all we've found necessary to use.

The Book of Virtues, by William Bennett. Available at bookstores everywhere.

Although we use this book for bedtime stories, it makes a good anthology of literature as well. Stories are grouped according to the particular virtues they emphasize, making it easy to select readings that reinforce your character training with your children. Fantastic collection!

Wordly Wise, by Kenneth Hodkinson and Joseph G. Ornato. Available through Educators Publishing Service.

This series of workbooks is a good vocabulary builder, offering different combinations of exercises to reinforce each word list covered.

MATHEMATICS

A Beka Books Traditional Arithmetic Series (grades 1–6). Available through A Beka Books.

This strong series provides a visually appealing, well-organized workbook approach to math instruction. Every page reviews old concepts as well as providing practice in the new skill learned. That the pages and problems are nice and varied helps alleviate boredom and anxiety for those children who dislike math—there's usually *something* on the page they like to do!

Math-It, by the Weimar Institute.

This program teaches "tricks" in addition, doubling, and multiplication that are designed to improve speed in mastering basic math facts. Kids easily make a game out of it while they get the practice they need.

RELIGION

We also use the *Faith and Life Series*, but in addition I rely heavily on Bible readings, saints' stories, and the liturgical calendar to convey to our children the fullness of our Faith in an age-appropriate way.

Family Prayer Time

After breakfast every morning, our family prays morning prayer together in the living room. We begin with a short morning offering, spontaneous prayer intentions from each child (including the two–year-old), and end with the Our Father. We follow this short prayer time with the Scripture readings for the day, including an explanation and discussion of how to live the teaching that day, and the story of the day's saint (read aloud by one of the children). We try to make Mass on a daily basis.

At lunchtime, we usually remember to say the Angelus with our grace.

Evening prayers offer another rich time to bring our children back into our Lord's presence. We say one decade of the rosary, make spontaneous prayers of thanks (again from all members of the family), and do a short "directed" examination of conscience for the children. For the examination of conscience, my husband or I pose certain questions for the children to reflect on silently, related to the day's events (for example, if it was a day filled with sibling squabbles, the conscience exam would ask if they acted charitably toward each other, gave in to anger, were slow to forgive, or carried a grudge). We conclude with the Act of Contrition and a blessing for each child.

SCIENCE

A Beka Books God's World Science Series (grades 1–6). Available through A Beka and Great Christian Books distributors. Science volumes for higher grades are available, but we haven't used them yet.

These books generally combine continuous review of basic science concepts, introducing more difficult material each year in a very systematic way. Easy to read, with good photographs in most volumes—your kids will probably like them. Sometimes the Protestant tone (such as an occasional focus on Protestant scientists) is a little off-putting. Generally, though, it's a good integration of the Christian outlook with science.

Usborne Books: We've used *Introduction to Chemistry*, *The Usborne Book of Science Experiments*, and *Mysteries and Marvels of Nature* as background reading material or for selected topics to complement our regular science program. Like most Usborne Books, these volumes are visually "cluttered" but appealing to kids. All the basic information is there and written in a kid-accessible manner.

Some Body: The Human Anatomy Game, from Aristoplay.

This game gives kids a "hands-on" way to figure out where all the organs are in the body. Even my six–year-old can do it! Game cards also provide brief descriptions of how each organ serves the body.

SPANISH

Spanish for Kids, tapes and book aimed at pre-K through grade 4. Available through OptimaLearning Company.

This program aims at verbal fluency and understanding of basic phrases and ideas. The tapes included with this program feature songs and dialogue and are very well done. Catchy music! This is a good first exposure to a language.

Appendix C

CURRICULUM SUPPLIERS

For an up-to-date listing of resources, please see the website of the National Association of Catholic Home Educators: www.nache.org.

Companies Referenced in Resource List

A Beka Book Publications, Pensacola Christian College, Box 18000, Pensacola, FL 32523–9160; telephone (904) 478–8480.

Addison Wesley Publishing Co., Jacob Way, Reading, MA 01867; telephone (800) 447–2226.

Alfred Publishing Co., Inc., 16380 Roscoe Blvd., P.O. Box 10003, Van Nuys, CA 91410–0003; telephone (818) 891–5999.

Apostolate for Family Consecration, John Paul II Holy Family Center, Seminary Rd., Rt. 2, P.O. Box 700, Bloomingdale, OH 43910–0151; telephone (614) 765–4301.

Aristoplay, Ltd., P.O. Box 7028, Ann Arbor, MI 48107; telephone (800) 634–7738.

Don Aslett's Cleaning Center, P.O. Box 39, 311 S. Fifth, Pocatello, ID 83204; telephone (800) 451–2402.

Audio-Visual Drawing Program, P.O. Box 50424, Irvine, CA 92619; telephone (949) 387-7444.

Barbour and Co., Inc., P.O. Box 719, Uhrichsville, OH 44683; telephone (614) 922–6045.

Bolchazy-Carducci Publishers, 1000 Brown St., Unit 101, Wauconda, IL 60084; telephone (708) 526–4344.

Creation Life Publishers, Inc., P.O. Box 1606, El Cajon, CA 92022.

Critical Thinking Skills Press and Software, P.O. Box 448, Pacific Grove, CA 93950–0448; telephone (408) 393–3288.

EDC Publishing, P.O. Box 470663, Tulsa, OK 74147; telephone (918) 622–4522.

Educational Insights, 19560 S. Rancho Way, Dominguez Hills, CA 90220; telephone (800) 933–3277.

Educators Publishing Service, Inc., 75 Moulton St., Cambridge, MA 02138; telephone (800) 225–5750.

Elijah Co., Rt. 2, Box 100–B, Crossville, TN 38555; telephone (615) 456–6284.

God's World Books, P.O. Box 2330, Asheville, NC 28802; telephone (800) 951–BOOK.

Golden Educational Center, P.O. Box 12, Bothell, WA 98041–0012; telephone (800) 800–1791.

Great Christian Books, 229 S. Bridge St., P.O. Box 8000, Elkton, MD 21922–8000; telephone (410) 392–0800.

Greenleaf Press, 1570 Old Laguardo Rd., Lebanon, TN 37087; telephone (615) 449–1617.

HEC Software, Inc., 60 N. Cutler Dr., no. 101, North Salt Lake, UT 84054; telephone (800) 333–0054.

Ignatius Press, P.O. Box 1339, Fort Collins, CO 80522; telephone (800) 651–1531.

Jeremy Tarcher, Inc., 9110 Sunset Blvd., Los Angeles, CA 90069.

Konos, P.O. Box 1534, Richardson, TX 75083; telephone (214) 669–8337.

Literacy Unlimited Publications, P.O. Box 278, Medina, WA 98039–0278.

Little Rock Scripture Study, Liturgical Press, St. John's Abbey, P.O. Box 7500, Collegeville, MN 56321–7500; telephone (800) 858–5434.

McDougal, Littell and Co., P.O. Box 8000, St. Charles, IL 60174; telephone (800) 225–3809.

Modern Curriculum Press, 13900 Prospect Rd., Cleveland, OH 44136; telephone (216) 238–7174.

Moss Music Group, Inc., 48 W. 38th St., New York, NY 10018; telephone (201) 894–8700.

National Writing Institute, 7946 Wright Rd., Niles, MI 49120; telephone (616) 684–4080.

Open Court Publishing Co., Peru, IL 61354; telephone (800) 435–6850.

OptimaLearning Language Land, 885 Olive Ave., Suite A, Novato, CA 94945; telephone (800) 672–1717.

Our Sunday Visitor, Huntington, IN 46750; telephone (219) 356–8400.

Parent–Child Press, P.O. Box 675, Hollidaysburg, PA 16648; telephone (814) 696–7512.

The Providence Project, 14566 N.W. 110th St., Whitewater, KS 67154; telephone (316) 799–2112.

Right at Home Productions, 7206 Claney Ct., Spokane, WA 99208.

Rod and Staff Publishers, Inc., Crockett, KY 41413; telephone (606) 522–4348.

Saxon Publishers, Inc., 1300 McGee, Suite 100, Norman, OK 73072; telephone (405) 329–7071.

Scholastic, Inc., 2931 E. McCarty St., Jefferson City, MO 65101; telephone (800) 325–6149.

Tom Snyder Productions, 90 Sherman St., Cambridge, MA 02140; telephone (617) 926–6000.

Spalding Education Foundation, 5930 W. Greenway, Suite 4, Glendale, AZ 85306; telephone (602) 547–2656.

Timberdoodle, E. 1610 Spencer Lake Rd., Shelton, WA 98584; telephone (206) 426–0672.

Weimar Institute, P.O. Box 486, Weimar, CA 95736; telephone (916) 637–4111.

Youth with a Mission, P.O. Box 55787, Seattle, WA 98155; telephone (206) 363–9844.

Zaner-Bloser, Inc., 2200 W. 5th Ave., P.O. Box 16764, Columbus, OH 43216–6764; telephone (614) 486–0221.

Packaged Curriculum Providers

Calvert School, Dept. 2CAT, 105 Tuscany Rd., Baltimore, MD 21210; telephone (410) 243–6030. Grades K–8. Not overtly Christian; classical in approach.

Kolbe Academy, 1600 F Street, Napa, CA 94559; telephone (707) 255–6412. Grades 1–12. They sell the syllabus and books needed per grade rather than a whole package. You design your own tests and gather other materials. Classical approach called Ignatian Education; lots of flexibility.

My Father's House, 5530 S. Orcas, Seattle, WA 98118; telephone (206) 725–9026. Educational materials by and for Catholic families. Lots of Montessori and Catholic history products and books.

Mother of Divine Grace, P.O. Box 1440, Ojai, CA 93024 or 1002 E. Ojai Ave., Ojai, CA 93023; telephone (805) 646–5818. Laura Berquist (author of *Designing Your Own Classical Curriculum*), director. Thoroughly Catholic and classical in approach, it offers full record keeping, including transcripts, consultation for customizing your child's curriculum (including which subjects to study and recommended resources) and experienced advice on getting the most out of your materials and the best out of your child. No grading but will provide general assessments of child's abilities.

Our Lady of the Rosary School, 105 E. Flaget Ave., Bardstown, KY 40004; telephone (502) 348–1338. Pre-K through grade 12. Each year includes teacher manuals and lesson plans; a variety of services are available, if you want them. Traditional Catholic educational materials used, including some out-of-print books.

Seton Home Study School, 1350 Progress Dr., Front Royal, VA 22630; telephone (540) 636–9990 or (540) 636–9996. Grades K–12. Curriculum includes a variety of Catholic and evangelical Christian books and workbooks needed, plus Seton detailed lesson guides; optional grading and record-keeping services are available. Most well established curriculum provider.

Appendix D

RECORD-KEEPING FORMS

The forms printed in this appendix may be enlarged and copied at your convenience. Feel free to adapt them to fit your particular needs. We suggest the use of such forms as these to simplify the challenging task of remembering from year to year the various accomplishments of your children in a number of areas: books read, projects completed, extracurricular activities (these are especially important when applying to college), and field trips. These record-keeping tools (based on forms developed by Kari Harrington) should also assist you by providing a focus for an activity and a place where you can jot down a brief evaluation.

WEEK OF					
SUBJECT					
MONDAY					
TUESDAY					
WEDNESDAY					
THURSDAY					
FRIDAY					

DAILY LESSON PLANS

READING LOG

BOOKS READ DURING YEAR

AUTHOR	BOOK TITLE	EVALUATION

PROJECT ASSIGNMENTS

SUBJECT / DATE DUE	PROJECT	COMMENTS

EXTRACURRICULAR ACTIVITIES Involvement in volunteer projects, sports, clubs, lessons, etc.

YEAR	ACTIVITY	INVOLVEMENT	HOURS / WEEK

DATE	FIELD TRIP	ACTIVITIES	COMMENTS

FIELD TRIP FORM

BIBLIOGRAPHY
HOME EDUCATION, GENERAL

Books

Adams, Jay E. *Back to the Blackboard*. Phillipsburg, NJ: Presbyterian and Reformed Publishing Co., 1982.

Alexander, Dan C., Jr. *Who's Ruining Our Schools?—The Case against the NEA Teacher Union*. Washington, DC: Save Our Schools Research and Education Foundation, 1986.

Beechick, Ruth. *Teaching Kindergartners—How to Understand and Instruct Fours & Fives*. Denver: Accent Books, 1980.

————. *You Can Teach Your Child Successfully, Grades 1–3*. Pollock Pines, CA: Arrow Press, 1988.

————. *You Can Teach Your Child Successfully, Grades 4–8*. Pollock Pines, CA: Arrow Press, 1988.

Berquist, Laura M. *Designing Your Own Classical Curriculum: A Guide to Catholic Home Education*, revised edition. Warsaw, N.D.: Bethlehem Books, 1994.

Blue, Ron, and Judy Blue. *Money Matters for Parents and Their Kids*. Pomona, CA: Focus on the Family, 1988.

Blumenfeld, Samuel L. *The New Illiterates—And How to Keep Your Child from Becoming One*. New Rochelle, NY: Arlington House, 1973.

————. *How to Tutor*. New Rochelle, NY: Arlington House, 1973.

Clark, Mary Kay. *Catholic Home Schooling—A Handbook for Parents*. Front Royal, VA: Seton Home Study School Press, 1993.

Crow, Alexis. *Home Education: Rights and Reasons*. Westchester, IL: Crossway Books, 1993.

Duffy, Cathy. *Christian Home Educators' Curriculum Manual*. Garden Grove, CA: Home Run Enterprises, 1990.

————. *Christian Home Educators' Curriculum Manual, Junior/Senior High*. Garden Grove, CA: Home Run Enterprises, 1992.

Durant, Penny Raife. *Prize-Winning Science Fair Projects*. New York: Scholastic, Inc., 1991.

Elkind, David. *The Hurried Child*. New York: Addison-Wesley, 1988.

————. *Miseducation—Preschoolers at Risk*. New York: Alfred A. Knopf, 1987.

Eyre, Linda, and Richard Eyre. *Teaching Your Children Values*. New York: Simon & Schuster, 1993.

Froehlich, Mary Ann. *Music Education in the Christian Home*. Brentwood, TN: Wolgemuth & Hyatt, Publishers, Inc., 1990.

Gabler, Mel, and Norma Gabler, with James C. Hefley. *What Are They Teaching Our Children?* Wheaton, IL: Victor Books, 1985.

Gatto, John Taylor. *Dumbing Us Down—The Hidden Curriculum of Compulsory Schooling*. Philadelphia: New Society Publishers, 1985.

Guterson, David. *Family Matters: Why Homeschooling Makes Sense*. New York: Harcourt, Brace, Jovanovich, 1992.

Hardon, John A., S.J. *The Faith—A Popular Guide Based on the Catechism of the Catholic Church*. Ann Arbor, MI: Servant Publications, 1995.

Harris, Gregg. *The Christian Homeschool*. Brentwood, TN: Wolgemuth & Hyatt Publishers, 1988.

Hefley, James C. *Textbooks on Trial*. Wheaton, IL: Victor Books, 1976.

Hensley, Sharon C. *Home Schooling Children with Special Needs*. Gresham, OR: Noble Publishing Associates, 1995.

Holt, John. *How Children Learn*. New York: Dell Publishing Co., Inc., 1967.

Hunt, Gladys. *Honey for a Child's Heart*. Grand Rapids, MI: Zondervan Publishing House, 1969.

Isaacs, David. *Character Building—A Guide for Parents and Teachers*. Kill Lane, Blackrock, County Dublin: Four Courts Press Limited, 1976.

Jones, Douglas. *Classical Education and the Home School*. Moscow, ID: Canon Press, 1995.

Kilpatrick, William. *Why Johnny Can't Tell Right from Wrong—Moral Illiteracy and the Case for Character Education*. New York: Simon & Schuster, 1992.

Klicka, Christopher J. *The Case for Home Schooling*. Washington, DC: Concerned Women for America, 1988.

————. *The Right Choice—The Incredible Failure of Public Education and the Rising Hope of Home Schooling*. Gresham, OR: Noble Publishing Associates, 1992.

Koster, John. *Reading, Writing, and Parents Who Care*. Wheaton, IL: Victor Books, 1991.

Kramer, Rita. *Ed School Follies: The Miseducation of America's Teachers*. New York: The Free Press, 1991.

Lopez, Diane. *Teaching Children*. Westchester, IL: Crossway Books, 1988.

Mason, Charlotte M. *Home Education*. 6 vols. 1935. Reprint: Wheaton, IL: Tyndale House, 1989.

Macaulay, Susan Schaeffer. *For the Children's Sake*. Westchester, IL: Crossway Books, 1984.

McEwan, Elaine K. *How to Raise a Reader*. Elgin, IL: David C. Cook Publishing Co., 1987.

Montessori, Maria. *The Montessori Method*. New York: Schocken Books, 1964.

Moore, Raymond S., and Dorothy N. Moore. *Better Late Than Early*. New York: Reader's Digest Press, 1975.

———. *Home Grown Kids*. Waco, TX: Word Books, 1981.

———. *Home School Burnout*. Brentwood, TN: Wolgemuth & Hyatt Publishers, 1988.

———. *Homespun Schools*. Waco, TX: Word Books, 1982.

———. *School Can Wait*. Berrien Springs, MI: Brigham Young University Press, 1979.

———. *The Successful Homeschool Family Handbook*. Nashville: Thomas Nelson Publishers, 1994.

Owen, Pat Hershey. *The Idea Book for Mothers*. Wheaton, IL: Tyndale House Publishers, Inc., 1981.

Peters, Edward N. *Home Schooling and the New Code of Canon Law*. Front Royal, VA: Christendom College Press, 1988.

Pride, Mary. *All the Way Home*. Westchester, IL: Crossway Books, 1989.

———. *The Big Book of Home Learning*. 4 vols. Wheaton, IL: Crossway Books, 1990.

Pride, Mary, and Bill Pride. *Pride's Guide to Computer Software*. Wheaton, IL: Crossway Books, 1992.

———. *The Way Home—Beyond Feminism, Back to Reality*. Westchester, IL: Crossway Books, 1985.

Ray, Dr. Brian D. *Marching to the Beat of Their Own Drum! A Profile of Home Education Research*. Paeonian Springs, VA: Home School Legal Defense Association, 1992.

Russell, William F. *Classics to Read Aloud to Your Children*. New York: Crown Publishers, Inc., 1984.

Sayers, Dorothy L. "The Lost Tools of Learning", essay in *A Matter of Eternity*. 1947. Reprint: Grand Rapids: Eerdmans Pub. Co., 1973.

Schlafly, Phyllis, ed. *Child Abuse in the Classroom*. Alton, IL: Pere Marquette Press, 1964.

Sowell, Thomas. *Inside American Education*. New York: The Free Press, 1993.

Tanquery, Adolphe. *The Spiritual Life*. Westminster, MD: The Newman Press, 1930.

Van Galen, Jane, and Mary Anne Pitman, eds. *Home Schooling: Political, Historical, and Pedagogical Perspectives*. Norwood, NJ: Ablex Publishing Corporation, 1991.

Vitz, Paul C. *Censorship: Evidence of Bias in Our Children's Textbooks*. Ann Arbor, MI: Servant Books, 1986.

Weiner, Harvey S., Ph.D. *Any Child Can Write*. New York: Bantam Books, 1990.

Whitehead, John W., and Wendell R. Bird. *Home Education and Constitutional Liberties*. Westchester, IL: Crossway Books, 1984.

Wilson, Elizabeth. *Books Children Love*. Westchester, IL: Crossway Books, 1987.

Magazines

Catholic Hearth. Rt. 2, Box 29A, Long Prairie, MN 56347.

The Catholic Home Educator. San Diego, CA. The National Association of Catholic Home Educators (NACHE), P.O. Box 420225, San Diego, CA 92142.

Cheerful Cherub. P.O. Box 262302, San Diego, CA 92196.

The Home School Court Report. Paeonian Springs, VA: Home School Legal Defense Association (HSLDA), Box 159, Paeonian Springs, VA 22129.

Homeschooling Today. P.O. Box 1425, Melrose, FL 32666.

Imitatores Familiae Sanctae. 3874 Forester Ct., San Jose, CA 95121.

In Review. Rt. 1, Box 137-A, Minto, ND 58261. (Review of good children's literature.)

My Friend. St. Paul Book and Media Center, 50 St. Paul's Ave., Boston, MA 02130.

Nazareth, A Catholic Family Journal. Box 56, Nahma, MI 49864.

Practical Homeschooling. P.O. Box 1250, Fenton, MO 63026–1850.

St. Joseph Messenger. 4597 School Section Rd., Cincinnati, OH 45211.

St. Paul's Family Magazine. 14780 W. 159th St., Olathe, KS 66062.

The Teaching Home. Box 20219, Portland, OR 97220.

Organizations and Networks

Apostolate for Family Consecration, John Paul II Holy Family Center, Seminary Rd., Rt. 2, Box 700, Bloomingdale, OH 43910; telephone (614) 765–4301. The Apostolate has resources such as videos for family holy hours, the Apostolate's Family Catechism, and several seven-day Holy Family Fests (a week of play, work, and prayer for families—an experience in Catholic community).

Catholics United for the Faith, 827 N. 4th St., Steubenville, OH 43952; telephone (614) 28FAITH. An international ·lay apostolate devoted to proclaiming the Catholic Faith in its fullness to the world and, in particular, to our children—the next generation of Catholics.

CRNET (Catholic Resource Network), Trinity Communications, P.O. Box 3610, Manassas, VA 22110. Customer service (703) 791–2576; modem (703) 791–4336; e-mail: http://www.crnet.org. CRNET is the largest Catholic telecommunications resource service in the world, providing authentic Catholic information and services 24 hours a day, including a "Home Education" forum.

Home School Legal Defense Association, Box 159, Paeonian Springs, VA 22129; telephone (540) 338–5600; fax (540) 338–2733 (for membership information and applications) and (540) 338–1952.

National Association of Catholic Home Educators, P.O. Box 2304, Elkton, MD 21922–2304. NACHE networks Catholic home educators across the country, publishes a quarterly journal, and sponsors regional and national Catholic home education conventions.

National Center for Home Education, branch of Home School Legal Defense Association (same address); telephone (540) 338–7600. This organization functions as an information clearing-house for home education.

St. Joseph's Covenant Keepers, Family Life Center International, P.O. Box 6060, Port Charlotte, FL 33949; telephone (941) 764–8565. Covenant Keepers is a movement of Catholic men calling other men to faithfulness to God, their spouse, and their family.

Traditions of Roman Catholic Homes (TORCH): 4425 Aaron Court, Cumming, GA 30040; e-mail: mrmunoz@bellsouth.net; website: www.catholic-homeschool.com. TORCH, a national network of Catholic home education support groups, publishes a monthly newsletter and provides resources and contacts for homeschoolers in North America.

BIBLIOGRAPHY
FAMILY LIFE

Homemaking Helps

Barnes, Emilie. *The Creative Home Organizer*. Eugene, OR: Harvest House Publishers, 1988.

———. *Survival for Busy Women*. Eugene, OR: Harvest House Publishers, 1986.

Bond, Jill. *Dinner's in the Freezer*. 3d ed. Lake Hamilton, FL: Reed Bond Books, 1993.

Covey, Stephen R. *The Seven Habits of Highly Effective People*. New York: Simon & Schuster, 1990. (A new breakthrough in time management!)

Hunter, Brenda. *Home by Choice—Understanding the Enduring Effects of a Mother's Love*. Sisters, OR: Multnomah Books, 1991.

Kippley, John F. *Sex and the Marriage Covenant*. Cincinnati, OH: Couple to Couple League International, Inc., 1991.

LeFever, Marlene D. *Creative Hospitality*. Wheaton, IL: Tyndale House Publishers, Inc., 1980.

Mains, Karen. *Open Heart, Open Home*. Elgin, IL: David C. Cook Publishing Co., 1976.

Schaeffer, Edith. *The Hidden Art of Homemaking—Creative Ideas for Enriching Everyday Life*. Wheaton, IL: Tyndale House Publishers Inc., 1971.

Schofield, Deniece. *Confessions of an Organized Housewife*. Cincinnati, OH: Writer's Digest Books, 1981.

Skoglund, Elizabeth R. *The Welcoming Hearth*. Wheaton, IL: Tyndale House Publishers, 1993.

Wilson, Mimi, and Mary Beth Lagerborg. *Once-a-Month Cooking*. 1982. Reprint: Colorado Springs, CO: Focus on the Family, 1986.

Young, Pam, and Peggy Jones. *Sidetracked Home Executives*. New York: Warner Books, 1981.

Parenting and Child Training

Allen, Dr. Roger, and Ron Rose. *Common Sense Discipline*. Fort Worth, TX: Sweet Publishing, 1986.

Blue, Ron, and Judy Blue. *Money Matters for Parents and Their Kids*. Pomona, CA: Focus on the Family, 1988.

Campbell, Ross, M.D. *How to Really Love Your Child*. Wheaton, IL: Victor Books, 1992.

———. *How to Really Love Your Teenager*. Wheaton, IL: Victor Books, 1993.

Dobson, Dr. James. *Dare to Discipline*. Wheaton, IL: Tyndale House Publishers, Inc.: 1970.

———. *Hide or Seek*. Old Tappan, NJ: Fleming H. Revell Co., 1974.

———. *The New Dare to Discipline*. Wheaton, IL: Tyndale House Publishers, 1992.

———. *The Strong-Willed Child*. Wheaton, IL: Tyndale House Publishers, Inc.: 1985.

Durfield, Richard C., Ph.D., and Renee Durfield. *Raising Them Chaste*. Minneapolis, MN: Bethany House Publishers, 1991.

Elliot, Elisabeth. *Passion and Purity*. Old Tappen, NJ: Fleming H. Revell Company, 1984.

Fugate, J. Richard. *What the Bible Says about . . . Child Training*. Garland, TX: Aletheia Publishers, Inc. 1980.

McCullough, Bonnie Runyan, and Susan Walker Monson. *401 Ways to Get Your Kids to Work at Home*. New York: St. Martin's Press, 1981.

McManus, Michael. *The Marriage Savers*. Grand Rapids, MI: Zondervan Publishing House, 1993.

Marshner, Connie. *Decent Exposure*. Brentwood, TN: Wolgemuth and Hyatt, Publishers, Inc., 1988.

Martin, Michaelann, Carol Puccio, and Zoe Romanowski. *Praying from the Hearth*. Huntington, IN: Our Sunday Visitor, 1996.

Medved, Michael. *Hollywood vs. America—Popular Culture and the War on Traditional Values*. New York: HarperCollins Publishers, 1992.

Moore, Raymond, and Dorothy Moore. *Home Built Discipline*. Nashville, TN: Thomas Nelson Publishers, 1987.

Rand, Ron. *For Fathers Who Aren't in Heaven*. Ventura, CA: Regal Books, 1986.

Smalley, Gary. *The Key to Your Child's Heart*. Waco, TX: Word Books Publishers, 1984.

Smalley, Gary, and John Trent, Ph.D. *The Blessing*. Nashville, TN: Thomas Nelson Publishers, 1986.

———. *The Gift of Honor*. Nashville, TN: Thomas Nelson Publishers, 1987.

———. *The Gift of the Blessing*. Nashville, TN: Thomas Nelson Publishers, 1993.

———. *The Hidden Value of a Man*. Colorado Springs, CO: Focus on the Family, 1992.

———. *Leaving the Lights On*. Sisters, OR: Multnomah Books, 1994.

———. *The Two Sides of Love*. Pomona, CA: Focus on the Family, 1990.

Trumbull, H. Clay. *Hints on Child Training.* Brentwood, TN: Wolgemuth & Hyatt, Publishers, Inc., 1989.

Ziglar, Zig. *Raising Positive Kids in a Negative World.* Nashville, TN: Thomas Nelson Publishers, 1985.

Spiritual Growth

Ball, Karen M., and Karen L. Tornberg. *Family Traditions That Last a Lifetime.* Wheaton, IL: Tyndale House Publishers, Inc., 1993.

Catholic Household Blessings and Prayers. Prepared by the Bishops' Committee on the Liturgy for the National Council of Catholic Bishops. Washington, DC: United States Catholic Conference, Inc., 1988.

Chervin, Ronda DeSola, and Carla Conley. *The Book of Catholic Customs and Traditions—Ideas for Families.* Ann Arbor, MI: Servant Publications, 1994.

Gill, Laurie Navar, and Teresa Zepeda. *Lent and Easter in the Christian Kitchen—Celebrating the Faith in the Home.* Part of a series, including the following: *The Forty Days of Lent for the Christian Family*, *The Fifty Days of Easter for the Christian Family*, and *Advent and Christmas for the Christian Family.* Gilhause Communications, 525 Shadowridge Dr., Ellisville, MO 63011–1707.

Hromas, Roberta. *52 Simple Ways to Teach Your Child to Pray.* Nashville, TN: Oliver Nelson Publishers, 1991.

Leifeld, Wendy. *Mothers of the Saints.* Ann Arbor, MI: Servant Publications, 1991.

MacDonald, Gordon. *Ordering Your Private World.* Nashville, TN: Thomas Nelson Publishers, 1984.

Mains, Karen Burton. *Making Sunday Special.* Waco, TX: Word Books Publishers, 1987.

Newland, Mary Reed. *The Year and Our Children—Planning the Family Activities for Christian Feasts and Seasons*. 1956. Reprint: San Diego, CA: Firefly Press, 1995.

Ortlund, Anne. *Disciplines of the Beautiful Woman*. Waco, TX: Word Books Publishers, 1977.

Rego, Fr. Richard J. *A Contemporary Guide to Conscience for the Sacrament of Confession*. St. Paul, MN: Leaflet Missal Company, 1990.

Trapp, Maria Augusta. *Around the Year with the Trapp Family*. New York: Pantheon Books, 1955.

Vitz, Evelyn Birge. *A Continual Feast*. San Francisco: Ignatius Press, 1991.

Weiser, Francis X. *The Easter Book*. New York: Harcourt, Brace and Co., 1954.

———. *The Holyday Book*. New York: Harcourt, Brace and Co., 1956.

Zimmerman, Martha. *Celebrate the Feasts*. Minneapolis, MN: Bethany House Publishers, 1960.

INDEX

Academics, applying the Faith in, 58–59, 62

Achievement, 97, 342; and educational approach, 8, 97; and educational background of parents, 25, 90–91, 91n. 5; and family income, 7, 7n. 7, 25; test results and home education, 7, 7n. 5, 13, 13n. 3, 15–18, 18n. 11, 184–85

ACT exam, 233, 234

Anointing of the Sick, as source of grace, 308–9, 310

Anxiety. *See* Fears; Stress

Aquila, Dominic, 34

Aristotle, 124

Art studies, resources for, 345

Augustine, Saint, 8

Authority: establishing and maintaining, 78–79, 87, 148; father's role in, 152–62; and parent as teacher, 87, 197, 204

Baptism, 305; reception of faith, hope, and love at, 319–20; as source of grace, 295–96, 309

Behavior problems, 21. *See also* Discipline

Bennett, William, *The Book of Virtues*, 166

Berquist, Laura, *Designing Your Own Classical Curriculum*, 131

Better Homes and Gardens (magazine), "When School Is at Home", 273

Better Late Than Early (D. Moore and R. Moore), 126–27

Bible studies: resources for, 332–33, 345–46. *See also* Scripture

Big Book of Home Learning, The (Pride), 181, 195

Bloom, Benjamin, 341

Blue, Judy, *Money Matters for Parents and Their Kids*, 219, 219n. 8

Blue, Ron, *Money Matters for Parents and Their Kids*, 219, 219n. 8

Book of Virtues, The (Bennett), 166

Burnout, 203; avoiding, 102–4, 281–84. *See also* Stress

Carnegie units, 341, 342

Casti Connubii, 5–6n. 2

Catechism of the Catholic Church, 52, 162, 213, 216, 334

Catholic Church: on chastity, 217, 223, 307; as Family of God, 43–46, 74, 301; mission of, 44, 55; and principle of subsidiarity, 35, 47, 274; as provider of education, 32, 34–36, 40, 42, 106; on role of parents in education, 5–6, 5–6n. 2, 33; on Scripture and Tradition in learning, 50–57; sense of community in, 71,

A page number followed by "n." indicates a footnote and includes the footnote number.